Mastering Xamarin Development

MW00451834

Build stunning, maintainable, cross-platform mobile application user interfaces with the power of Xamarin

Steven F. Daniel

BIRMINGHAM - MUMBAI

Mastering Xamarin UI Development

Copyright © 2017 Packt Publishing

All rights reserved. No part of this book may be reproduced, stored in a retrieval system, or transmitted in any form or by any means, without the prior written permission of the publisher, except in the case of brief quotations embedded in critical articles or reviews.

Every effort has been made in the preparation of this book to ensure the accuracy of the information presented. However, the information contained in this book is sold without warranty, either express or implied. Neither the author, nor Packt Publishing, and its dealers and distributors will be held liable for any damages caused or alleged to be caused directly or indirectly by this book.

Packt Publishing has endeavored to provide trademark information about all of the companies and products mentioned in this book by the appropriate use of capitals. However, Packt Publishing cannot guarantee the accuracy of this information.

First published: January 2017

Production reference: 1130117

Published by Packt Publishing Ltd.
Livery Place
35 Livery Street
Birmingham
B3 2PB, UK.
ISBN 978-1-78646-200-8

www.packtpub.com

Credits

Author

Steven F. Daniel

Reviewers

Lance McCarthy

Engin Polat

Commissioning Editor

Amarabha Banerjee

Acquisition Editor

Shweta Pant

Content Development Editor

Priyanka Mehta

Technical Editor

Abhishek Sharma

Copy Editor

Safis Editing

Project Coordinator

Izzat Contractor

Proofreader

Safis Editing

Indexer

Tejal Daruwale Soni

Graphics

Abhinash Sahu

Production Coordinator

Deepika Naik

About the Author

Steven F. Daniel is the CEO and founder of GENIESOFT STUDIOS, a software development company based in Melbourne, Victoria, that focuses primarily on developing games and business applications for the iOS, Android, and Mac OS X platforms. He is an experienced software developer with more than 17 years of experience in developing desktop and web-based applications for several companies and startups.

Steven is extremely passionate about making people employable by helping them bridge the gap between using their existing skills in iOS, Android, and Xamarin to get the job done. To achieve this, he writes books to help novice and advanced programmers succeed within the industry. Steven is extremely passionate about, and loves being at the forefront of, technology. He is a member of the SQL Server Special Interest Group (SQLSIG), Melbourne CocoaHeads, and the Java Community. He was the cofounder and Chief Technology Officer (CTO) at SoftMpire Pty Ltd., a company that is focused primarily on developing business applications for the iOS and Android platforms.

Steven is the author of various book titles, some of which are as follows:

- Apple Watch App Development
- Android Wearable Programming
- Xcode 4 Cookbook
- iPad Enterprise Application Development Blueprints
- iOS 5 Essentials
- Xcode 4 iOS Development Beginner's Guide

Check out his blog at http://www.geniesoftstudios.com/blog/, or follow him on twitter at http://twitter.com/GenieSoftStudio.

Acknowledgments

No book is the product of just the author; he just happens to be the one with his name on the cover. Several people contributed to the success of this book, and it would take more space than thanking each one individually.

I would personally like to thank three special people who have been an inspiration and who have provided me with so much support during the writing of this book, Reshma Raman, my Senior Acquisition Editor, who is the reason that this book exists; Shweta Pant, my Acquisition Editor; and Priyanka Mehta for her understanding and support, as well as her brilliant suggestive approaches during the chapter rewrites. I would like to thank each of you for everything, and making the writing process enjoyable.

Lastly, to my reviewers, thank you so much for your valued suggestions and improvements to make this book what it is; I am truly grateful to each one of you.

Thank you also to the entire PACKT Publishing team for working so diligently to help bring out a high-quality product. Finally, a big shout out to the engineers at Xamarin, Inc. for creating Xamarin Studio and the Mono Platform to provide developers with the tools to create fun and sophisticated applications with the power of Xamarin.Forms.

Finally, I would like to thank all my friends for their support, understanding, and encouragement during the book writing process. I am extremely grateful to have you as my friends, and it is a privilege to know each one of you.

About the Reviewers

Lance McCarthy is an exceptional community leader with an acute expertise for all things .NET and C#, especially on the XAML stack, including WPF, Silverlight, Windows Phone, and Windows store apps. He is very helpful online, guiding and answering questions from Microsoft developers on Twitter as @lancewmccarthy; he blogs on his own time as well, with a strong focus on Windows Universal apps, at `WinPlatform.wordpress.com`. He organizes and hosts events in the Boston area, such as user group nights, mini-code camps, and full hackathons.

During the day, Lance is a senior technical support engineer at Telerik, where he supports developers with their Classic Windows, Universal Windows, web and mobile (Xamarin, Android and iOS native) application development.

On the side, Lance writes blog posts for `blogs.windows.com/buildingapps/`, creates resources for developers (tutorials, sample source code, tips of the week, and so on), and helps the developer community in any way possible.

Previously, Lance worked for Nokia and Microsoft as a Developer Ambassador, where he sought out and engaged developers through outreach programs and provides them with technical support and resources to make them successful on the Windows platforms.

Lance was also an assistant professor at Harvard University, helping students build, market, and publish successful Windows Phone apps. He has also appeared on podcasts, such as the Windows Developer Show, has been a technical editor for publications and books, has won several app building contests and hackathons (including first place in the Microsoft Build 2013 hackathon), and is a published developer with over a million downloads in the Windows Store.

Some of the books that he has reviewed are as follows:

- Netdunio Home Automation Projects by Matt Cavanaugh
- Mastering Cross-Platform Development with Xamarin by Can Bilgin
- Begin to Code with C# by Rob Miles

Engin Polat has been involved in many large and medium-scale projects on .NET technologies as a developer, architect, and consulting, and he has won many awards since 1999. Since 2008, he has been training many large enterprises in Turkey on Windows development, web development, distributed application development, software architecture, mobile development, cloud development, and so on. Apart from this, he organizes seminars and events in many universities in Turkey about .NET technologies, Windows platform development, cloud development, web development, game development, and so on. He shares his experiences on his personal blog (`http://www.engin polat.com`). He has MCP, MCAD, MCSD, MCDBA, and MCT certifications. Since 2012, he is recognized as a Windows Development MVP by Microsoft; since 2017, he is recognized as a Visual Studio and Development Technologies MVP too. Between 2013 and 2015, he was recognized as a Nokia Developer Champion--very few people in the world are given this award. Since 2015, he has been recognized as a Regional Director by Microsoft.

He has reviewed a few books for Packt, some of which are as follows:

- Mastering Cross-Platform Development with Xamarin
- Xamarin Blueprints
- Xamarin 4 by Example

I'd like to thank my dear wife, Yeliz, and my beautiful daughter, Melis Ada, for all the support they gave me while I was working on this book project.

I also want to extend a warm welcome to the newest member of my family, my dear son, Utku Ege.

www.PacktPub.com

For support files and downloads related to your book, please visit www.PacktPub.com.

Did you know that Packt offers eBook versions of every book published, with PDF and ePub files available? You can upgrade to the eBook version at www.PacktPub.com and as a print book customer, you are entitled to a discount on the eBook copy. Get in touch with us at service@packtpub.com for more details.

At www.PacktPub.com, you can also read a collection of free technical articles, sign up for a range of free newsletters and receive exclusive discounts and offers on Packt books and eBooks.

https://www.packtpub.com/mapt

Get the most in-demand software skills with Mapt. Mapt gives you full access to all Packt books and video courses, as well as industry-leading tools to help you plan your personal development and advance your career.

Why subscribe?

- Fully searchable across every book published by Packt
- Copy and paste, print, and bookmark content
- On demand and accessible via a web browser

Customer Feedback

Thank you for purchasing this Packt book. We take our commitment to improving our content and products to meet your needs seriously--that's why your feedback is so valuable. Whatever your feelings about your purchase, please consider leaving a review on this book's Amazon page. Not only will this help us, more importantly it will also help others in the community to make an informed decision about the resources that they invest in to learn. You can also review for us on a regular basis by joining our reviewers' club. **If you're interested in joining, or would like to learn more about the benefits we offer, please contact us**: customerreviews@packtpub.com.

To my favorite uncle, Benjamin Jacob Daniel, thank you for always making me smile and for inspiring me to work hard and achieve my dreams; you are a true inspiration and I couldn't have done this without your love, support, and guidance. Thank you.

As always, to Chan Ban Guan, for the continued patience, encouragement, and support, and most of all for believing in me during the writing of this book. I would like to thank my family for their continued love and support, and for always believing in me throughout the writing of this book.

This book would not have been possible without your love and understanding and I would like to thank you from the bottom of my heart.

Table of Contents

Preface

Xamarin is the most powerful cross-platform mobile development framework. If you are interested in creating stunning user interfaces for the iOS and Android mobile platforms using the power of Xamarin and Xamarin.Forms, then this is your ticket.

This book will provide you with the practical skills required to develop real-world Xamarin applications. You will learn how to implement user interface structures and layouts, create customized elements, and write C# scripts to customize layouts. You'll learn how to create User Interface layouts from scratch and customize these layouts to suit your needs by using Data Templates and Custom Renderers.

You'll be introduced to the architecture behind the Model-View-ViewModel (MVVM) pattern, and how to implement this within your application so that you can navigate between each of your ViewModels and ContentPages.

We will then move on to discuss more advanced topics, such as how to incorporate platform-specific features within your apps that are dependent on the mobile platform being run, and you will learn how to properly perform location updates, whether the application's state is in the foreground or background, by registering the app as a background-necessary application.

We discuss more advanced topics, such as working with Microsoft Azure App services to create your very first cloud-based backend HTTP web service to handle communication between the cloud and the app, by creating a DataService API that will allow our app to consume the API so that it can retrieve, store, and delete walk trail information from the cloud.

We will also cover how you can work with the Facebook SDK to incorporate social networking features to obtain information about a Facebook user, as well as post information to their Facebook wall and use the Open Graph API to retrieve certain information about the user.

Moving on, you will learn how to use third-party libraries, such as the Razor template engine, which allows you to create your own HTML5 templates, within the Xamarin Studio environment to build a book library Hybrid solution that uses the SQLite.Net library to store, update, retrieve, and delete information within a SQLite local database. You'll also implement key data binding techniques that will make your user interfaces dynamic and create personalized animations and visual effects within your user interfaces using custom renderers and the PlatformEffects API to customize and change the appearance of control elements.

At the end of this book, you will learn how to create and run unit tests using the NUnit and UITest testing frameworks right within the Xamarin Studio IDE. You'll learn how to write unit tests for your ViewModels that will essentially test the business logic to validate that everything is working correctly, before moving on to test the user interface portion using automated UI testing.

In this book, I have tried my best to keep the code simple and easy to understand by providing a step-by-step approach, with lots of screenshots at each step to make it easier to follow. You will soon master the different aspects of Xamarin.Forms, and the technology and skills needed to create your own applications for the Xamarin.Forms platform.

Feel free to contact me at support@geniesoftstudios.com with any queries, or just drop me an e-mail to say a friendly "Hello".

What this book covers

Chapter 1, *Creating the TrackMyWalks Native App*, focuses on how to set up a basic cross-platform native app structure using Xamarin.Forms before proceeding with adding new, and updating existing, packages within your solution.

You'll learn how to create C# classes that will act as the model for our app, and will create content pages that will form the user interface. We will also cover the differences between developing apps using Xamarin Studio and Microsoft Visual Studio.

Chapter 2, *MVVM and Data Binding*, introduces you to the architecture behind the MVVM pattern, and how you can implement this within your application by adding new Views and the associated Models.

You'll learn how to create the underlying C# class files that will act as the ViewModels for your app, and update existing content pages to data-bind with the ViewModels to represent the information that will be displayed within the user interface for our application.

Chapter 3, *Navigating within the MVVM Model - The Xamarin.Forms Way*, builds upon your working knowledge of the MVVM design pattern architecture to show you how you can navigate through the ViewModels by creating a C# class that acts as the navigation service for our app, and updates our existing WalkBaseViewModel class to include additional abstract class methods each of our ViewModels will inherit; in turn, you'll update content pages to bind with the ViewModels to allow navigation between these Views to happen.

Chapter 4, *Adding Location-Based Features within Your App*, focuses on how you can incorporate platform-specific features within the TrackMyWalks app, which is dependent on the mobile platform, by creating a location service C# class that will include several class methods for both the iOS and Android platforms.

You'll learn how to properly perform location updates whether the application's state is in the foreground or background by registering the app as a background-necessary application.

Chapter 5, *Customizing the User Interface*, shows you how you can work with DataTemplates to lay out your views neatly within your applications user interface by creating a C# class. You'll get accustomed to working with platform-specific APIs to extend the default behavior of Xamarin.Forms controls using custom renderers to create a custom picker, before moving on to learn how to use the Xamarin.Forms Effects API to customize the appearance and styling of native control elements for each platform by implementing a CustomRenderer class.

Finally, you will learn how to manipulate the visual appearance of data bound using value and image converters.

Chapter 6, *Working with Razor Templates*, introduces you to the Razor HTML templating engine, and how you can use it to create a hybrid mobile solution. You'll learn how to build a book library mobile solution using the power of Razor templates, how to create and use models within your application, and how to connect this up to a SQLite database to store, retrieve, update, and delete book details.

Chapter 7, *Incorporating API Data Access using Microsoft Azure App Services*, shows you how you can use Microsoft Azure App services to create your very first live, cloud-based backend HTTP web service to handle all the communication between the cloud and the app. You'll learn how to create a DataService API that will allow the app to consume the API so that it can retrieve, store, and delete walk trail information from the cloud, all from within the TrackMyWalks app.

Chapter 8, *Making our App Social – Using the Facebook API*, shows you how you can use both Xamarin.Auth and the Facebook SDK to incorporate social networking features within the TrackMyWalks app to obtain information about a Facebook user, as well as post information to their Facebook wall.

You'll learn how to create a sign-in page that allows users to log in to your app using their Facebook credentials, and how to create a FacebookApiUser class that will be used to store information about the logged-in user, and use the Open Graph API to retrieve certain information about the user.

Finally, you will see how you can leverage the Facebook library to post walk data to your Facebook profile page, so you can show off your Walk Trail progress to your friends and/or work colleagues.

Chapter 9, *Unit Testing your Xamarin.Forms App using the NUnit and UITest Frameworks*, focuses on showing you how to create and run unit tests using the NUnit and UITest testing frameworks right within the Xamarin Studio IDE. You'll learn how to write unit tests for our ViewModels that will essentially test the business logic to validate that everything is working correctly before testing the user interface's portion using automated UI testing.

Chapter 10, *Packaging and Deploying your Xamarin.Forms Applications*, focuses on how to submit your TrackMyWalks iOS app to the Apple App Store, and share your creations with the rest of the community. You'll learn the steps required to set up your iOS development team, as well as certificates for both development and distribution, and you will learn how to create the necessary provisioning profiles for both your development and distribution builds and create the necessary app IDs for your application.

Finally, you will learn how to register your iOS devices so that your users can download and test your apps on their iOS devices and learn how to prepare your TrackMyWalks iOS app for submission to iTunes Connect using the Xamarin Studio IDE.

What you need for this book

The minimum requirement for this book is an Intel-based Macintosh computer running OS X El Capitan 10.11. We will be using Xamarin Studio 6.1.2, which is the Integrated Development Environment (IDE) used for creating Xamarin.Forms applications using C#, as well as Xcode 8.2.1 to compile our iOS app and run this within the simulator.

Almost all the projects that you create with the help of this book will work and run on the iOS simulator. However, some projects will require an iOS or Android device to work correctly. You can download the latest versions of Xamarin Studio and Xcode at:

Xamarin Studio: http://xamarin.com/download

Xcode: https://itunes.apple.com/au/app/xcode/id497799835?mt=12

Who this book is for

This book is intended for developers who have a working experience of application development principles, as well as a basic knowledge of Xamarin and C# coding and wish to expand their knowledge and develop applications using Xamarin.Forms. It is assumed that you are familiar with Object-Oriented Programming (OOP), and have some experience developing C# applications using Xamarin Studio.

Conventions

In this book, you will find a number of text styles that distinguish between different kinds of information. Here are some examples of these styles and an explanation of their meaning.

Code words in text, database table names, folder names, filenames, file extensions, pathnames, dummy URLs, user input, and Twitter handles are shown as follows: "One thing you will notice is that our solution contains a file called TrackMyWalks.cs which is part of the TrackMyWalks Portable Class Library."

A block of code is set as follows:

```
//
//  WalkEntryViewModel.cs
//  TrackMyWalks ViewModels
//
//  Created by Steven F. Daniel on 22/08/2016.
//  Copyright © 2016 GENIESOFT STUDIOS. All rights reserved.
//  using TrackMyWalks.Models;
    using TrackMyWalks.ViewModels;
    using Xamarin.Forms;
    namespace TrackMyWalks
    {
        public class WalkEntryViewModel : WalkBaseViewModel
        {
```

When we wish to draw your attention to a particular part of a code block, the relevant lines or items are set in bold:

```
//
//  WalksPage.cs
//  TrackMyWalks
//
//  Created by Steven F. Daniel on 04/08/2016.
//  Copyright © 2016 GENIESOFT STUDIOS. All rights reserved.
//
using System.Collections.Generic;
using Xamarin.Forms;
using TrackMyWalks.Models;
using TrackMyWalks.ViewModels;
namespace TrackMyWalks
{
    public class WalksPage : ContentPage
    {
        public WalksPage()
        {
```

Any command-line input or output is written as follows:

```
Last login: Sun Nov 6 10:48:41 on console
GENIESOFT-MAC-Mini:~ stevendaniel$ curl
https://trackmywalks.azurewebsites.net/tables/walkentries
--header "ZUMO-API-VERSION:2.0.0"
```

New terms and **important words** are shown in bold. Words that you see on the screen, for example, in menus or dialog boxes, appear in the text like this: "if you click on the **Proceed With ...** button, it will navigate to the walks **Trail Details** page where you can begin your trail, by clicking on the **Begin this Trail** button."

Warnings or important notes appear in a box like this.

Tips and tricks appear like this.

Reader feedback

Feedback from our readers is always welcome. Let us know what you think about this book-what you liked or disliked. Reader feedback is important for us as it helps us develop titles that you will really get the most out of. To send us general feedback, simply e-mail feedback@packtpub.com, and mention the book's title in the subject of your message. If there is a topic that you have expertise in and you are interested in either writing or contributing to a book, see our author guide at www.packtpub.com/authors.

Customer support

Now that you are the proud owner of a Packt book, we have a number of things to help you to get the most from your purchase.

Downloading the example code

You can download the example code files for this book from your account at http://www.packtpub.com. If you purchased this book elsewhere, you can visit http://www.packtpub.com/support and register to have the files e-mailed directly to you.

You can download the code files by following these steps:

1. Log in or register to our website using your e-mail address and password.
2. Hover the mouse pointer on the **SUPPORT** tab at the top.
3. Click on **Code Downloads & Errata**.
4. Enter the name of the book in the **Search** box.
5. Select the book for which you're looking to download the code files.
6. Choose from the drop-down menu where you purchased this book from.
7. Click on **Code Download**.

Once the file is downloaded, please make sure that you unzip or extract the folder using the latest version of:

- WinRAR / 7-Zip for Windows
- Zipeg / iZip / UnRarX for Mac
- 7-Zip / PeaZip for Linux

The code bundle for the book is also hosted on GitHub at `https://github.com/PacktPubl ishing/Mastering-Xamarin-UI-Development`. We also have other code bundles from our rich catalog of books and videos available at `https://github.com/PacktPublishing/`. Check them out!

Errata

Although we have taken every care to ensure the accuracy of our content, mistakes do happen. If you find a mistake in one of our books-maybe a mistake in the text or the code- we would be grateful if you could report this to us. By doing so, you can save other readers from frustration and help us improve subsequent versions of this book. If you find any errata, please report them by visiting `http://www.packtpub.com/submit-errata`, selecting your book, clicking on the **Errata Submission Form** link, and entering the details of your errata. Once your errata are verified, your submission will be accepted and the errata will be uploaded to our website or added to any list of existing errata under the Errata section of that title.

To view the previously submitted errata, go to `https://www.packtpub.com/books/conten t/support` and enter the name of the book in the search field. The required information will appear under the **Errata** section.

Piracy

Piracy of copyrighted material on the Internet is an ongoing problem across all media. At Packt, we take the protection of our copyright and licenses very seriously. If you come across any illegal copies of our works in any form on the Internet, please provide us with the location address or website name immediately so that we can pursue a remedy.

Please contact us at `copyright@packtpub.com` with a link to the suspected pirated material.

We appreciate your help in protecting our authors and our ability to bring you valuable content.

Questions

If you have a problem with any aspect of this book, you can contact us at `questions@packtpub.com`, and we will do our best to address the problem.

1

Creating the TrackMyWalks Native App

Since **Xamarin** made its appearance several years ago, developers have been delighted with being able to create native mobile applications that target non-Microsoft platforms, and with having the option of developing apps using either C# or F# programming languages, which enables developers to distribute their app ideas on iOS and Android platforms.

As you progress through this book, you will learn how to apply best practice principles when developing cross-platform mobile applications and design patterns using the `Xamarin.Forms` platform, which allows developers to build cross-platform user interface layouts that can be shared across Android, iOS, and Windows Phone mobile platforms.

Since each of these apps can be written using a single programming language, it makes sense to write a single codebase that would compile and build separate apps for each of these different platforms.

This chapter will begin by setting up a basic structure of an app built using `Xamarin.Forms`, which will be the foundation for the subsequent chapters, where we will continually build upon this, applying new concepts. In this chapter, you will see how to create an initial cross-platform native app using `Xamarin.Forms` and how to go about adding new, and updating existing, packages within your solution.

You'll learn how to create C# classes that will act as the model for our app, as well as creating content pages that will form the user interface. To end the chapter, you will learn about the differences between developing apps using Xamarin Studio and/or Microsoft Visual Studio.

This chapter will cover the following points:

- Creating the Xamarin.Forms `TrackMyWalks` mobile app solution
- Updating the `TrackMyWalks` solution packages using the `NuGet` package manager
- Creating the `TrackMyWalks` data model
- Creating the `ContentPages` for the `TrackMyWalks` solution
- Understanding the differences between Xamarin Studio and Visual Studio

Creating the TrackMyWalks solution

In this section, we will take a look at how we can go about creating a new `Xamarin.Forms` solution for the first time. We will begin by developing the basic structure for our application, as well as by adding the necessary entity models and designing the user interface files.

Before we can proceed, we need to create our `TrackMyWalks` project. It is very simple to create this using Xamarin Studio. Simply follow the steps listed below:

1. Launch the Xamarin Studio application. You will be presented with the following screen:

2. Next, click on the **New Solution...** button, or alternatively choose the **File | New | Solution...** or simply press *Shift + Command + N*.

3. Next, choose the **Forms App** option which is located under the **Multiplatform | App** section. Ensure you have selected **C#** as the programming language to use:

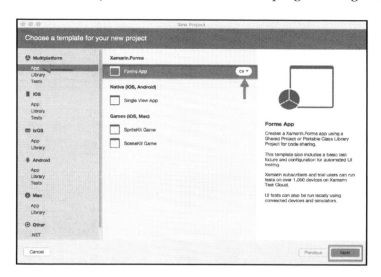

4. Next, enter `TrackMyWalks` to use as the name for your app in the **App Name** field.

5. Then, specify a name for the **Organization Identifier** field.

6. Next, ensure that both the **Android** and **iOS** checkboxes have been selected in the **Target Platforms** fields.

7. Then, ensure that the **Use Portable Class Library** option has been selected in the **Shared Code** section, as shown in the following screenshot.

The difference between using a Portable Class Library versus a Shared Library is essentially that a Portable Class Library enables developers to write code once, so that it can be used within different platform projects such as Websites, Android, and iOS. A Shared Library enables developers to copy all the files within the library project to all the projects that are contained within the solution during compilation for the various platforms that will use it.

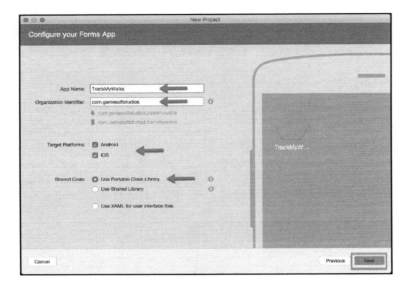

The **Organization Identifier** option for your app needs to be unique. Xamarin Studio recommends that you use the reverse domain style (for example, `com.domainName.appName`).

8. Next, ensure that the **Use XAML for user interface files** option has not been selected.

9. Then, click on the **Next** button to proceed to the next step in the wizard.

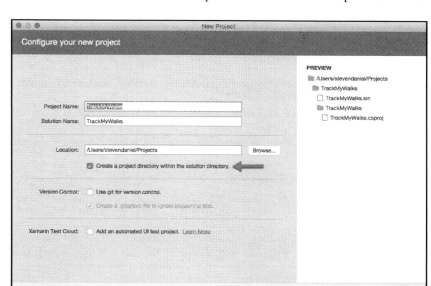

10. Next, ensure that the **Create a project directory within the solution directory.** checkbox has been selected.
11. Then, click on the **Create** button to save your project to the specified location.

Once your project has been created, you will be presented with the Xamarin development environment along with several project files that the template has created for you, as shown in the following screenshot:

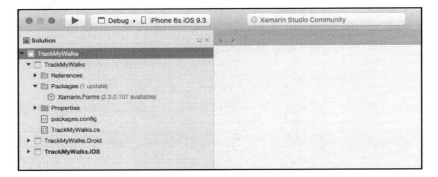

As you can see from the preceding screenshot, the TrackMyWalks solution has been divided into three main areas. The following table provides a brief description of what each area is used for:

Platform specific project	Description
TrackMyWalks	This is the **Portable Class Library** (**PCL**) project that will be responsible for acting as the main architectural layer for the TrackMyWalks solution. This project contains all of the business logic, data objects, Xamarin.FormsPages, views, and other non-platform specific code. Any code that you create within this project can be shared across multiple platform-specific projects.
TrackMyWalks.Droid	This project is an Android specific project that contains all of the code and assets required to build and deploy the Android app contained within the solution. By default, this project contains a reference to the TrackMyWalks Portable Class Library.
TrackMyWalks.iOS	This project is an iOS specific project that contains all of the code and assets required to build and deploy the iOS app contained within the solution. By default, this project contains a reference to the TrackMyWalks Portable Class Library.

One thing you will notice is that our solution contains a file called `TrackMyWalks.cs` which is part of the `TrackMyWalks` Portable Class Library. The `TrackMyWalks.cs` file contains a class named `App` that inherits from the `Xamarin.Forms.Application` class hierarchy, as can be seen in the following code snippet:

```
//
//   TrackMyWalks.cs
//   TrackMyWalks
//
//   Created by Steven F. Daniel on 04/08/2016.
//   Copyright © 2016 GENIESOFT STUDIOS. All rights reserved.
//
using Xamarin.Forms;

namespace TrackMyWalks
{
    public class App : Application
    {
        public App()
        {
// The root page of your application
            var content = new ContentPage
            {
                Title = "TrackMyWalks",
                  Content = new StackLayout {
                      VerticalOptions = LayoutOptions.Center,
                        Children = { new Label {
                            HorizontalTextAlignment =
                            TextAlignment.Center,
                            Text = "Welcome to Xamarin Forms!"
                        }
                    }
                }
            };

            MainPage = new NavigationPage(content);
        }

        protected override void OnStart()
        {
            // Handle when your app starts
        }
        protected override void OnSleep()
        {
            // Handle when your app sleeps
        }
        protected override void OnResume()
        {
```

```
                        // Handle when your app resumes
            }
        }
    }
```

The `App` constructor method sets up the `MainPage` property to a new instance of the `ContentPage` that will simply display some default text as created by the project wizard. Throughout this chapter, we will be building the initial user interface page views and then modifying the `MainPage` property for our `App` class, contained within the `TrackMyWalks.cs` file.

Updating the TrackMyWalks solution packages

In this section, we will take a look at how to update the `Xamarin.Forms` packages contained within our `TrackMyWalks` solution. Basically, you will notice that each project contained within our solution contains a `Packages` folder.

The `Xamarin.Forms` package is essentially a `NuGet` package that gets automatically included in our solution whenever we specify that we want to create a `Xamarin.FormsApp` project template.

From time to time, you will notice that Xamarin will notify you whenever a package is out of date and needs to be updated to ensure that you are running the latest version.

 A `NuGet` package, is essentially the package manager for the Microsoft Development Platform that contains the client tools that provide the capability for producing and consuming .NET packages.

Let's take a look at how to go about updating the NuGet packages within our TrackMyWalks solution to ensure that we are running the latest Xamarin.Forms packages. Perform the following steps:

1. Right-click on the TrackMyWalks solution and choose the **Update NuGet Packages** menu option, as shown in the following screenshot:

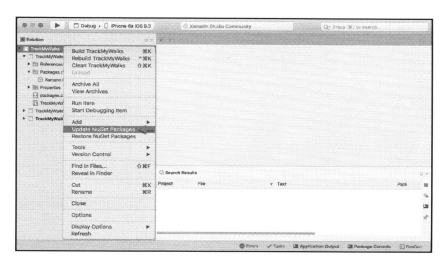

Once you have selected this option, Xamarin Studio will proceed to update each package that is contained within the TrackMyWalks solution for each of the platform-specific projects, and will display a progress indicator similar to the one shown in the following screenshot:

During the package update process, some packages that are contained as part of each platform-specific project require you to accept their license terms prior to installing, which is shown in the following screenshot:

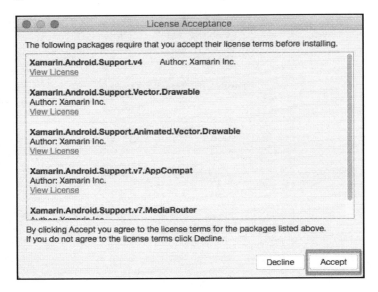

2. Click on the **Accept** button to accept the license terms and conditions for the packages displayed within the dialog box and to install the packages, as shown in the preceding screenshot.

Now that you have successfully updated the Xamarin.Forms packages within your solution, we can now proceed with building the user interface files for the TrackMyWalks solution.

Creating the TrackMyWalks model

In this section, we will proceed to create our **TrackMyWalks** model that will represent our walk entries. As we progress throughout this chapter, we will see how we can use this model to set up and initialize some walk entries for our main **WalksPage** using a ListView control so that we can display walk entry for each row within the ListView.

Let's take a look at how we can achieve this, by following the steps below:

1. Create a new folder within the `TrackMyWalks` Portable Class Library project solution, called `Models` as shown in the following screenshot:

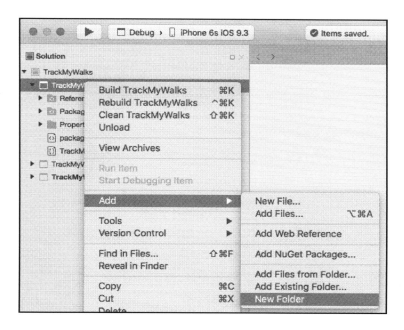

2. Next, create a new class file within the `Models` folder, as shown in the following screenshot:

3. Then, choose the **Empty Class** option under the **General** section and enter in `WalkEntries` for the name of the new class file to be created as shown in the following screenshot:

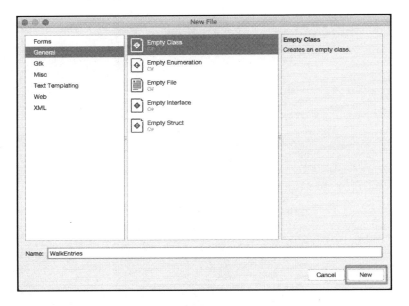

4. Next, click on the **New** button to allow the wizard to proceed and create the new file, as shown in the preceding screenshot.

Congratulations, you have created your first folder and C# class file for our solution. We can now proceed with adding the property descriptors that will be used to define our model.

5. Ensure that the `WalkEntries.cs` file is displayed, then locate the `WalkEntries` class constructor and enter the following highlighted code sections:

```
//
//  WalkEntries.cs
//  TrackMyWalks
//
//  Created by Steven F. Daniel on 04/08/2016.
//  Copyright © 2016 GENIESOFT STUDIOS. All rights reserved.
//

namespace TrackMyWalks.Models
{
    public class WalkEntries
```

```
        {
                public string Title { get; set; }
                public string Notes { get; set; }
                public double Longitude { get; set; }
                public double Latitude { get; set; }
                public double Kilometers { get; set; }
                public string Difficulty { get; set; }
                public double Distance { get; set; }
                public string ImageUrl { get; set; }
        }
}
```

In the preceding code snippet, we have successfully defined the model that will be used to represent our walk entries. In the next section, we will use this model to set up and initialize some walk entries for our main `WalksPage` using a `ListView` control, then use a `DataTemplate` to describe how the model data should be displayed for each row within the `ListView`.

Creating the walks main page

As mentioned in the previous section, the `WalksPage` will essentially serve as the main entry point for our application. We will use our `WalkEntries` model to populate some static walks information data, then display this information within a `ListView` control using a `DataTemplate`. So let's get started by following these steps:

1. Firstly, create a new folder within the `TrackMyWalks` Portable Class Library project solution called `Pages`, as you did in the previous section.
2. Next, from the **New File** screen, select the **Forms** section within the left section pane.
3. Then, select the **Forms ContentPage** option in the right pane.

4. Next, enter `WalksPage` for the name of the new class to be created.

5. Finally, click on the **New** button, as shown in the following screenshot:

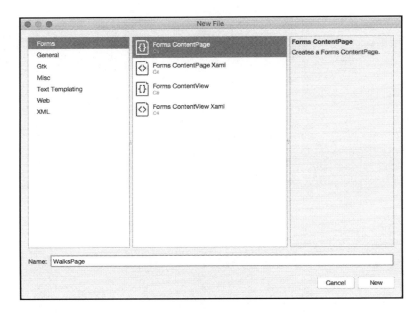

6. Next, ensure that the `WalksPage.cs` file is displayed within the code editor and enter in the following highlighted code sections.

```
//
// WalksPage.cs
// TrackMyWalks
//
// Created by Steven F. Daniel on 04/08/2016.
// Copyright © 2016 GENIESOFT STUDIOS. All rights reserved.
//
using System.Collections.Generic;
using Xamarin.Forms;
using TrackMyWalks.Models;

namespace TrackMyWalks
{
 public class WalksPage : ContentPage
 {
 public WalksPage()
 {
 var newWalkItem = new ToolbarItem
 {
```

```
Text = "Add Walk"
};
newWalkItem.Clicked += (sender, e) =>
{
 Navigation.PushAsync(new WalkEntryPage());
};

ToolbarItems.Add(newWalkItem);

var walkItems = new List<WalkEntries>
{
new WalkEntries {
Title = "10 Mile Brook Trail, Margaret River",
Notes = "The 10 Mile Brook Trail starts in the Rotary Park
near Old Kate, a preserved steam " +
 "engine at the northern edge of Margaret River. ",
Latitude = -33.9727604,
Longitude = 115.0861599,
Kilometers = 7.5,
Distance = 0,
Difficulty= "Medium",
ImageUrl = "http://trailswa.com.au/media/cache/media/
images/trails/_mid/FullSizeRender1_600_480_c1.jpg"
},
new WalkEntries {
Title = "Ancient Empire Walk, Valley of the Giants",
Notes = "The Ancient Empire is a 450 metre walk trail
that takes you around and through some of " +
 "the giant tingle trees including the most popular
of the gnarled veterans, known as Grandma Tingle.",
 Latitude = -34.9749188,
 Longitude = 117.3560796,
 Kilometers = 450,
 Distance = 0,
 Difficulty = "Hard",
 ImageUrl = "http://trailswa.com.au/media/cache/media/
images/trails/_mid/Ancient_Empire_534_480_c1.jpg"
 },
 };

 var itemTemplate = new DataTemplate(typeof(ImageCell));
 itemTemplate.SetBinding(TextCell.TextProperty, "Title");
 itemTemplate.SetBinding(TextCell.DetailProperty, "Notes");
 itemTemplate.SetBinding(ImageCell.ImageSourceProperty,
   "ImageUrl");

 var walksList = new ListView {
```

```
            HasUnevenRows = true,
            ItemTemplate = itemTemplate,
            ItemsSource = walkItems,
            SeparatorColor = Color.FromHex("#ddd"),
            };

    // Set up our event handler
    walksList.ItemTapped += (object sender,
    ItemTappedEventArgs e) =>
    {
    var item = (WalkEntries)e.Item;
    if (item == null) return;
    Navigation.PushAsync(new WalkTrailPage(item));
    item = null;
    };
    Content = walksList;
    }
    }
}
```

In the preceding code snippet, we began by declaring our `newWalkItem` variable that instantiates from the `ToolbarItem` class which will be used to attach a new **Add Walk** button to the main toolbar of the base `ContentPage.ToolbarItems` collection to provide a way for users to add new walk trail information within the app.

Next, we create an event for our new `WalkItem` using the `Clicked` event of the `ToolbarItem` class, which will be used to navigate to the new `WalksEntryPage`.

In our next step, we declare a new variable `walkItems` that is a collection of list items to store each of our walk entries within our model and then use the `DataTemplate` class to describe how we want our model data to be displayed within each of the rows declared within the `ListView`.

Finally, we set up an event handler for our `ListView` that will be used to move to the `WalksTrailPage` to display information about the item selected.

Creating the new walk entry content page

In this section, we will begin building the user interface for our new `WalkEntryPage`. This page is called when the user clicks on the **Add Walk** button from the main page and will be used to allow the user a means of adding new walk information to be used within the application.

There are a number of ways you can go about presenting this information to collect data. For the purpose of this app, we will be using a `TableView`, but you could quite easily use a `StackLayout` and present this information as a series of `Labels` and `EntryCells`.

Let's begin by creating the new `WalkEntryPage` by performing the following steps:

1. Create a new `ContentPage` called `WalkEntryPage`, as you did in the section entitled *Creating the walks main page*, located within this chapter.
2. Next, ensure that the `WalkEntryPage.cs` file is displayed within the code editor and enter in the following highlighted code sections:

```
//
// WalkEntryPage.cs
// TrackMyWalks
//
// Created by Steven F. Daniel on 04/08/2016.
// Copyright © 2016 GENIESOFT STUDIOS. All rights reserved.
//
using Xamarin.Forms;
using TrackMyWalks.Models;
using System.Collections.Generic;

namespace TrackMyWalks
{
 public class WalkEntryPage : ContentPage
 {
 public WalkEntryPage()
 {
 // Set the Content Page Title
 Title = "New Walk Entry";

 // Define our New Walk Entry fields
  var walkTitle = new EntryCell
 {
  Label = "Title:",
Placeholder = "Trail Title"
 };
var walkNotes = new EntryCell
```

```
{
Label = "Notes:",
Placeholder = "Description"
};
var walkLatitude = new EntryCell
{
Label = "Latitude:",
Placeholder = "Latitude",
Keyboard = Keyboard.Numeric
};
var walkLongitude = new EntryCell
{
Label = "Longitude:",
Placeholder = "Longitude",
Keyboard = Keyboard.Numeric
};
var walkKilometers = new EntryCell
{
Label = "Kilometers:",
Placeholder ="Kilometers",
Keyboard = Keyboard.Numeric
};
var walkDifficulty = new EntryCell
{
Label = "Difficulty Level:",
Placeholder ="Walk Difficulty"
};
var walkImageUrl = new EntryCell
{
Label = "ImageUrl:",
Placeholder ="Image URL"
};

// Define our TableView
Content = new TableView
{
Intent = TableIntent.Form,
Root = new TableRoot
{
new TableSection()
{
walkTitle,
walkNotes,
walkLatitude,
walkLongitude,
walkKilometers,
walkDifficulty,
walkImageUrl
```

```
    }
    }
  };
  var saveWalkItem = new ToolbarItem {
  Text = "Save"
  };
  saveWalkItem.Clicked += (sender, e) => {
  Navigation.PopToRootAsync(true);
  };

  ToolbarItems.Add(saveWalkItem);
    }
    }
}
```

In the preceding code snippet, we began by declaring a number of EntryCell labels for our user interface to capture information entered by the user for–Title, Notes, Latitude, Longitude, Kilometers, Difficulty and ImageURL. As you progress through this book, you will learn how to customize the look and feel of the EntryCells by creating a customized platform-specific picker for the Walk Difficulty and Kilometers.

Next, we define our TableView and add each of our EntryCell fields to the TableSection property of the TableView control. Each TableSection that is defined within a TableView consists of a heading and one or more ViewCells, which, in our case, are the EntryCell fields.

Finally, we declare and add a ToolbarItem called saveWalkItem to our ContentPageToolbarItems collection, then create an event that, when clicked, will save the walk information entered to the main walks page. Obviously, we will be refactoring the new WalkEntryPage throughout this book, which, when the **Save** button is pressed, will actually send this information to the server using a RESTful API and refresh the main TrackMyWalks page.

Creating the walk trail content page

In this section, we will begin building the user interface for our WalksTrailPage. This page is called when the user clicks on an entry within the ListView on our TrackMyWalks main content page and will be used to display information associated with the chosen trail:

1. Create a new ContentPage called WalkTrailPage as you did in the section entitled *Creating the walks main page,* located within this chapter.

2. Next, ensure that the WalkTrailPage.cs file is displayed within the code editor and enter the following highlighted code sections:

```csharp
//
// WalkTrailPage.cs
// TrackMyWalks
//
// Created by Steven F. Daniel on 04/08/2016.
// Copyright © 2016 GENIESOFT STUDIOS. All rights reserved.
//
using Xamarin.Forms;
using TrackMyWalks.Models;

namespace TrackMyWalks
{
 public class WalkTrailPage : ContentPage
 {
 public WalkTrailPage(WalkEntries walkItem)
 {
 Title = "Walks Trail";

 var beginTrailWalk = new Button
 {
 BackgroundColor = Color.FromHex("#008080"),
 TextColor = Color.White,
 Text = "Begin this Trail"
 };

 // Set up our event handler
 beginTrailWalk.Clicked += (sender, e) =>
 {
 if (walkItem == null) return;
 Navigation.PushAsync(new DistanceTravelledPage (walkItem));
 Navigation.RemovePage(this);
 walkItem = null;
 };
 var walkTrailImage = new Image()
 {
```

```
Aspect = Aspect.AspectFill,
Source = walkItem.ImageUrl
};

var trailNameLabel = new Label()
{
FontSize = 28,
FontAttributes = FontAttributes.Bold,
TextColor = Color.Black,
Text = walkItem.Title
};

var trailKilometersLabel = new Label()
{
FontAttributes = FontAttributes.Bold,
FontSize = 12,
TextColor = Color.Black,
Text = $"Length: { walkItem.Kilometers } km"
};

var trailDifficultyLabel = new Label()
{
FontAttributes = FontAttributes.Bold,
FontSize = 12,
TextColor = Color.Black,
Text = $"Difficulty: { walkItem.Difficulty } "
};

var trailFullDescription = new Label()
{
FontSize = 11,
TextColor = Color.Black,
Text = $"{ walkItem.Notes }",
HorizontalOptions = LayoutOptions.FillAndExpand
};

this.Content = new ScrollView
{
Padding = 10,
Content = new StackLayout
{
Orientation = StackOrientation.Vertical,
HorizontalOptions = LayoutOptions.FillAndExpand,
Children =
{
walkTrailImage,
trailNameLabel,
trailKilometersLabel,
```

```
                    trailDifficultyLabel,
                    trailFullDescription,
                    beginTrailWalk
                    }
                    }
                    };
                    }
                    }
                    }
```

In the preceding code snippet, we began by importing our `TrackMyWalks.Models` class as we will be using this to extract the information passed in from our `WalksPage`.

Next, we declare our `beginTrailWalk` variable that inherits from the `Button` class; then we set up the `Clicked` event of the `Button` class, which will be used to navigate to the `DistanceTravelledPage` content page when clicked to display information about our trail after removing our walks trail content page from the `NavigationPage` hierarchy.

In the next step, we declare an image variable `walkTrailImage` and set the `Source` property of the image to be the image of the selected `walkItem` from the `ListView`. We then declare and initialize a number of label objects that will contain the `walkItem` information that has been passed from the `WalksPage` content page `ListView` control and displayed.

Next, we define a `ScrollView` control that is part of the `Xamarin.Forms.Core` base class, then add each of our form `Image` and `Label` fields to the `StackLayout` control. The `ScrollView` control is a fantastic control that allows our `ContentPage` to scroll its contents should the information be too big to fit within the actual device's screen real estate.

Adding the Xamarin.Forms.Maps NuGet package

In this section, we will need to add the `Xamarin.Forms.Maps` NuGet package to our core project, as well as for each of the platform-specific projects for both iOS and Android platforms. This package is required in order to use the `Xamarin.FormsMap` control in the `DistanceTravelled` content page that we will be building in the next section.

1. Right-click on the `TrackMyWalks` solution and choose the **Add Packages...** menu option, as shown in the following screenshot:

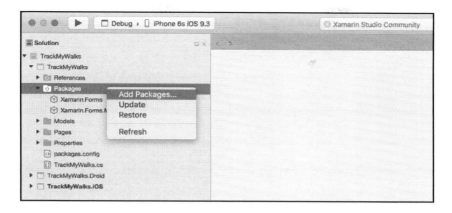

2. This will display the **Add Packages** dialog. Enter in maps within the **Search** dialog and then select and click the **Xamarin.Forms.Maps** option within the list, as shown in the following screenshot:

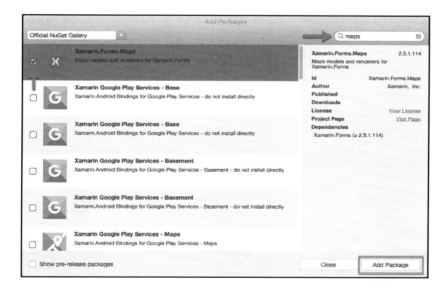

3. Finally, click on the **Add Package** button to add the `Xamarin.Forms.Maps` NuGet package to the `TrackMyWalks` core solution.

4. Repeat the same process to add the `Xamarin.Forms.Maps` NuGet package for both the iOS and Android projects that are contained within the `TrackMyWalks` solution.

Now that you have added the `NuGet` Package for the `Xamarin.Forms Map`, we can begin to utilize this control within the `DistanceTravelled` content page that we will be covering in the next section.

Creating the DistanceTravelledPage content page

In this section, we will begin building the user interface for our `DistanceTravelledPage` content page. This page is called when the user clicks on the **Begin this Trail** button from the `WalksTrailPage` content page, which will be used to display information about the chosen trail, as well as placing a pin placeholder within the `Xamarin.Forms.Maps` control and calculating the distance travelled, and time taken:

1. Create a new `ContentPage` called `DistanceTravelledPage` as you did in the previous section.

2. Next, ensure that the `DistanceTravelledPage.cs` file is displayed within the code editor and enter the following highlighted code sections:

```
//
//   DistanceTravelledPage.cs
//   TrackMyWalks
//
//   Created by Steven F. Daniel on 04/08/2016.
//   Copyright © 2016 GENIESOFT STUDIOS. All rights reserved.
//
using Xamarin.Forms;
using Xamarin.Forms.Maps;
using TrackMyWalks.Models;

namespace TrackMyWalks
{
    public class DistanceTravelledPage : ContentPage
    {
```

3. Then, update the `DistanceTravelledPage` method constructor to include the `walkItem` parameter for the chosen walk, as shown by the following highlighted code sections:

```
public DistanceTravelledPage(WalkEntries walkItem)
{
    Title = "Distance Travelled";
```

4. Next, we declare a `trailMap` variable that will point to an instance of the `Xamarin.Forms.Maps` control to create a placeholder pin marker within the map control. Using the latitude and longitude coordinates, enter the following highlighted code sections:

```
// Instantiate our map object
var trailMap = new Map();
// Place a pin on the map for the chosen walk type
trailMap.Pins.Add(new Pin
{
    Type = PinType.Place,
    Label = walkItem.Title,
    Position = new Position(walkItem.Latitude, walkItem.Longitude)
});
// Center the map around the list of walks entry's location
trailMap.MoveToRegion(MapSpan.FromCenterAndRadius(new
  Position(walkItem.Latitude, walkItem.Longitude),
  Distance.FromKilometers(1.0)));
```

5. Then, we declare a number of `Label` objects that contain our `walkItem` information, which has been passed from the `WalkTrailPage` content page so that we can trail related information. Enter in the following highlighted code sections:

```
var trailNameLabel = new Label()
{
    FontSize = 18,
    FontAttributes = FontAttributes.Bold,
    TextColor = Color.Black,
    Text = walkItem.Title
};
var trailDistanceTravelledLabel = new Label()
{
    FontAttributes = FontAttributes.Bold,
    FontSize = 20,
    TextColor = Color.Black,
    Text = "Distance Travelled",
    HorizontalTextAlignment = TextAlignment.Center
```

```
    };
    var totalDistanceTaken = new Label()
    {
        FontAttributes = FontAttributes.Bold,
        FontSize = 20,
        TextColor = Color.Black,
        Text = $"{ walkItem.Distance } km",
        HorizontalTextAlignment = TextAlignment.Center
    };
    var totalTimeTakenLabel = new Label()
    {
        FontAttributes = FontAttributes.Bold,
        FontSize = 20,
        TextColor = Color.Black,
        Text = "Time Taken:",
        HorizontalTextAlignment = TextAlignment.Center
    };
    var totalTimeTaken = new Label()
    {
        FontAttributes = FontAttributes.Bold,
        FontSize = 20,
        TextColor = Color.Black,
        Text = "0h 0m 0s",
        HorizontalTextAlignment = TextAlignment.Center
    };
```

6. Next, we declare our `walksHomeButton` variable that inherits from the Button class and proceed to set up our click handler, which will be used to navigate our app to the main `WalksPage` content page when clicked. Enter the following highlighted code sections:

```
var walksHomeButton = new Button
{
    BackgroundColor = Color.FromHex("#008080"),
    TextColor = Color.White,
    Text = "End this Trail"
};
 // Set up our event handler
 walksHomeButton.Clicked += (sender, e) =>
 {
     if (walkItem == null) return;
     Navigation.PopToRootAsync(true);
     walkItem = null;
 };
```

7. Then, we define a `ScrollView` control that is part of the `Xamarin.Forms.Core` base class and proceed to add each of our form `Button` and `Label` fields to the `StackLayout` control. Enter the following highlighted code sections:

```
this.Content = new ScrollView
{
    Padding = 10,
    Content = new StackLayout
    {
        Orientation = StackOrientation.Vertical,
        HorizontalOptions = LayoutOptions.FillAndExpand,
        Children = {
            trailMap,
            trailNameLabel,
            trailDistanceTravelledLabel,
            totalDistanceTaken,
            totalTimeTakenLabel,
            totalTimeTaken,
            walksHomeButton
        }
    }
    };
    }
    }
}
```

In the preceding code snippet, we began by importing our `TrackMyWalks.Models` class as we will be using this to extract the information passed in from our `WalksPage`. The `Xamarin.Forms.Maps` NuGet package is a cross-platform library that allows developers to display and annotate information within the map. We will be using this control to create a pin placeholder within the map control, along with additional details associated with the trail.

Next, we declare our `trailMap` variable that points to an instance of the `Xamarin.Forms.Maps` control and create a placeholder pin marker within the map containing the details for the chosen trail, then center in on the map to show the area for our walks location, derived by the `latitude` and `longitude` coordinates. We then declare and initialize a number of `Label` objects that contain the `walkItem` information that has been passed from the `WalkTrailPage` content page and declare our `walksHomeButton` variable that inherits from the `Button` class, then set up the `Clicked` event for the `Button` class, which will be used to navigate back to the `TrackMyWalks` when clicked.

Finally, we define a `ScrollView` control that is part of the `Xamarin.Forms.Core` base class, then add each of our form `Button` and `Label` fields to the `StackLayout` control.

In our next section, we will need to initialize the `Xamarin.Forms.Maps` NuGet package library within each of our platform-specific start up classes (for example, `AppDelegate.cs` for iOS and `MainActivity.cs` for Android). Let's take a look at how we can achieve this by following the steps below.

1. Ensure that the `AppDelegate.cs` file is displayed within the code editor and enter the following highlighted code sections:

```
//
// AppDelegate.cs
// TrackMyWalks
//
// Created by Steven F. Daniel on 04/08/2016.
// Copyright © 2016 GENIESOFT STUDIOS. All rights reserved.
//
using Foundation;
using UIKit;

namespace TrackMyWalks.iOS
{
    [Register("AppDelegate")]
    public partial class AppDelegate :
global::Xamarin.Forms.Platform.iOS.FormsApplicationDelegate
    {
        public override bool FinishedLaunching(UIApplication app,
NSDictionary options)
        {
            global::Xamarin.Forms.Forms.Init();
            Xamarin.FormsMaps.Init();
            LoadApplication(new App());
            return base.FinishedLaunching(app, options);
        }
    }
}
```

In the preceding code snippet, we began by initializing our `AppDelegate` class to use the `Xamarin.Forms.Maps` library, by adding the `Xamarin.FormsMaps.Init` which initializes the `Xamarin.Forms` platform, so that our `TrackMyWalks` solution can use the maps. If this is omitted from this class, the `DistanceTravelledPage` content page will not display the map and will not work as expected.

For more information on Xamarin.Forms.Maps library, as well as the various types of different classes available, please refer to the Xamarin developer documentation at https://developer.xamarin.com/api/name space/Xamarin.Forms.Maps/.

Creating the Splash screen content page

In this section, we will begin building the user interface for our Splash page which will only be used for the Android platform, since iOS already contains a method of achieving this. The splash page will simply display the default Xamarin icon, but as we progress throughout this book, we will be refactoring this page to include a more suitable image for our app:

1. Create a new ContentPage called SplashPage as you did in the previous section.

2. Next, ensure that the SplashPage.cs file is displayed within the code editor and enter the following highlighted code sections:

```
//
//    SplashPage.cs
//    TrackMyWalks
//
//    Created by Steven F. Daniel on 04/08/2016.
//    Copyright © 2016 GENIESOFT STUDIOS. All rights reserved.
//
using System;
using System.Threading.Tasks;
using Xamarin.Forms;

namespace TrackMyWalks
{
    public class SplashPage : ContentPage
    {
```

3. Then, locate the SplashPage constructor method and enter the following highlighted code sections:

```
public SplashPage()
{
    AbsoluteLayout splashLayout = new AbsoluteLayout
    {
    HeightRequest = 600
    };
```

```
      var image = new Image()
  {
    Source = ImageSource.FromFile("icon.png"),
    Aspect = Aspect.AspectFill,
  };

  AbsoluteLayout.SetLayoutFlags(image, AbsoluteLayoutFlags.All);
  AbsoluteLayout.SetLayoutBounds(image, new Rectangle(0f, 0f,
    1f, 1f));

  splashLayout.Children.Add(image);

  Content = new StackLayout()
  {
    Children = { splashLayout }
  };
  }
```

4. Next, locate the OnAppearing method and enter the following highlighted code sections:

```
  protected override async void OnAppearing()
  {
    base.OnAppearing();

  // Delay for a few seconds on the splash screen
  await Task.Delay(3000);

  // Instantiate a NavigationPage with the MainPage
  var navPage = new NavigationPage(new WalksPage()
  {
    Title = "Track My Walks"
  });
    Application.Current.MainPage = navPage;
    }
  }
  }
```

In the preceding code snippet, we began by importing our System.Threading.Tasks class. This class will be used to perform a slight delay to allow our user to see the splash screen, as defined within the OnAppearing class method.

We then create a `splashLayout` variable of type `AbsoluteLayout` that will be used to position and size each of the child elements proportionally within our view, and then set the `HeightRequest` property.

Next, we declare an `image` variable that inherits from the `Image` class; then assign the `Source` property to the image that we would like to use and set the images `Aspect` property so that the image fills the view.

In our final steps, we define values for both of the `LayoutFlags` and `LayoutBounds` properties on the `AbsoluteLayout` class so that the image resizes within the view. Then we add our `splashLayout` to the content page using the `StackLayout` control. Finally, we override the `OnAppearing` class method of the `Xamarin.Forms.Page` page life cycle, which gets called immediately prior to the page becoming visible on the screen, and then specify a delay of three seconds prior to instantiating a new instance of the `NavigationPage`, which will call our `WalksPage` to be the main content root page.

Updating the Xamarin.Forms App class

In this section, we need to initialize the `App` class of `Xamarin.Forms` library to call our `SplashPage` and set the root page for our application if the detected OS device is Android. Let's take a look at how we can achieve this:

1. Open the `TrackMyWalks.cs` located within the `TrackMyWalks` group and ensure that it is displayed within the code editor.
2. Next, locate the `App` method and enter the following highlighted code sections, as shown in the following code snippet:

```
//
//   TrackMyWalks.cs
//   TrackMyWalks
//
//   Created by Steven F. Daniel on 04/08/2016.
//   Copyright ©2016 GENIESOFT STUDIOS. All rights reserved.
//
using Xamarin.Forms;

namespace TrackMyWalks
{
    public class App : Application
    {
        public App()
        {
            // Check the Target OS Platform
```

```
if (Device.OS == TargetPlatform.Android)
{
    MainPage = new SplashPage();
}
else
{
    // The root page of your application
    var navPage = new NavigationPage(new TrackMyWalks.
     WalksPage()
     {
         Title = "Track My Walks"
     });
    MainPage = navPage;
}
        }
    }
}
```

In the preceding code snippet, we began checking the `Device.OS` class to determine what OS `Xamarin.Forms` is running on, then used the `TargetPlatform` class to determine whether our app is being run on Google'sAndroid OS platform. If our app is running on Android, we set the `App` constructor methods `MainPage` to a new instance of the `ContentPage` that will simply use the `SplashPage` as the root page. Alternatively, we create a new instance of the `NavigationPage` class and set this to our `WalksPage` to be the main content root page for our `ContentPage`.

Differences between Xamarin Studio and Visual Studio

When developing cross-platform mobile apps, you currently have a choice of using either Xamarin Studio or Microsoft's Visual Studio development environments. It is worth noting that, although the screenshots and example code used throughout this book have been developed using Xamarin Studio running on an Apple Macintosh computer, the code should compile fine on a Windows machine running Microsoft Visual Studio 2015.

However, there are some differences that you need to be aware of before embarking on the journey of building your mobile development solutions. If you are running Xamarin Studio on a Windows machine, you will get an Android project solution whenever you create a new Xamarin.Forms solution.

If you want to integrate and develop apps for Windows Phone, you will need to ensure that you are running Microsoft Visual Studio on a Windows machine. When developing apps for iOS applications, you will need to prepare your Mac to be the Xamarin build host by firstly enabling **Remote Login** on your Mac within the **System Preferences** section, and then selecting the Mac to be the build host from within the Microsoft Visual Studio environment on your Windows machine.

 For more information on how to prepare your Mac to be the Xamarin build host, refer to the Xamarin developer documentation at https://dev eloper.xamarin.com/guides/ios/getting_started/installation/win dows/connecting-to-mac/.

Now that you have an understanding of the differences between Xamarin Studio and Microsoft Visual Studio, our next step is to compile, build and run the TrackMyWalks application within the iOS simulator.

Running the TrackMyWalks app using the simulator

In this section, we will take a look at how to compile and run the TrackMyWalks application. You have the option of choosing to run your application using an actual device, or choosing from a list of simulators available for an iOS device.

The version number of the simulator is dependent on the version of the iOS SDK that is installed on your computer. Perform the following steps:

1. To run the app, choose your preferred device from the list of available iOS simulators and select the **Run** menu option, as shown in the following screenshot:

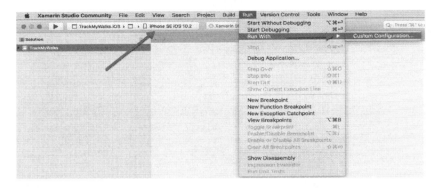

2. Next, choose the **Run With** sub-menu item, and then choose the **Custom Configuration...** then click on the **Run** button from the **Custom Parameters** dialog, as shown in the following screenshot:

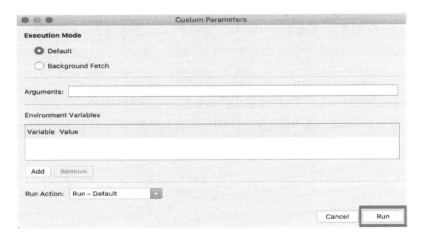

3. Alternatively, you can also build and run the `TrackMyWalks` application by pressing Command + Return key combinations.

When the compilation is complete, the iOS simulator will appear automatically and the `TrackMyWalks` application will be displayed, as shown in the following screenshot:

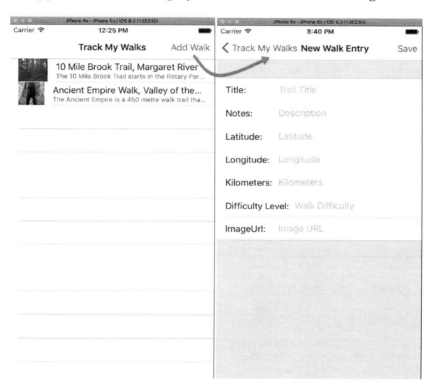

As you can see from the preceding screenshot, this currently displays a list of static walk trail entries, that are displayed within our `ListView`. When the user clicks on the **Add Walk** button link, this will display the new `WalkEntry` content page, so they can begin entering new Walk trail information.

Currently, this page doesn't save entered information, but as we progress throughout this book, we will be refactoring these pages to allow for this to happen. Upon clicking the **Save** button, the user will be redirected back to the main **Track My Walks** page.

The preceding screenshot shows you the navigation flow between each of the pages when a trail has been selected from the list, with the final screen showing the distance travelled page along with the placeholder pin marker showing the trail location within the map view.

Congratulations, you have successfully built the foundation for the `TrackMyWalks` application, as well as the user interface for each of the content pages that will be used by our app. As we progress through this book, we will be enhancing our app to include better architectural design patterns, nicer looking user interface elements, as well as real-time data being synchronized through the use of RESTful web service APIs.

Summary

In this chapter we explored how to go about creating a `Xamarin.Forms` cross-platform application for both iOS and Android platforms. We then moved on to building a series of content pages with static data.

Next, we looked at how to use the default `Xamarin.Forms` navigation APIs to help move between each of the content pages, which we will refactor quite a bit when we cover this in `Chapter 3`, *Navigating within the MVVM Model – The Xamarin.Forms Way* to use a more flexible, customized navigation service. Finally, we talked about some of the differences between using Xamarin Studio and Microsoft Visual Studio for development, before running our `TrackMyWalks` app within the simulator.

In the next chapter, you will learn about the concepts behind the **Model-View-View-Model** (**MVVM**) pattern architecture, how to implement the MVVM model within your application, and the process of how to add new ViewModels to your Xamarin solution.

2
MVVM and Data Binding

In the previous chapter, we explored how to go about creating a native `Xamarin.Forms` cross-platform application for both the iOS and Android platforms, and learned how to add new packages to your solution using the NuGet package manager. We also looked at how to go about adding and creating several ContentPages to your solution, as well as how to run and test your app within the simulator.

The Model-View-View Model (MVVM) architectural pattern was invented with the Extensible Application Markup Language (XAML) in mind that was created by Microsoft back in 2008 and is particularly well suited for use with the MVVM application architectural pattern, because it enforces a separation of the XAML user interface from the underlying data model through a class that will act as a connection between both the View and the Model. The View and the ViewModel can then be connected through data bindings that have been defined within the XAML file.

XAML has also been integrated into the `Xamarin.Forms` platform that allows for the creation of cross-platform, natively-based programming interfaces for iOS, Android, and Windows Phone mobile devices. This allows developers to define user interfaces using all the `Xamarin.Forms` views, layouts, and pages, as well as custom classes.

XAML enforces the separation between the application's user interface from the underlying data, through a class that will act as the communication layer between the View and the ViewModel, which are connected through data-bindings that are defined in either the XAML or underlying code file, along with the binding context for the View, that points to an instance of the ViewModel.

This chapter will begin by introducing you to the architecture behind the MVVM pattern architecture, and how you can implement these within your application, by adding new Views and the associated Models.

You'll learn how to create the underlying C# class files that will act as the ViewModels for our app, as well as updating the existing content pages to data-bind with the ViewModels to represent the information that will be displayed within the user-interface for our application.

This chapter will cover the following points:

- Understanding the MVVM pattern architecture and data-binding
- Implementing the MVVM base model within the `TrackMyWalks` solution
- Implementing the MVVM ViewModels within the app
- Implementing the MVVM data-bindings to our user interface pages

Understanding the MVVM pattern architecture

In this section we will be taking a look at the MVVM pattern architecture and the communication between the components that make up the architecture.

The MVVM design pattern is designed to control the separation between the user interfaces (views), the ViewModels that contain the actual binding to the **Model,** and the models that contain the actual structure of the entities representing information stored on a database or from a web service.

The following screenshot shows the communication between each of the components contained within the MVVM design pattern architecture:

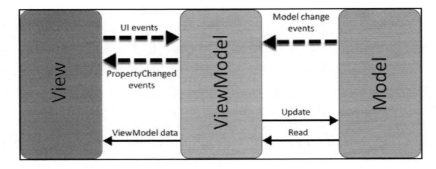

pattern is divided into three main areas, as you can see from the ...ot, and these are explained in the following table:

	escription
	The **Model** is basically a representation of business related entities used by an application, and is responsible for fetching data from either a database, or web service, and then de-serialized to the entities contained within the **Model**.
	The **View** component of the MVVM model basically represents the actual screens that make up the application, along with any custom control components, and control elements, such as buttons, labels, and text fields. The views contained within the MVVM pattern are platform-specific and are dependent on the platform APIs that are used to render the information that is contained within the application's user interface.
ViewModel	The **ViewModel** essentially controls, and manipulates the views by acting as their main data context. The **ViewModel** contains a series of properties that are bound to the information contained within each **Model**. Those properties are then bound to each of the views to represent this information within the user interface. ViewModels can also contain command objects that provide action-based events that can trigger the execution of event methods that occur within the **View**. For example, when the user taps on a toolbar item, or a button. ViewModels generally implement the `INotifyPropertyChanged` and `INotifyCollectionChanged` interfaces. Such a class fires a `PropertyChanged` and `INotifyCollectionChanged` event whenever a collection has changed (such as, adding an item, removing an item, or when a change occurs to one of the items, properties) changes. The data binding mechanism in `Xamarin.Forms` attaches a handler to this `PropertyChanged` and `CollectionChanged` events so it can be notified when a property changes and keep the target updated with the new value.

Now that you have a good understanding of the components that are contained within MVVM design pattern architecture, we can begin to create our entity models and update our user interface files.

In `Xamarin.Forms`, the term View is used to describe form controls, such as buttons and labels, and uses the term **Page** to describe the user interface or screen. Whereas, in MVVM, Views are used to describe the user interface, or screen.

Implementing the MVVM ViewModels within your app

In this section, we will begin by setting up the basic structure for our `TrackMyWalks` solution to include the folder that will be used to represent our ViewModels. Let's take a look at the following steps to achieve this:

1. Launch the Xamarin Studio application and ensure that the `TrackMyWalks` solution is loaded within the Xamarin Studio IDE.

2. Next, create a new folder within the `TrackMyWalks` PCL project, called `ViewModels` as shown in the following screenshot:

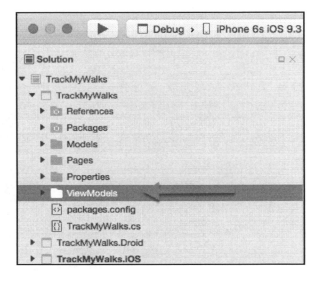

Creating the WalkBaseViewModel for the TrackMyWalks app

In this section, we will begin by creating a base MVVM ViewModel that will be used by each of our ViewModels when we create these, the Views (pages) will then implement those ViewModels and use them as their `BindingContext`.

 We will start by creating a base ViewModel class that will essentially be an **abstract** class, containing basic functionality that each of our ViewModels will inherit from, and will implement the `INotifyPropertyChanged` Interface.

Let's take a look at how we can achieve this, by following these steps:

1. Create an empty class within the `ViewModels` folder, shown in the following screenshot:

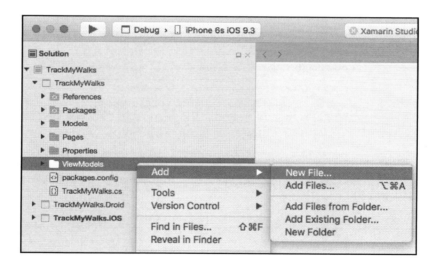

2. Next, choose the **Empty Class** option located within the **General** section, and enter in `WalkBaseViewModel` for the name of the new class file to be created, as shown in the following screenshot:

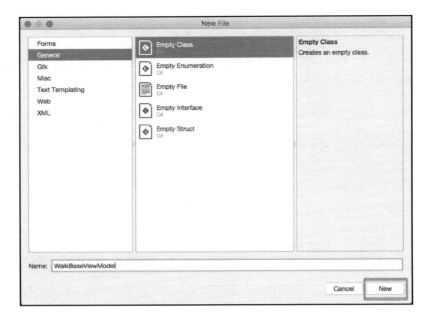

3. Next, click on the **New** button to allow the wizard to proceed and create the new empty class file, as shown in the preceding screenshot.

Up until this point, all we have done is create our `WalkBaseViewModel` class file. This abstract class will act as the base ViewModel class that will contain the basic functionality that each of our ViewModels will inherit from.

As we start to build the base class, you will see that it contains a couple of members and it will implement the `INotifyPropertyChangedInterface`. As we progress through this book, we will build to this class, which will be used by the `TrackMyWalks` application. To proceed with creating the base ViewModel class, perform the following step as shown:

4. Ensure that the `WalkBaseViewModel.cs` file is displayed within the code editor, and enter in the following code snippet:

```
//
// WalkBaseViewModel.cs
// TrackMyWalks Base ViewModel
```

```
//
// Created by Steven F. Daniel on 22/08/2016.
// Copyright © 2016 GENIESOFT STUDIOS. All rights reserved.
//
using System.ComponentModel;
using System.Runtime.CompilerServices;

namespace TrackMyWalks.ViewModels
{
 public abstract class WalkBaseViewModel :
   INotifyPropertyChanged
 {
 protected WalkBaseViewModel()
 {
 }

 public event PropertyChangedEventHandler PropertyChanged;

 protected virtual void OnPropertyChanged
   ([CallerMemberName] string propertyName = null)
 {
 var handler = PropertyChanged;
 if (handler != null)
 {
 handler(this, new PropertyChangedEventArgs(propertyName));
 }
 }
 }
}
```

In the preceding code snippet, we begin by creating a new `abstract` class for our `WalkBaseViewModel` that implements from the `INotifyPropertyChanged` interface class, which allows the View or page to be notified whenever properties contained within the ViewModel have changed. Next, we declare a variable `PropertyChanged` that inherits from the `PropertyChangedEventHandler` that will be used to indicate whenever properties on the object have changed. Finally, within the `OnPropertyChanged` method, this will be called when it has determined that a change has occurred on a property within the ViewModel from a child class.

The `INotifyPropertyChanged` interface is used to notify clients, typically binding clients, when the value of a property has changed.

Implementing the WalksPageViewModel

In the previous section, we built our base class ViewModel for our `TrackMyWalks` application. This will act as the main class that will allow our View or pages to be notified whenever changes to properties within the ViewModel have been made.

In this section, we will need to begin building the ViewModel for our `WalksPage`. This model will be used to store the `WalkEntries`, which will later be used and displayed within the `ListView` on the `WalksPage` content page.

Let's take a look at how we can achieve this by following these steps:

1. First, create a new class file within the `ViewModels` folder called `WalksPageViewModel`, as you did in the previous section, entitled *Creating the WalkBaseViewModel* located within this chapter.

2. Next, ensure that the `WalksPageViewModel.cs` file is displayed within the code editor, and enter in the following code snippet:

```
//
//  WalksPageViewModel.cs
//  TrackMyWalks ViewModels
//
//  Created by Steven F. Daniel on 22/08/2016.
//  Copyright © 2016 GENIESOFT STUDIOS. All rights reserved.
//
using System.Collections.ObjectModel;
using TrackMyWalks.Models;

namespace TrackMyWalks.ViewModels
{
    public class WalksPageViewModel : WalkBaseViewModel
    {
        ObservableCollection<WalkEntries> _walkEntries;

        public ObservableCollection<WalkEntries> walkEntries
        {
            get { return _walkEntries; }
            set { _walkEntries = value;
              OnPropertyChanged();
            }
        }
    }
```

In the preceding code snippet, we begin by ensuring that our ViewModel inherits from the `WalkBaseViewModel` class. Next, we create an `ObservableCollection` variable `_walkEntries` which is very useful when you want to know when the collection has changed, and an event is triggered that will tell the user what entries have been added or removed from the `WalkEntries` model.

In our next step, we create the `ObservableCollection` constructor `WalkEntries`, that is defined within the `System.Collections.ObjectModel` class, and accepts a `List` parameter containing our `WalkEntries` model. The `WalkEntries` property will be used to bind to the `ItemSource` property of the `ListView` within the `WalksMainPage`. Finally, we define the getter (`get`) and setter (`set`) methods that will return and set the content of our `_walkEntries` when it has been determined whether a property has been modified or not.

3. Next, locate the `WalksPageViewModel` class constructor, and enter the following highlighted code sections:

```
public WalksPageViewModel()
{
walkEntries = new ObservableCollection<WalkEntries>() {
new WalkEntries {
Title = "10 Mile Brook Trail, Margaret River",
Notes = "The 10 Mile Brook Trail starts in the
 Rotary Park near Old Kate, a preserved steam " +
 "engine at the northern edge of Margaret River. ",
Latitude = -33.9727604,
Longitude = 115.0861599,
Kilometers = 7.5,
Distance = 0,
Difficulty = "Medium",
ImageUrl = "http://trailswa.com.au/media/
 cache/media/images/trails/_mid/" +
  "FullSizeRender1_600_480_c1.jpg"
},
new WalkEntries {
Title = "Ancient Empire Walk, Valley of the Giants",
Notes = "The Ancient Empire is a 450 metre walk trail
that takes you around and through some of " +
"the giant tingle trees including the most popular of
 the gnarled veterans, known as " + "Grandma Tingle.",
Latitude = -34.9749188,
Longitude = 117.3560796,
Kilometers = 450,
Distance = 0,
Difficulty = "Hard",
```

```
        ImageUrl = "http://trailswa.com.au/media/cache/media/
         images/trails/_mid/" + "Ancient_Empire_534_480_c1.jpg"
        },
        };
        }
      }
}
```

In the preceding code snippet, we began by creating a new `ObservableCollection` for our `walkEntries` method and then added each of the walk list items that we would like to store within our Model. As each item is added, the `ObservableCollection`, constructor is called, and the setter (`set`) method is invoked to add the item, then the `INotifyPropertyChanged` event will be triggered to notify that a change has occurred.

Updating the walks main page to use the MVVM model

Now that we have created the MVVM ViewModel that will be used for our main `WalksPage`, we need to modify the Walks main page. In this section, we will be taking a look at how to bind the `WalksPageBindingContext` to the `WalksPageViewModel` so that the walk entry details can be displayed.

Let's take a look at how we can achieve this, by following these steps:

1. Ensure that the `WalksPage.cs` file is displayed within the code editor, and enter in the following highlighted code sections:

```
//
//  WalksPage.cs
//  TrackMyWalks
//
//  Created by Steven F. Daniel on 04/08/2016.
//  Copyright © 2016 GENIESOFT STUDIOS. All rights reserved.
//
using System.Collections.Generic;
using Xamarin.Forms;
using TrackMyWalks.Models;
using TrackMyWalks.ViewModels;

namespace TrackMyWalks
{
    public class WalksPage : ContentPage
```

```
    {
        public WalksPage()
        {
            var newWalkItem = new ToolbarItem
            {
                Text = "Add Walk"
            };

            // Set up our click event handler
            newWalkItem.Clicked += (sender, e) =>
            {
                Navigation.PushAsync(new WalkEntryPage());
            };

            // Add the ToolBar item to our ToolBar
            ToolbarItems.Add(newWalkItem);
```

2. Next, we need to declare and create a new `BindingContext` instance for the `WalksPage`, and set this to a new instance of the `WalksPageViewModel` so that it knows where to get the `WalkEntries` so that we can populate these within the `ListView`. Proceed and enter in the following highlighted code sections:

```
// Declare and initialize our Model Binding Context
BindingContext = new WalksPageViewModel();

// Define our Item Template
var itemTemplate = new DataTemplate(typeof(ImageCell));
itemTemplate.SetBinding(TextCell.TextProperty, "Title");
itemTemplate.SetBinding(TextCell.DetailProperty, "Notes");
itemTemplate.SetBinding(ImageCell.ImageSourceProperty,
    "ImageUrl");
```

3. Then, change the way in which our `ListView` gets the `WalkEntries` variable items, by updating the `ListView` class and setting the binding property for the walk entries, by initializing the `ItemsView<Cell>.ItemsSourceProperty` property and using the `SetBinding` method to bind the contents. Proceed and enter in the following highlighted code sections:

```
var walksList = new ListView
{ HasUnevenRows = true,
  ItemTemplate = itemTemplate,
  SeparatorColor = Color.FromHex("#ddd"),
};
// Set the Binding property for our walks Entries
walksList.SetBinding(ItemsView<Cell>.ItemsSourceProperty,
  "walkEntries");
```

```
        // Initialize our event Handler to use when the item is tapped
        walksList.ItemTapped += (object sender, ItemTappedEventArgs e) =>
        {
             var item = (WalkEntries)e.Item;
             if (item == null) return;
             Navigation.PushAsync(new WalkTrailPage(item));
             item = null;
        };
        Content = walksList;
        }
    }
}
```

In this section, we looked at the steps involved in modifying our `WalksPage` so that it can take advantage of our `WalksPageViewModel`. We looked at how to set our content page to an instance of our `WalksPageViewModel` so that it knows where to get the list of walk entries to be used and displayed within the `ListView` control. The `SetBinding` property creates and applies a binding to a specific property. As you can see, by using ViewModels within your application, you can see that the result is both clean and elegant, and makes your code a lot more readable when supporting code modifications.

Implementing the walks entry page ViewModel

We have created the ViewModel that will be used by our `WalksPage` so that the walk entries can be displayed within the `ListView` control. The next step is to build the ViewModel that will be used to create new walk entries and have this information saved back to our `WalkBaseViewModel`, which we will be covering in a later chapter as we progress through this book.

In this section, we will be taking a look at the steps required to create the ViewModel for our `WalksEntryViewModel` so that we can initialize, and capture information entered within this screen.

Let's take a look at how we can achieve this, by following these steps:

1. Create a new class file within the `ViewModels` folder called `WalksEntryViewModel`, as you did in the previous section, entitled *Creating the WalkBaseViewModel* located within this chapter.

2. Next, ensure that the `WalksEntryViewModel.cs` file is displayed within the code editor, and enter in the following code snippet.

```
//
//   WalkEntryViewModel.cs
//   TrackMyWalks ViewModels
//
//   Created by Steven F. Daniel on 22/08/2016.
//   Copyright © 2016 GENIESOFT STUDIOS. All rights reserved.
//
using TrackMyWalks.Models;
using TrackMyWalks.ViewModels;
using Xamarin.Forms;

namespace TrackMyWalks.ViewModels
{
    public class WalkEntryViewModel : WalkBaseViewModel
    {
```

3. Then, create the following `Title` property and its associated getters and setter qualifiers. The `OnPropertyChanged` method, as we mentioned previously, will be called when our property determines that the contents have been changed. A call is made to the `SaveCommand.ChangeCanExecute` method that will validate the form fields, and then determine whether the `SaveToolBarItem` should be enabled or not to allow the user to save the walk entry details. Proceed and enter in the following code snippet:

```
string _title;
public string Title
{
    get { return _title; }
    set
    {
        _title = value;
        OnPropertyChanged();
        SaveCommand.ChangeCanExecute();
    }
}
```

4. Next, create the remaining ViewModel properties and the associated getters and setter qualifiers that will be used to bind the values entered on the `WalkEntryPage`, as shown in the following code snippets:

```
string _notes;
public string Notes
{
    get { return _notes; }
    set
    {
```

```
            _notes = value;
            OnPropertyChanged();
        }
    }

    double _latitude;
    public double Latitude
    {
        get { return _latitude; }
        set
        {
            _latitude = value;
            OnPropertyChanged();
        }
    }

    double _longitude;
    public double Longitude
    {
        get { return _longitude; }
        set
        {
            _longitude = value;
            OnPropertyChanged();
        }
    }

    double _kilometers;
    public double Kilometers
    {
        get { return _kilometers; }
        set
        {
            _kilometers = value;
            OnPropertyChanged();
        }
    }

    string _difficulty;
    public string Difficulty
    {
        get { return _difficulty; }
        set
        {
            _difficulty = value;
            OnPropertyChanged();
        }
    }
```

```
double _distance;
public double Distance
{
    get { return _distance; }
    set
    {
        _distance = value;
        OnPropertyChanged();
    }
}

string _imageUrl;
public string ImageUrl
{
    get { return _imageUrl; }
    set
    {
        _imageUrl = value;
        OnPropertyChanged();
    }
}
```

5. Next, we need to initialize our ViewModel class constructor with default values for our `Title`, `Difficulty` and `Distance` properties. Locate the `WalkEntryViewModel` class constructor, and enter the following highlighted code sections:

```
public WalkEntryViewModel()
{
    Title = "New Walk";
    Difficulty = "Easy";
    Distance = 1.0;
}
```

6. Then, we need to create a `Command` property for our class. This will be used within our `WalkEntryPage` and will be used to bind to the `SaveToolBarItem`. The `Command` property will run an action upon being pressed, then execute a class instance method to determine whether the command can be executed. Proceed and enter the following highlighted code sections:

```
Command _saveCommand;
public Command SaveCommand
{
    get
    {
        return _saveCommand ?? (_saveCommand = new
```

```
        Command(ExecuteSaveCommand, ValidateFormDetails));
    }
}
```

7. Next, we need to create the `ExecuteSaveCommand` instance method. This will be used to store the walk information that we enter, which will be written to each of the properties as defined within the `WalkEntries` model. The saving portion will not be covered in this chapter, as this will be covered in a later chapter. For now, proceed and enter in the following highlighted code sections:

```
void ExecuteSaveCommand()
{
    var newWalkItem = new WalkEntries
    {
        Title = this.Title,
        Notes = this.Notes,
        Latitude = this.Latitude,
        Longitude = this.Longitude,
        Kilometers = this.Kilometers,
        Difficulty = this.Difficulty,
        Distance = this.Distance,
        ImageUrl = this.ImageUrl
    };
    // Here, we will save the details entered in a later chapter.
}
```

8. Finally, create the `ValidateFormDetails` instance method. This will be used to determine whether or not we can save our new walk information. This method is pretty basic, but you could add additional checks depending on your needs. For this example, we'll use the `IsNullOrWhiteSpace` method on the `string` class, and pass in the `Title` property, which checks to see if the `Title` property contains any blank spaces, or is an empty field. To proceed, enter in the following highlighted code section:

```
// method to check for any form errors
bool ValidateFormDetails()
{
    return !string.IsNullOrWhiteSpace(Title);
}
}
}
```

In this section, we began by ensuring that our ViewModel inherits from the `WalkBaseViewModel` class and then moved on to create a `Title` property and its associated getters and setter qualifiers. We also created the `OnPropertyChanged` method, as we defined previously so that it will be called when the property determines that the contents have been changed.

Next, we added a reference to the method `SaveCommand.ChangeCanExecute` that will validate the form fields to determine if the `SaveToolBarItem` should be enabled to allow the user to save the walk entry details. We then created the remaining properties for our ViewModel with their associated getters and setters, which will be used to bind the values entered on the `WalkEntryPage`.

In the next steps, we initialized the class constructor with default values for the `Title`, `Difficulty` and `Distance` properties and then created a `Command` property to our class so that it can be used within the `WalkEntryPage` and will be used to bind to the `SaveToolBarItem`.

Finally, we needed to create the `ExecuteSaveCommand` instance method so that it can store our walk information to each of the properties as defined within the `WalkEntries` model.

Updating the WalksEntryPage to use the MVVM model

In this section, we need to bind our model binding context `BindingContext` to the `WalkEntryViewModel` so that the new walk information that will be entered within this page can be stored within the `WalkEntries` model. Let's take a look at how we can achieve this, by following these steps:

1. Ensure that the `WalkEntryPage.cs` file is displayed within the code editor.

```
//
//  WalkEntryPage.cs
//  TrackMyWalks
//
//  Created by Steven F. Daniel on 04/08/2016.
//  Copyright © 2016 GENIESOFT STUDIOS. All rights reserved.
//
using Xamarin.Forms;
using TrackMyWalks.Models;
using System.Collections.Generic;

namespace TrackMyWalks
{
    public class WalkEntryPage : ContentPage
```

```
{
    public WalkEntryPage()
    {
        // Set the Content Page Title
        Title = "New Walk Entry";
```

2. Next, we need to declare and create a new `BindingContext` instance for the `WalksEntryPage`, and set this to a new instance of the `WalkEntryViewModel` so that it knows where to get the `WalkEntries` so that we can bind it to the associated properties contained within our model. Proceed and enter in the following highlighted code sections:

```
// Declare and initialize our Model Binding Context
BindingContext = new WalkEntryViewModel();
```

3. Next, create the remaining `EntryCell` objects, as well as the `SetBinding` properties to their matched property name as contained within the ViewModel, as shown in the following code snippets:

```
// Define our New Walk Entry fields
var walkTitle = new EntryCell
{
    Label = "Title:",
    Placeholder = "Trail Title"
};
walkTitle.SetBinding(EntryCell.TextProperty, "Title",
  BindingMode.TwoWay);

var walkNotes = new EntryCell
{
    Label = "Notes:",
    Placeholder = "Description"
};
walkNotes.SetBinding(EntryCell.TextProperty, "Notes",
 BindingMode.TwoWay);

var walkLatitude = new EntryCell
{
    Label = "Latitude:",
    Placeholder = "Latitude",
    Keyboard = Keyboard.Numeric
};
walkLatitude.SetBinding(EntryCell.TextProperty,
  "Latitude", BindingMode.TwoWay);

var walkLongitude = new EntryCell
{
```

```csharp
        Label = "Longitude:",
        Placeholder = "Longitude",
        Keyboard = Keyboard.Numeric
};
walkLongitude.SetBinding(EntryCell.TextProperty,
    "Longitude", BindingMode.TwoWay);

var walkKilometers = new EntryCell
{
    Label = "Kilometers:",
    Placeholder = "Kilometers",
    Keyboard = Keyboard.Numeric
};
walkKilometers.SetBinding(EntryCell.TextProperty,
    "Kilometers", BindingMode.TwoWay);

var walkDifficulty = new EntryCell
{
    Label = "Difficulty Level:",
    Placeholder = "Walk Difficulty"
};
walkDifficulty.SetBinding(EntryCell.TextProperty,
    "Difficulty", BindingMode.TwoWay);

var walkImageUrl = new EntryCell
    Label = "ImageUrl:",
    Placeholder = "Image URL"
};
walkImageUrl.SetBinding(EntryCell.TextProperty,
    "ImageUrl", BindingMode.TwoWay);

// Define our TableView
Content = new TableView
{
    Intent = TableIntent.Form,
    Root = new TableRoot
    {
        new TableSection()
        {
            walkTitle,
            walkNotes,
            walkLatitude,
            walkLongitude,
            walkKilometers,
            walkDifficulty,
            walkImageUrl
        }
    }
```

```
        };
        var saveWalkItem = new ToolbarItem
        {
            Text = "Save"
        };

        saveWalkItem.SetBinding(MenuItem.CommandProperty,
          "SaveCommand");

        ToolbarItems.Add(saveWalkItem);

        saveWalkItem.Clicked += (sender, e) =>
        {
            Navigation.PopToRootAsync(true);
        };
    }
  }
}
```

In this section, we looked at the steps involved in modifying our `WalksEntryPage` so that it can take advantage of our `WalksEntryViewModel`. We looked at how to set the content page to an instance of the `WalksEntryViewModel` so that it points to the `WalkEntries` model. We then used the `SetBinding` method on each of our `EntryCells` so that it can bind to the appropriate ViewModel property. Finally, we updated the `SaveToolbarItem` on the `WalkEntryPage` to bind to the `WalksEntryViewModelSaveCommand` property.

The following table provides a brief description of the different binding types, and when these should be used within your applications:

Binding mode	Description
OneWay	This type of binding indicates that the binding should only propagate changes from source (usually the ViewModel) to target (the `BindableObject`). This is the default mode for most `BindableProperty` values.
OneWayToSource	This type of binding indicates that the binding only propagates changes from the target `BindableObject` to the ViewModel and is mainly used for read-only `BindableProperty` values.
TwoWay	This type of binding indicates that the binding should propagate the changes from the ViewModel to the target `BindableObject` in both directions.

One thing to notice is that, if you don't specify a value for the `BindingMode` property, it will use the default `BindingMode.OneWay` which is defined in the `BindableProperty.DefaultBindingMode` property.

Implementing the walk trail page ViewModel

In this section, we will be taking a look at the steps required to create the ViewModel for our `WalksTrailViewModel` so that we can obtain the walk entry information associated with the chosen walk that has been selected from the main `WalksPage`.

Let's take a look at how we can achieve this, by following these steps:

1. Create a new class file within the `ViewModels` folder called `WalksTrailViewModel`, as you did in the previous section entitled *Creating the WalkBaseViewModel*, located within this chapter.

2. Next, ensure that the `WalksTrailViewModel.cs` file is displayed within the code editor, and enter the following code snippet:

```
//
//  WalksTrailViewModel.cs
//  TrackMyWalks ViewModels
//
//  Created by Steven F. Daniel on 22/08/2016.
//  Copyright © 2016 GENIESOFT STUDIOS. All rights reserved.
//
using TrackMyWalks.Models;

namespace TrackMyWalks.ViewModels
{
    public class WalksTrailViewModel : WalkBaseViewModel

    {
        WalkEntries _walkEntry;

        public WalkEntries WalkEntry
        {
            get { return _walkEntry; }
            set
            {
                _walkEntry = value;
                OnPropertyChanged();
            }
        }

        public WalksTrailViewModel(WalkEntries walkEntry)
```

```
            {
                WalkEntry = walkEntry;
            }
        }
    }
```

In this section, we began by ensuring that our ViewModel inherits from the `WalkBaseViewModel` class and then we created an `WalkEntries` variable _walkEntries that will be used to store our `WalkEntries`. Next, we created a `WalkEntry` property and its associated getters and setter qualifiers and the `OnPropertyChanged` method, so that it will be called when our property determines that the contents have been changed. In the final step, we created the `WalksTrailViewModel` constructor, that accepts a `List` parameter containing our `WalkEntries` model.

Updating the WalksTrailPage to use the MVVM model

In this section we need to bind our model binding context `BindingContext` to the `WalksTrailViewModel` so that the walk information details will be displayed from the `WalkEntries` model when a walk has been clicked on within the main `WalksPage`. Let's take a look at how we can achieve this, by following these steps:

1. Ensure that the `WalkTrailPage.cs` file is displayed within the code editor, and enter in the following highlighted code sections:

```
//
//   WalkTrailPage.cs
//   TrackMyWalks
//
//   Created by Steven F. Daniel on 04/08/2016.
//   Copyright © 2016 GENIESOFT STUDIOS. All rights reserved.
//
using Xamarin.Forms;
using TrackMyWalks.Models;
using TrackMyWalks.ViewModels;

namespace TrackMyWalks
{
    public class WalkTrailPage : ContentPage
    {
        public WalkTrailPage(WalkEntries walkItem)
        {
            Title = "Walks Trail";
```

2. Next, we need to declare and create a new `BindingContext` instance for the `WalksTrailPage`, and set this to a new instance of the `WalksTrailViewModel` so that it knows where to get the `WalkEntries` so that we can bind it to the associated properties contained within our Model and display this within the View. Proceed and enter the following highlighted code sections:

```
// Declare and initialize our Model Binding Context
BindingContext = new WalksTrailViewModel(walkItem);

var beginTrailWalk = new Button
{
    BackgroundColor = Color.FromHex("#008080"),
    TextColor = Color.White,
    Text = "Begin this Trail"
};

// Declare and initialize our Event Handler
beginTrailWalk.Clicked += (sender, e) =>
{
    if (walkItem == null) return;
    Navigation.PushAsync(new DistanceTravelled(walkItem));
    Navigation.RemovePage(this);
    walkItem = null;
};
```

3. Next, create the remaining `Image` and `Label` control objects, as well as the `SetBinding` properties to their matched property name as contained within the ViewModel, as shown in the following code snippets:

```
var walkTrailImage = new Image()
{
    Aspect = Aspect.AspectFill
};
walkTrailImage.SetBinding(Image.SourceProperty,
  "WalkEntry.ImageUrl");

var trailNameLabel = new Label()
{
    FontSize = 28,
    FontAttributes = FontAttributes.Bold,
    TextColor = Color.Black
};
trailNameLabel.SetBinding(Label.TextProperty,
  "WalkEntry.Title");

var trailKilometersLabel = new Label()
```

[69]

```
    {
        FontAttributes = FontAttributes.Bold,
        FontSize = 12,
        TextColor = Color.Black,
    };
        trailKilometersLabel.SetBinding(Label.TextProperty,
        "WalkEntry.Kilometers", stringFormat: "Length: {0} km");

var trailDifficultyLabel = new Label()
    {
        FontAttributes = FontAttributes.Bold,
        FontSize = 12,
        TextColor = Color.Black
    };
        trailDifficultyLabel.SetBinding(Label.TextProperty,
        "WalkEntry.Difficulty", stringFormat: "Difficulty: {0}");

var trailFullDescription = new Label()
    {
        FontSize = 11,
        TextColor = Color.Black,
        HorizontalOptions = LayoutOptions.FillAndExpand
    };
        trailFullDescription.SetBinding(Label.TextProperty,
         "WalkEntry.Notes");

this.Content = new ScrollView
    {
        Padding = 10,
        Content = new StackLayout
        {
            Orientation = StackOrientation.Vertical,
            HorizontalOptions = LayoutOptions.FillAndExpand,
            Children =
            {
            walkTrailImage,
            trailNameLabel,
            trailKilometersLabel,
            trailDifficultyLabel,
            trailFullDescription,
            beginTrailWalk
            }
        }
    };
    }
    }
}
```

In this section, we looked at the steps involved in modifying our `WalksTrailPage` so that it can take advantage of the `WalksTrailViewModel`. We looked at how to set the content page to an instance of our `WalksTrailViewModel` so that it knows where to get the list of walk entries to be used and displayed within our `StackLayout` control. We used the `SetBinding` property to create and bind each of our model values to a specific property.

Finally, we defined a `ScrollView` control, then added each of our form `Image` and `Label` fields to the `StackLayout` control.

Implementing the DistanceTravelledViewModel

In this section, we will be taking a look at the steps required to create the ViewModel for our `DistTravelledViewModel` so that we can calculate how long the chosen walk from the main `WalksPage` took to complete.

Let's take a look at how we can achieve this, by following these steps:

1. Create a new class file within the `ViewModels` folder called `DistTravelledViewModel`, as you did in the previous section entitled *Creating the WalkBaseViewModel*, located within this chapter.

2. Next, ensure that the `DistTravelledViewModel.cs` file is displayed within the code editor, and enter the following code snippet:

```
//
//  DistTravelledViewModel.cs
//  TrackMyWalks ViewModels
//
//  Created by Steven F. Daniel on 22/08/2016.
//  Copyright © 2016 GENIESOFT STUDIOS. All rights reserved.
//
using TrackMyWalks.Models;
using TrackMyWalks.ViewModels;

namespace TrackMyWalks.ViewModels
{
    public class DistTravelledViewModel : WalkBaseViewModel
    {
        WalkEntries _walkEntry;
```

3. Then, create the following `WalkEntry` property and its associated getters and

setter qualifiers. The `OnPropertyChanged` method, as we mentioned previously, will be called when our property determines that the contents have been changed. Proceed and enter in the following code snippet:

```
public WalkEntries WalkEntry
{
    get { return _walkEntry; }
    set
    {
        _walkEntry = value;
        OnPropertyChanged();
    }
}
```

4. Next, create the remaining ViewModel properties and the associated getters and setter qualifiers that will be used to bind the values entered on the `DistanceTravelledPage`, as shown in the following code snippets:

```
double _travelled;
public double Travelled
{
    get { return _travelled; }
    set
    {
        _travelled = value;
        OnPropertyChanged();
    }
}

double _hours;
public double Hours
{
    get { return _hours; }
    set
    {
        _hours = value;
        OnPropertyChanged();
    }
}

double _minutes;
public double Minutes
{
    get { return _minutes; }
    set
    {
        _minutes = value;
```

```
            OnPropertyChanged();
        }
    }

    double _seconds;
    public double Seconds
    {
        get { return _seconds; }
        set
        {
            _seconds = value;
            OnPropertyChanged();
        }
    }

    public string TimeTaken
    {
        get
        {
            return string.Format("{0:00}:{1:00}:{2:00}", this.Hours,
                this.Minutes, this.Seconds);
        }
    }

    public DistTravelledViewModel(WalkEntries walkEntry)
    {
        this.Hours = 0;
        this.Minutes = 0;
        this.Seconds = 0;
        this.Travelled = 100;

        WalkEntry = walkEntry;
    }
  }
}
```

In this section, we began by ensuring that our ViewModel inherits from the WalkBaseViewModel class and then we created an WalkEntries variable _walkEntries that will be used to store our WalkEntries.

Next, we created a WalkEntry property and its associated getters and setter qualifiers and the OnPropertyChanged method, so that it will be called when our property determines that the contents have been changed.

In our final step, we created the `DistTravelledViewModel` constructor, that accepts a `List` parameter containing our `WalkEntries` model, prior to initializing our class constructor with default values for the `Hours`, `Minutes`, `Seconds`, and `Travelled` properties.

Updating the DistanceTravelledPage to use the MVVM model

In this section we need to bind our model binding context `BindingContext` to the `DistTravelledViewModel` so that the walk information details and the calculations of distance travelled will be displayed from the `WalkEntries` model.

Let's take a look at how we can achieve this, by following these steps:

1. Ensure that the `DistanceTravelledPage.cs` file is displayed within the code editor.

   ```
   //
   //  DistanceTravelledPage.cs
   //  TrackMyWalks
   //
   //  Created by Steven F. Daniel on 04/08/2016.
   //  Copyright © 2016 GENIESOFT STUDIOS. All rights reserved.
   //
   using Xamarin.Forms;
   using Xamarin.Forms.Maps;
   using TrackMyWalks.Models;

   namespace TrackMyWalks
   {
       public class DistanceTravelledPage : ContentPage
       {
   ```

2. Next, we need to update the map to get its values from the `DistTravelledViewModel` so that it correctly plots these within the map view. We need to do this because the `Xamarin.Forms.Map` control doesn't provide support for binding directly to the map, so we have to set these directly within our ViewModel instead. Therefore, we need to create a private `_viewModel` variable within the content page to return the value from the page's `BindingContext`.

3. Proceed and enter the following highlighted code sections:

```
DistTravelledViewModel _viewModel
{
  get { return BindingContext as DistTravelledViewModel; }
}

public DistanceTravelledPage(WalkEntries walkItem)
{
Title = "Distance Travelled";
```

4. Next, create a new `BindingContext` instance for the `DistanceTravelledPage`, and set this to a new instance of the `DistTravelledViewModel` so that it knows where to get the `WalkEntries` to bind it to the associated properties contained within our model and display this within the View. Proceed and enter in the following highlighted code sections:

```
// Declare and initialize our Model Binding Context
   BindingContext = new DistTravelledViewModel(walkItem);

// Instantiate our map object
   var trailMap = new Map();
```

5. Next, update the map to grab the name of the chosen walk and the `Latitude` and `Longitude` values from the `DistTravelledViewModel`. Proceed and enter the following highlighted code sections:

```
// Place a pin on the map for the chosen walk type
trailMap.Pins.Add(new Pin
{
  Type = PinType.Place,
  Label = _viewModel.WalkEntry.Title,
  Position = new Position(_viewModel.WalkEntry.Latitude,
  _viewModel.WalkEntry.Longitude)
});

// Center the map around the list of walks entry's location
   trailMap.MoveToRegion(MapSpan.FromCenterAndRadius(new
   Position(_viewModel.WalkEntry.Latitude,
   _viewModel.WalkEntry.Longitude),
   Distance.FromKilometers(1.0)));
```

6. Next, create the remaining `Label` control objects, as well as the `SetBinding` properties to their matched property name as contained within the ViewModel, as shown in the following code snippets:

```
var trailNameLabel = new Label()
{
    FontSize = 18,
    FontAttributes = FontAttributes.Bold,
    TextColor = Color.Black,
    HorizontalTextAlignment = TextAlignment.Center
};
trailNameLabel.SetBinding(Label.TextProperty,
 "WalkEntry.Title");

var trailDistanceTravelledLabel = new Label()
{
    FontAttributes = FontAttributes.Bold,
    FontSize = 20,
    TextColor = Color.Black,
    HorizontalTextAlignment = TextAlignment.Center
};

trailDistanceTravelledLabel.SetBinding(Label.TextProperty,
 "Travelled", stringFormat: "Distance Travelled: {0} km");

var totalTimeTakenLabel = new Label()
{
    FontAttributes = FontAttributes.Bold,
    FontSize = 20,
    TextColor = Color.Black,
    HorizontalTextAlignment = TextAlignment.Center
};

totalTimeTakenLabel.SetBinding(Label.TextProperty, "TimeTaken",
 stringFormat: "Time Taken: {0}");

var walksHomeButton = new Button
{
    BackgroundColor = Color.FromHex("#008080"),
    TextColor = Color.White,
    Text = "End this Trail"
};

// Set up our event handler
walksHomeButton.Clicked += (sender, e) =>
{
    if (walkItem == null) return;
```

```
            Navigation.PopToRootAsync(true);
            walkItem = null;
    };

    this.Content = new ScrollView
    {
        Padding = 10,
        Content = new StackLayout
        {
            Orientation = StackOrientation.Vertical,
            HorizontalOptions = LayoutOptions.FillAndExpand,
            Children = {
            trailMap,
            trailNameLabel,
            trailDistanceTravelledLabel,
            totalTimeTakenLabel,
            walksHomeButton
            }
        }
    };
    }
  }
}
```

In this section, we looked at the steps involved in modifying the DistanceTraveledPage so that it can take advantage of the DistTravelledViewModel. We looked at how to set the content page to an instance of our DistTravelledViewModel. We used the SetBinding property to create and bind each of our model values to a specific property. Finally, we defined a ScrollView control, then added each of the form Image and Label fields to the StackLayout control.

Now that you have created all of the MVVM ViewModels and have updated the associated content pages, our next step is to finally build and run the TrackMyWalks application within the iOS simulator.

When compilation completes, the iOS Simulator will appear automatically and the `TrackMyWalks` application will be displayed, as shown in the following screenshot:

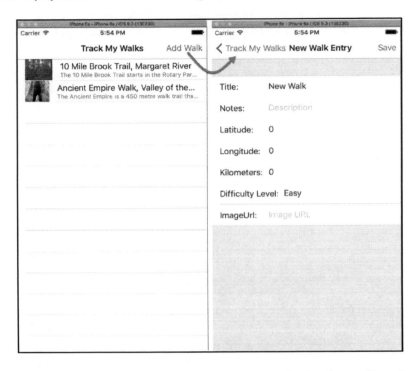

As you can see from the preceding screenshot, this currently displays a list of static trail entries, that are displayed within the `ListView`. When the user clicks on the **Add Walk** button link, this will display the **New Walk Entry** content page.

As you can see from the **New Walk Entry** screen, we have successfully binded each of the `EntryCell` properties to our `WalkEntryViewModel` and have displayed this information beside each of the content page properties. If you clear out the information associated with the `Title` property, you will notice that the **Save** button will dim. This is because the `ValidateFormDetails` instance method performs a check, then the `SaveCommand` command event is triggered, and handles it accordingly.

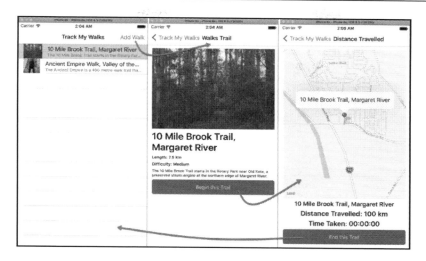

The preceding screenshot shows you the navigation flow between each of the pages when a trail has been selected from the list, with the final screen showing the **Distance Travelled** page along with the placeholder pin marker showing the trail location within the map view.

Summary

In this chapter, we updated our `TrackMyWalks` application and created a number of ViewModels. We then removed and migrated our data and logic from each of our pages, then added binding to those pages so that they point directly to the ViewModels associated with the page.

In the next chapter, you will learn about the different navigation techniques that can be used within the MVVM model architecture, to navigate between ViewModels by creating and implementing a navigation service between each of the Views, so that you can easily navigate between them.

3
Navigating within the MVVM Model - The Xamarin.Forms Way

Up to this point, you have seen how to incorporate the MVVM architectural pattern into your applications, so that it enforces the separation between the application's user interface, or presentation layer, from the underlying data. This is done by using a class that acts as the communication layer between both the View and the ViewModel, and is connected through data bindings along with the binding context for the View, pointing to an instance of the ViewModel.

In this chapter, you will see how you can leverage what you already know about the MVVM design pattern, and we will learn how to move navigation into the ViewModels. You'll learn how to create a C# class that will act as the navigation service for our app, as well as how to update our existing `WalkBaseViewModel` class file. This will include a number of abstract class methods that each of our ViewModels will inherit, and in turn update the content pages to bind with the ViewModels to allow navigation between these Views to happen.

This chapter will cover the following topics:

- Understanding the `Xamarin.Forms` Navigation API pattern architecture
- Creating a navigation service using the `Xamarin.Forms.Navigation` class
- Updating the `TrackMyWalks` application to use the navigation service
- Updating the MVVM ViewModels to use the navigation service interface
- Updating the user interface content pages to use the updated MVVM ViewModels

Understanding the Xamarin.Forms Navigation API

In this section, we will take a look at the `Xamarin.Forms` Navigation API pattern architecture and gain an understanding into the different types of navigation patterns that are available.

The `Xamarin.Forms` Navigation API is exposed through the `Xamarin.Forms.INavigation` interface, and is implemented via the `Navigation` property. The `Navigation` property can be called from any `Xamarin.Forms` object, typically the `Xamarin.Forms.Page` that inherits from the `ContentPage` class that is part of the `Xamarin.Forms.Core` assembly.

The `Xamarin.Forms` Navigation API supports two different types of navigation–hierarchical and modal, and these are explained in the following table:

Navigation page	Description
Hierarchical	The hierarchical navigation type is essentially a stack-based navigation pattern that enables users to move iteratively through each of the screens within the hierarchy, and then navigate back out again, one screen at a time, removing them from the navigation stack.
Modal	The modal navigation type is a single pop-up or screen that interrupts the hierarchical navigation by requiring the user to respond to an action, prior to the screen or popup from being dismissed.

The hierarchical navigation pattern provides a means of navigating through the navigational structure and is typically the most used. This involves the user tapping their way forward through a series of pages, and then navigating backwards through the stack using the navigation methods on Android or iOS devices.

The following screenshot shows the process when moving from one page to another within the hierarchical navigation model, and popping pages from the `NavigationStack`. Whenever a new page is pushed onto the navigation stack, this will become the active page.

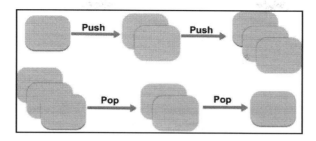

Alternatively, when you want to return back to the previous page, the application will start by popping the current page from the navigation stack, and the new topmost page will then become the active page. The modal navigation pattern displays a page on top of the current page that prevents the user from any interaction from the page underneath it, and provides the user with choices for what they want to do before the modal page can be closed.

The INavigation interface, which is part of the Xamarin.Forms.NavigationPage, implements and exposes two separate read-only properties–NavigationStack and ModalStack. This will allow you to view both the hierarchical and modal navigation stacks.

The Xamarin.FormsINavigation interface provides you with several methods that will allow you to asynchronously push (add) and pop (remove) pages onto the navigation and modal stacks, and these are explained in the table below:

Navigation methods	Description
PushAsync(Page page)	This method adds a new page at the top of the NavigationStack that enables users to move deeper within the screen hierarchy.
PopAsync()	This method allows you to navigate back through the NavigationStack to the previous page, if one has been previously added to the NavigationStack.
PushModalAsync(Page page)	This method allows you to display a page modally when you need to either display some informational information or request information from the user. A good example of a modal page would be a sign-on page, where you need to get user credentials.
PopModalAsync()	This method will dismiss the currently displayed modal page and return you to the page displayed underneath.

As well as the above mentioned navigation methods, the `Xamarin.Forms.INavigation` interface provides you with a number of additional methods that will help you manipulate the `NavigationStack`, and these are explained in the following table:

Navigation methods	Description
`InsertPageBefore(Page page, Page before)`	This method allows you to insert a page before a specific page that has already been added to the `NavigationStack`.
`RemovePage(Page page)`	This method allows you to remove a specific page within the `NavigationStack`.
`PopToRootAsync()`	This method navigates you back to the first page that is contained within the `NavigationStack` whilst removing all of the other pages that are contained within the `NavigationStack`.

Now that you have a good understanding of the components that are contained within the Navigation API pattern architecture, we can begin to take a look at some of the different approaches to navigating between pages and ViewModels.

Differences between the navigation and ViewModel approaches

In this section, we will take a look at the approaches when performing navigation within ViewModels contained within an `Xamarin.Forms` solution. When performing navigation within your ViewModels, there are a couple of approaches that you should consider before going down this path. An approach would be to use the page navigation approach, which involves navigating to another page using a direct reference to that page.

The page navigation approach can be accomplished in `Xamarin.Forms` by essentially passing the current `INavigation` instance into a ViewModel's object constructor, which will force the ViewModel to use the `Xamarin.Forms` default navigation mechanism to navigate to other pages.

If you wanted to use the ViewModel approach to navigate to a page using the associated pages ViewModel, you would need to form some sort of mapping between each of the pages, as well as their associated ViewModels. This would be done by creating a dictionary or key-value type property in the navigation service that will maintain a one-to-one mapping for each of the pages and their type.

In MVVM, actions taken by the user on a particular page are bound to commands that are part of the pages, ViewModel, and so this process needs to be thought through differently when navigating to another page, or even the previous page, when performing tasks such as saving data or updating a maps location. As such, we need to rethink how to achieve navigation that leverages the MVVM design pattern within our app, so that it can be controlled by the ViewModels and not by the underlying pages.

When using the ViewModels to handle the navigation, this alleviates the need for a ViewModel to have any dependencies on the specific implementation of a page, and because the ViewModel doesn't navigate directly to a page via the ContentPage's ViewModel, this means that when you implement this approach, there is a need for a relationship or mapping to be done between each of the pages and their associated `ViewModels`.

In the next section, we will be taking a look at how to navigate through our `TrackMyWalks` app by creating a navigation service that will include ViewModel and page type mappings.

Implementing the navigation service within your app

In this section, we will begin by setting up the basic structure for our `TrackMyWalks` solution to include the folder that will be used to represent our `Services`. Let's take a look at how we can achieve this, by performing following the steps:

1. Launch the Xamarin Studio application and ensure that the `TrackMyWalks` solution is loaded within the Xamarin Studio IDE.

2. Next, create a new folder within the `TrackMyWalks` Portable Class Library project, called `Services`, as shown in the following screenshot:

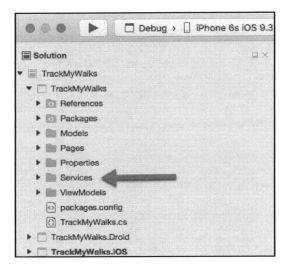

Now that we have created the folder structure that will be used to store our navigation services, we can begin to start building the `Navigation Service Interface` class that will be used by our `Navigation Service` class and in turn used by our ViewModels.

Creating the navigation service interface for the TrackMyWalks app

In this section, we will begin by creating a navigation service interface class that will extend from the `Xamarin.Forms` navigation abstraction layer. This is so that we can perform ViewModel to ViewModel navigation within our MVVM design pattern, and in turn bind with our content pages to allow navigation between these Views to happen.

We will first need to define the interface for our navigation service, as this will contain and define its methods, and will make it a lot easier if we ever wanted to add new method implementations for our service, without the need to change each of our ViewModels.

Let's take a look at how we can achieve this, by performing the following steps:

1. Create an empty class within the `Services` folder, as shown in the following screenshot:

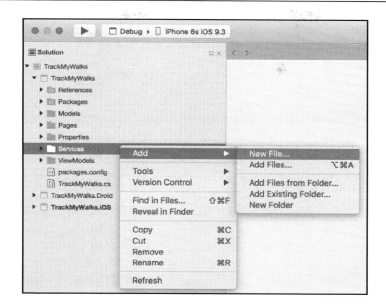

2. Next, choose the **Empty Interface** option located within the **General** section, and enter in IWalkNavService for the name of the new interface file to create, as shown in the following screenshot:

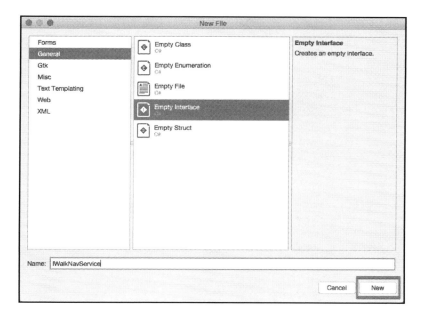

3. Next, click on the **New** button to allow the wizard to proceed and create the new empty class file, as shown in the preceding screenshot.

Up until this point, all we have done is create our `IWalkNavService` class file. This Interface class will be used and will act as the base `NavigationService` class that each of our ViewModels will inherit from. As we start to build the `Navigation Service Interface` class, you will see that it contains a couple of class members that will be used by our content pages and ViewModels, as we will be using this as our base class within our ViewModels used by the `TrackMyWalks` application.

To proceed with creating the base `IWalkNavService` interface, ensure that the `IWalkNavService.cs` file is displayed within the code editor, and enter in the following code snippet:

```
//
//  IWalkNavService.cs
//  TrackMyWalks Navigation Service Interface
//
//  Created by Steven F. Daniel on 03/09/2016.
//  Copyright © 2016 GENIESOFT STUDIOS. All rights reserved.
//
using System.Threading.Tasks;
using TrackMyWalks.ViewModels;

namespace TrackMyWalks.Services
{
    public interface IWalkNavService
    {
        // Navigate back to the Previous page in
         the NavigationStack
        Task PreviousPage();

        // Navigate to the first page within
         the NavigationStack
        Task BackToMainPage();

        // Navigate to a particular ViewModel within
         our MVVM Model,
        // and pass a parameter
        Task NavigateToViewModel<ViewModel,
            TParameter>(TParameter parameter)
            where ViewModel : WalkBaseViewModel;
    }
}
```

In the preceding code snippet, we started by creating a new Interface class for our

IWalkNavService that allows the ability to navigate to each of our ViewModels, as well as navigating back to the PreviousPage method, and back to the first page within our hierarchical model, as determined by the BackToMainPage method.

 An interface contains only the methods, properties, and event signature definitions. Any class that implements the interface must implement all members of the interface that are specified in the interface definition.

The NavigateToViewModel method declares a generic type which is used to restrict the ViewModel to its use to objects of the WalkBaseViewModel base class, and a strongly-typed TParameter parameter to be passed along with the navigation.

 The term **strongly-typed** means that, if a variable has been declared of a specific type (string, integer, or defined as a user-defined type), it cannot be assigned a value of a different type later on, as this will result in the compiler notifying you of an error. An example would be: int i = 10; i = "Ten"

The Task class is essentially used to handle asynchronous operations. This is done by ensuring that the asynchronous method you initiated will eventually finish, thus completing the task. The Task object is used to return back information once it has finished by returning back a Task object almost instantaneously, although the underlying work within the method would likely finish later.

To handle this, you can use the await keyword to wait for the task to complete which will block the current thread and wait until the asynchronous method has completed.

Creating a navigation service to navigate within our ViewModels

In the previous section, we created our base interface class for our navigation service and defined a number of different methods, which will be used to navigate within our MVVM ViewModel.

These will be used by each of our ViewModels, and the Views (pages) will implement these ViewModels and use them as their `BindingContext`.

Let's take a look at how we can achieve this, by performing the following the steps:

1. Create an empty class within the `Services` folder, as shown in the next screenshot.

2. Next, choose the **Empty Class** option located within the **General** section, and enter in `WalkNavService` for the name of the new class file to create, as shown in the following screenshot:

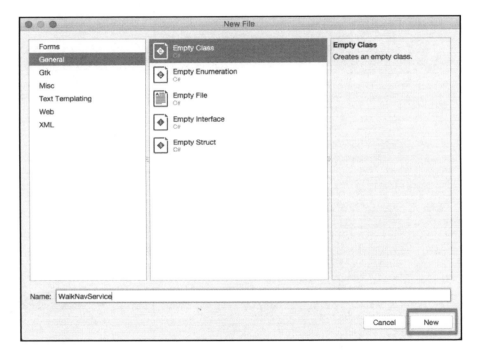

3. Next, click on the **New** button to allow the wizard to proceed and create the new empty class file, as shown in the preceding screenshot.

4. Up until this point, all we have done is create our `WalkNavService` class file. This class will be used and will act as the base `NavigationService` class that will contain the functionality required that each of our ViewModels will inherit from, in order to navigate between each of the ViewModels within our MVVM model.

5. As we start to build our `Navigation` class, you will see that it contains a number of method members that will be used to enable navigation between each of our ViewModels and it will implement the `IWalkNavService` Interface. To proceed with creating the base `WalkNavService` class, perform the following steps:

6. Ensure that the `WalkNavService.cs` file is displayed within the code editor, and enter in the following code snippet:

```
//
//   WalkNavService.cs
//   TrackMyWalks Navigation Service Class
//
//   Created by Steven F. Daniel on 03/09/2016.
//   Copyright © 2016 GENIESOFT STUDIOS. All rights reserved.
//
using System;
using Xamarin.Forms;
using System.Collections.Generic;
using System.Threading.Tasks;
using System.Reflection;
using System.Linq;
using TrackMyWalks.ViewModels;
using TrackMyWalks.Services;
```

First, we need to initialize our navigation class to be marked as a dependency, by adding the `Dependency` metadata attribute so that it can be resolved by the `Xamarin.FormsDependencyService` class. This will enable so that it to find and use our method implementation as defined by our interface.

7. Next, we also need to need to ensure that our `WalkNavService` class inherits from the `IWalkNavService` navigation interface class, so that it can access the method getters and setters. Proceed and enter in the following code snippet as shown here:

```
[assembly: Dependency(typeof(WalkNavService))]
namespace TrackMyWalks.Services
{
    public class WalkNavService : IWalkNavService
    {
```

8. Next, we need to create a public `INavigation` property named `navigation`. The `navigation` property will provide our class with a reference to the current `Xamarin.Forms.INavigation` instance, and this will need to be set when the navigation service is first initialized. We will see how this is done as we progress through updating our `TrackMyWalks` app. Proceed and enter in the following code snippet:

```
public INavigation navigation { get; set; }
```

9. Then we need to register the navigation service to handle ContentPage to ViewModel mappings by declaring a dictionary `_viewMapping` property variable that inherits from the `IDictionary` interface. Proceed and enter in the following code snippet:

```
readonly IDictionary<Type, Type> _viewMapping =
    new Dictionary<Type, Type>();
```

10. Next, we need to declare a new method called `RegisterViewMapping` which will be used to populate our ViewModel and `ContentPage` (View) within the `_viewMapping` dictionary property object. Proceed and enter in the following code sections:

```
// Register our ViewModel and View within our Dictionary
public void RegisterViewMapping(Type viewModel, Type view)
{
    _viewMapping.Add(viewModel, view);
}
```

11. Then, we need to create the `PreviousPage` instance method for our `WalkNavService` class. This will be used to navigate back to the previous page contained within our `NavigationStack`, by first checking the `NavigationStack` property of the `navigation` property `INavigation` interface to ensure that it is not null and that we have more than one ViewModel contained within our `NavigationStack` to navigate back to. If we don't perform this check, it could result in our application crashing. Finally, we use the `PopAsync` method to remove the last view added to our `NavigationStack`, thus returning back to the previous ViewModel. Proceed and enter in the following code sections:

```
// Instance method that allows us to move back to the
// previous page.
public async Task PreviousPage()
{
```

```
// Check to see if we can move back to the previous page
if (navigation.NavigationStack != null &&
    navigation.NavigationStack.Count > 0)
{
    await navigation.PopAsync(true);
}
}
```

12. Next, we need to create the `BackToMainPage` instance method for our `WalkNavService` class. This will be used to take us back to the first `ContentPage` contained within our `NavigationStack`. We use the `PopToRootAsync` method of our `navigation` property and use the `await` operator to wait until the task completes, before removing all ViewModels contained within our `NavigationStack` and returning back a `Task` object. Proceed and enter the following code:

```
// Instance method that takes us back to the main
// Root WalksPage
public async Task BackToMainPage()
{
    await navigation.PopToRootAsync(true);
}
```

13. Then, we need to create the `NavigateToViewModel` instance method for our `WalkNavService` class. This will be used to navigate to a specific ViewModel that is contained within our `_viewMapping` dictionary object. Next, we use the `TryGetValue` method of the `_viewMapping` dictionary object to check to see if our ViewModel does indeed exist within our dictionary, and return the name of the ViewModel.

14. The name of the returned view will be stored within the `viewType` object, and we then use the `PushAsync` method to navigate to that view. Finally, we set the `BindingContext` for the last pushed view that is contained within our `NavigationStack`, and then navigate to the view, passing in any parameters required. Proceed and enter in the following code sections:

```
// Instance method that navigates to a specific ViewModel
// within our dictionary viewMapping
public async Task NavigateToViewModel<ViewModel,
    WalkParam>(WalkParam parameter)
    where ViewModel : WalkBaseViewModel
{
    Type viewType;

    if (_viewMapping.TryGetValue(typeof(ViewModel), out
```

```
      viewType))
{
  var constructor = viewType.GetTypeInfo()
  .DeclaredConstructors
  .FirstOrDefault(dc => dc.GetParameters()
  .Count() <= 0);

    var view = constructor.Invoke(null) as Page;
    await navigation.PushAsync(view, true);
}

if (navigation.NavigationStack.Last().BindingContext is
    WalkBaseViewModel<WalkParam>)
    await ((WalkBaseViewModel<WalkParam>)(
    navigation.NavigationStack.Last().BindingContext)).
    Init(parameter);
}
}
}
```

In the preceding code snippet, we began by ensuring that our `WalkNavService` class inherits from our `IWalkNavService` class, and then moved on to create a `navigation` property that inherits from our `INavigation` class. We then created its associated getter and setter qualifiers.

Finally, we created the instance methods required for our `WalkNavService` class.

Updating the WalkBaseViewModel to use our navigation service

In this section we will proceed to update our `WalkBaseViewModel` class to include references to our `IWalkNavService`. Since our `WalkBaseViewModel` inherits and is used by each of our `ViewModels`, it makes sense to place it within this class. That way, if we need to add additional methods, we can just add them within this class. To proceed, perform the following steps:

1. Ensure that the `WalkBaseViewModel.cs` file is displayed within the code editor, and enter in the following code snippet:

```
//
//  WalkBaseViewModel.cs
//  TrackMyWalks Base ViewModel
//
```

```
//   Created by Steven F. Daniel on 22/08/2016.
//   Copyright © 2016 GENIESOFT STUDIOS. All rights reserved.
//
using System.ComponentModel;
using System.Runtime.CompilerServices;
using System.Threading.Tasks; using TrackMyWalks.Services;

namespace TrackMyWalks.ViewModels
{
    public abstract class WalkBaseViewModel : INotifyPropertyChanged
    {
```

2. Next, we need to create a protected `IWalkNavService` property named `NavService`. The `NavService` property will provide our class with a reference to the current `navigation` instance that is contained within our `IWalkNavService` interface class. Proceed and enter in the following code section:

```
protected IWalkNavService NavService { get; private set; }
```

3. Then, we need to modify the class constructor and declare a `navService` parameter that inherits from our `IWalkNavService` interface class. Next, we set the `NavService` property for our `WalkBaseViewModel` base class, to an instance of the `navService` parameter. Proceed and enter in the following highlighted code sections:

```
protected WalkBaseViewModel(IWalkNavService navService)
{
    NavService = navService;
}
```

4. Next, we need to create the `Init` abstract method for our `WalkBaseViewModel` class that returns back an asynchronous `Task` object. This will be used to initialize our `WalkBaseViewModel`. Proceed and enter in the following highlighted code sections:

```
public abstract Task Init();

public event PropertyChangedEventHandler PropertyChanged;

protected virtual void OnPropertyChanged(
  [CallerMemberName] string propertyName = null)
{
    var handler = PropertyChanged;
    if (handler != null)
```

[95]

```
    {
        handler(this, new PropertyChangedEventArgs(propertyName));
    }
  }
}
```

5. Then, we need to create a secondary abstract class for our `WalkBaseViewModel` that inherits from the `WalkBaseViewModel` and defines a generic-typed `TParameter` object. We then proceed to overload the `WalkBaseViewModel` class constructor, and set this class to inherit from our `navService` base class. Proceed and enter in the following highlighted code sections:

```
public abstract class WalkBaseViewModel<WalkParam> :
  WalkBaseViewModel
{
    protected WalkBaseViewModel(IWalkNavService navService) :
      base(navService)
    {
    }
```

6. Next, we need to override the `Init` method for our `WalkBaseViewModel<WalkParam>` that accepts a default `WalkParam` value for our `walkDetails` model. Proceed and enter in the following highlighted code sections:

```
public override async Task Init()
{
    await Init(default(WalkParam));
}
public abstract Task Init(WalkParam walkDetails);
  }
}
```

In the preceding code snippet, we began by creating a `NavService` property that inherits from our `IWalkNavService` class, and then created its associated getter and setter qualifiers.

Next, we update the `WalkBaseViewModel` class constructor to set the `NavService` property to an instance of our `navService`, before creating our `Init` abstraction method that will be used to initialize our class.

In the next step, we create a new abstract class for our `WalkBaseViewModel` that implements from the `WalkBaseViewModel` class, and then overloads our class constructor so that it inherits from our `navService` class.

Next, we'll override the `Init` method for our `WalkBaseViewModel<WalkParam>` that accepts a default `WalkParam` value for our `walkDetails` model.

Updating the walks main page ViewModel and navigation service

We have created our `IWalkNavService` Interface class and updated the `NavService` class to include all of the necessary class instance methods. We also made some changes to our `WalkBaseViewModel` class to inherit from our `IWalkNavService` navigation service. We have also included an additional abstraction class that will be used to initialize our `WalkBaseViewModel` when navigating between `ViewModels` within our MVVM model.

Our next step is to modify the walks main page. In this section, we will be taking a look at how to update our `WalksPageViewModel` so that it can take advantage of our navigation service.

Let's take a look at how we can achieve this, by performing the following steps:

1. Ensure that the `WalksPageViewModel.cs` file is displayed within the code editor, and enter in the following highlighted code sections:

```
//
//  WalksPageViewModel.cs
//  TrackMyWalks ViewModels
//
//  Created by Steven F. Daniel on 22/08/2016.
//  Copyright © 2016 GENIESOFT STUDIOS. All rights reserved.
//
using System;
using System.Collections.ObjectModel;
using System.Threading.Tasks;
using TrackMyWalks.Models;
using TrackMyWalks.Services;
using Xamarin.Forms;

namespace TrackMyWalks.ViewModels
{
    public class WalksPageViewModel : WalkBaseViewModel
    {
        ObservableCollection<WalkEntries> _walkEntries;
```

```
public ObservableCollection<WalkEntries> walkEntries
{
    get { return _walkEntries; }
    set
    {
        _walkEntries = value;
        OnPropertyChanged();
    }
}
```

2. Now we need to modify the `WalksPageViewModel` class constructor, which will need to include a parameter `navService` that is included within our `IWalkNavService` interface class. Then we need to set the ViewModel's class constructor to access all instance class members contained within the `navService` within the `WalksPageViewModel` by using the `base` keyword. We then set up an `ObservableCollection` called `walkEntries`. This accepts a list parameter containing our `WalkEntries` model, which will be used to determine whenever the collection has changed within the `WalkEntries` model.

3. Next, we create the `Init` method within our `WalksPageView` model, and a method called `LoadWalkDetails` to populate the `WalkDetails`. Proceed and enter in the following highlighted code sections:

```
public WalksPageViewModel(IWalkNavService navService) :
  base(navService)
{
        walkEntries = new ObservableCollection<WalkEntries>();
}
public override async Task Init()
{
    await LoadWalkDetails();
}
```

4. Next, we need to create a new `async` method called `LoadWalkDetails` that will be used to add each of the walk entries within our model. We use the `Task.Factory.StartNew` to start and execute our task, and then proceed to populate each of our lists of `WalkEntries` asynchronously. We then use and specify the `await` keyword to wait until our `Task` completes. Proceed and enter in the following highlighted code sections:

```
public async Task LoadWalkDetails()
{
    await Task.Factory.StartNew(() =>
    {
        walkEntries = new ObservableCollection<WalkEntries>() {
```

```
      new WalkEntries {
          Title = "10 Mile Brook Trail, Margaret River",
          Notes = "The 10 Mile Brook Trail starts in the
          Rotary Park near Old Kate, a preserved steam " +
          "engine at the northern edge of Margaret River. ",
              Latitude = -33.9727604,
              Longitude = 115.0861599,
              Kilometers = 7.5,
              Distance = 0,
              Difficulty = "Medium",
              ImageUrl =
                "http://trailswa.com.au/media/cache/media/images/
                  trails/_mid/" +"FullSizeRender1_600_480_c1.jpg"
      },
      new WalkEntries
      {
          Title = "Ancient Empire Walk, Valley of the Giants",
          Notes = "The Ancient Empire is a 450 metre walk trail
          that takes you around and through some of " +
          "the giant tingle trees including the most popular
           of the gnarled veterans, known as " +
            "Grandma Tingle.",
              Latitude = -34.9749188,
              Longitude = 117.3560796,
              Kilometers = 450,
              Distance = 0,
              Difficulty = "Hard",
              ImageUrl ="http://trailswa.com.au/media/cache
                /media/images/trails/_mid/" +
                "Ancient_Empire_534_480_c1.jpg"
      },
      };
  });
}
```

5. Next, we need to create a Command property for our class. This will be used within our WalksPage and will be used to bind to the Add WalkToolBarItem. The Command property will run an action upon being pressed, and then execute a class instance method, to determine whether the command can be executed. Proceed and enter in the following highlighted code sections:

```
Command _createNewWalk;
public Command CreateNewWalk
{
    get
    {
        return _createNewWalk
```

```
        ?? (_createNewWalk =
        new Command(async () =>
        await NavService.NavigateToViewModel<WalkEntryViewMod
        el, WalkEntries>(null)));
    }
}
```

6. Then, create a `Command` property to our class. This will be used within the
   `WalksPage` and will be used to handle clicks on a walk item within the
   `ListView`. The `Command` property will run an action upon being pressed, and
   then execute a class instance method to determine whether the command can be
   executed or not, prior to navigating to the `WalksTrailViewModel` and passing
   in the `trailDetails` for the chosen walk within the `ListView`. Proceed and
   enter in the following highlighted code sections:

```
Command<WalkEntries> _trailDetails;
public Command<WalkEntries> WalkTrailDetails
{
    get
    {
        return _trailDetails ?? (_trailDetails =
          new Command<WalkEntries>(async (trailDetails) =>
           await NavService.NavigateToViewModel
            <WalksTrailViewModel, WalkEntries>(trailDetails)));
    }
  }
 }
}
```

Now that we have modified our `WalksPageViewModel` to include the navigation service
class, which will be used by our main `WalksPage`, our next step is to modify our walks
main page so that it points to a reference of our `WalksPageViewModel`, and ensures that all
of the necessary `Command` bindings and `BindingContext`s have been set up correctly.

Updating the walks main page to use the updated ViewModel

Now that we have modified our MVVM ViewModel to take advantage of the navigation
service, we need to modify our walks main page to bind the `WalksPageBindingContext`
to the `WalksPageViewModel` so that the walk entry details can be displayed and all of the
navigational aspects are working as expected.

Let's take a look at how we can achieve this, by performing the following steps:

1. Ensure that the `WalksPage.cs` file is displayed within the code editor, and enter in the following highlighted code sections:

```
//
//   WalksPage.cs
//   TrackMyWalks
//
//   Created by Steven F. Daniel on 04/08/2016.
//   Copyright © 2016 GENIESOFT STUDIOS. All rights reserved.
//
using System.Collections.Generic;
using Xamarin.Forms;
using TrackMyWalks.Models;
using TrackMyWalks.ViewModels;
using TrackMyWalks.Services;


namespace TrackMyWalks
{
    public class WalksPage : ContentPage
    {
```

2. Next, we need to create a new private property named _viewModel within our `WalksPage` class. This is of the `WalksPageViewModel` type, and will essentially provide us with access to the ContentPage's `BindingContext` object. Proceed and enter in the following highlighted code sections:

```
WalksPageViewModel _viewModel {
    get { return BindingContext as WalksPageViewModel;
    }
}

public WalksPage()
{
    var newWalkItem = new ToolbarItem
    {
        Text = "Add Walk"
    };
```

3. Then, we need to set up a `Binding` to the `Command` property that we defined within our `WalksPageViewModel` class. This will be called when the user chooses the **Add Walk** button. Proceed and enter in the following highlighted code sections:

```
// Set up our Binding click event handler
  newWalkItem.SetBinding(ToolbarItem.CommandProperty,
  "CreateNewWalk");

// Add the ToolBar item to our ToolBar
ToolbarItems.Add(newWalkItem);
```

4. Next, we need to declare and initialize our `WalksPageViewModelBindingContext` to include our `IWalkNavService` constructor, which is used by the `WalkBaseViewModel` class, and is retrieved from the `Xamarin.Forms DependencyService` class. Proceed and enter in the following highlighted code sections:

```
// Declare and initialize our Model Binding Context
  BindingContext = new WalksPageViewModel(DependencyService.Get
  <IWalkNavService>());
// Define our Item Template
var itemTemplate = new DataTemplate(typeof(ImageCell));
itemTemplate.SetBinding(TextCell.TextProperty, "Title");
itemTemplate.SetBinding(TextCell.DetailProperty, "Notes");
itemTemplate.SetBinding(ImageCell.ImageSourceProperty, "ImageUrl");

    var walksList = new ListView
    {
        HasUnevenRows = true,
        ItemTemplate = itemTemplate,
        SeparatorColor = Color.FromHex("#ddd"),
    };

    // Set the Binding property for our walks Entries
    walksList.SetBinding(ItemsView<Cell>.ItemsSourceProperty,
    "walkEntries");
```

5. Then, we need to change the way in which an item gets selected from the `ListView`. We need to make a call to the `WalksTrailDetails` command that is included within our `WalksPageViewModel` class, so that it can navigate to the `WalksTrailViewModel`, whilst passing in the chosen item from within the `ListView`. Proceed and enter the following highlighted code sections:

```
// Initialize our event Handler to use when
```

```
   the item is tapped
walksList.ItemTapped += (object sender,
 ItemTappedEventArgs e) =>
{
    var item = (WalkEntries)e.Item;
    if (item == null) return;
    _viewModel.WalkTrailDetails.Execute(item);
    item = null;
};
   Content = walksList;
}
```

6. Finally, we need to create an OnAppearing instance method of the navigation hierarchy that will be used to display our WalksEntries prior to the ViewModel appearing on screen.

7. We need to ensure that our ViewModel has been properly initialized by checking to see that it isn't null, prior to calling the Init method of our WalksPageViewModel. Proceed and enter the following highlighted code sections:

```
protected override async void OnAppearing()
{
   base.OnAppearing();  // Initialize our WalksPageViewModel
   if (_viewModel != null)
   await _viewModel.Init();
 }
}
}
```

In this section, we looked at the steps involved in modifying the WalksPage so that it can take advantage of our updated WalksPageViewModel. We looked at how to set the content page to an instance of the WalksPageViewModel so that it knows where to get the list of walk entries. The list will be used and displayed within the ListView control, and will then update the BindingContext property for the WalksPage to point to an instance of the IWalkNavService interface. As you can see, by using a navigation service within your ViewModels, it makes navigating between each of the ViewModels quite easy.

Updating the walks entry page ViewModel and navigation service

Now that we have modified the MVVM ViewModel that will be used for the main `WalksPage`, our next step is to begin modifying the `WalkEntryViewModel` to take advantage of the navigation service, which will be used to create new walk entries, and save this information back to the `WalkBaseViewModel`. This will be covered in a later chapter as we progress throughout this book.

Let's take a look at how we can achieve this, by performing the following steps:

1. Ensure that the `WalkEntryViewModel.cs` file is displayed within the code editor, and enter in the following highlighted code sections:

```
//
//  WalkEntryViewModel.cs
//  TrackMyWalks ViewModels
//
//  Created by Steven F. Daniel on 22/08/2016.
//  Copyright © 2016 GENIESOFT STUDIOS. All rights reserved.
//
using System;
using System.Diagnostics.Contracts;
using System.Threading.Tasks;
using TrackMyWalks.Models;
using TrackMyWalks.Services;
using TrackMyWalks.ViewModels;
using Xamarin.Forms;

namespace TrackMyWalks.ViewModels
{
    public class WalkEntryViewModel : WalkBaseViewModel
    {
        string _title;
        public string Title
        {
            get { return _title; }
            set
            {
                _title = value;
                OnPropertyChanged();
                SaveCommand.ChangeCanExecute();
            }
        }

        string _notes;
```

```
public string Notes
{
    get { return _notes; }
    set
    {
        _notes = value;
        OnPropertyChanged();
    }
}

double _latitude;
public double Latitude
{
    get { return _latitude; }
    set
    {
        _latitude = value;
        OnPropertyChanged();
    }
}

double _longitude;
public double Longitude
{
    get { return _longitude; }
    set
    {
        _longitude = value;
        OnPropertyChanged();
    }
}

double _kilometers;
public double Kilometers
{
    get { return _kilometers; }
    set
    {
        _kilometers = value;
        OnPropertyChanged();
    }
}

string _difficulty;
public string Difficulty
{
    get { return _difficulty; }
    set
```

```
        {
            _difficulty = value;
            OnPropertyChanged();
        }
    }

    double _distance;
    public double Distance
    {
        get { return _distance; }
        set
        {
            _distance = value;
            OnPropertyChanged();
        }
    }

    string _imageUrl;
    public string ImageUrl
    {
        get { return _imageUrl; }
        set
        {
            _imageUrl = value;
            OnPropertyChanged();
        }
    }
```

2. In the next step, we need to modify the `WalksEntryViewModel` class constructor which will now need to include a parameter `navService` that is included within the `IWalkNavService` interface class. Then we'll set the ViewModel's class constructor to access all instance class members contained within the `navService` within the `WalksEntryViewModel`, by using the `base` keyword. Next, we'll initialize the constructor with default values for our `Title`, `Difficulty` and `Distance` properties.

3. Locate the `WalkEntryViewModel` class constructor, and enter the following highlighted code sections:

```
public WalkEntryViewModel(IWalkNavService navService) :
 base(navService)
{
    Title = "New Walk";
    Difficulty = "Easy";
    Distance = 1.0;
}
```

4. Next, we need to modify the `SaveCommand` command property to include the `async` and `await` keywords. This command property will be used to bind to the `SaveToolBarItem` and will run an action upon being pressed. It will then execute a class instance method to determine whether the command can be executed. Proceed and enter in the following highlighted code sections:

```
Command _saveCommand;
public Command SaveCommand
{
    get
    {
        return _saveCommand ?? (_saveCommand =
        new Command(async () => await ExecuteSaveCommand(),
        ValidateFormDetails));
    }
}
```

5. Next, we locate and modify the `ExecuteSaveCommand` instance method to include the `async Task` keywords to the method definition, and then include a reference to our `PreviousPage` method that is defined within our `IWalkNavService` interface to allow our `WalkEntryPage` to be dismissed upon the user clicking on the **Save** button. Proceed and enter in the following highlighted code sections:

```
async Task ExecuteSaveCommand()
{
var newWalkItem = new WalkEntries
{
Title = this.Title,
Notes = this.Notes,
Latitude = this.Latitude,
Longitude = this.Longitude,
Kilometers = this.Kilometers,
Difficulty = this.Difficulty,
Distance = this.Distance,
ImageUrl = this.ImageUrl
};

// Here, we will save the details entered in a later chapter.
await NavService.PreviousPage();
}

// method to check for any form errors
bool ValidateFormDetails()
{
 return !string.IsNullOrWhiteSpace(Title);
```

```
        }
```

6. Finally, create the `Init` method within the `WalkEntryViewModel`. This will be used to initialize the `WalkEntryPage` when it is called. We use the `Task.Factory.StartNew` method to give the ViewModel enough time to display the page on screen, prior to initializing the `ContentPage` contents. Proceed and enter in the following highlighted code sections:

```
public override async Task Init()
{
await Task.Factory.StartNew(() =>
{
Title = "New Walk";
Difficulty = "Easy";
Distance = 1.0;
});
}
}
}
```

In this section, we began by ensuring that our ViewModel inherits from the `WalkBaseViewModel` class and then modifies the `WalksEntryViewModel` class constructor to include the parameter `navService` which is included within the `IWalkNavService` interface class. In our next step, we'll initialize the class constructor with default values for the `Title`, `Difficulty`, and `Distance` properties and then modify the `SaveCommand` command method to include a reference to the `NavService.PreviousPage` method. This is declared within the `IWalkNavService` interface class to allow our `WalkEntryPage` to navigate back to the previous calling page when the Save button is clicked.

Updating the WalksEntryPage to use the updated ViewModel

In this section, we need to bind our model binding context, `BindingContext`, to the `WalkEntryViewModel` so that the new walk information, which will be entered within this page, can be stored within the `WalkEntries` model. Let's take a look at how we can achieve this, by performing the following steps:

1. Ensure that the `WalkEntryPage.cs` file is displayed within the code editor, and enter in the following highlighted code sections:

```
//
//   WalkEntryPage.cs
//   TrackMyWalks
//
//   Created by Steven F. Daniel on 04/08/2016.
//   Copyright © 2016 GENIESOFT STUDIOS. All rights reserved.
//
using Xamarin.Forms;
using TrackMyWalks.Models;
using System.Collections.Generic;

namespace TrackMyWalks
{
    public class WalkEntryPage : ContentPage
    {
```

2. Next, we need to create a new private property named `_viewModel` within the `WalkEntryPage` class that is of the `WalksEntryViewModel` type, and which will essentially provide us with access to the ContentPage's `BindingContext` object. Proceed and enter in the following highlighted code sections:

```
WalkEntryViewModel _viewModel
{
    get
    { return BindingContext as WalkEntryViewModel;
    }
}

public WalkEntryPage()
{
    // Set the Content Page Title
    Title = "New Walk Entry";
```

3. Next, we need to declare and initialize our
   `WalkEntryViewModelBindingContext` to include the `IWalkNavService`
   constructor, which is used by the `WalkBaseViewModel` class, and is retrieved
   from the `Xamarin.FormsDependencyService` class. Proceed and enter in the
   following highlighted code sections:

```
// Declare and initialize our Model Binding Context
   BindingContext = new WalkEntryViewModel(
   DependencyService.Get<IWalkNavService>());

    // Define our New Walk Entry fields
    var walkTitle = new EntryCell
    {
        Label = "Title:",
        Placeholder = "Trail Title"
    };
    walkTitle.SetBinding(EntryCell.TextProperty,
    "Title", BindingMode.TwoWay);

    var walkNotes = new EntryCell
    {
        Label = "Notes:",
        Placeholder = "Description"
    };
    walkNotes.SetBinding(EntryCell.TextProperty,
    "Notes", BindingMode.TwoWay);

    var walkLatitude = new EntryCell
    {
        Label = "Latitude:",
        Placeholder = "Latitude",
        Keyboard = Keyboard.Numeric
    };
    walkLatitude.SetBinding(EntryCell.TextProperty,
    "Latitude", BindingMode.TwoWay);

    var walkLongitude = new EntryCell
    {
        Label = "Longitude:",
        Placeholder = "Longitude",
        Keyboard = Keyboard.Numeric
    };
    walkLongitude.SetBinding(EntryCell.TextProperty,
    "Longitude", BindingMode.TwoWay);

    var walkKilometers = new EntryCell
    {
```

```
        Label = "Kilometers:",
        Placeholder = "Kilometers",
        Keyboard = Keyboard.Numeric
};
walkKilometers.SetBinding(EntryCell.TextProperty,
"Kilometers", BindingMode.TwoWay);

var walkDifficulty = new EntryCell
{
    Label = "Difficulty Level:",
    Placeholder = "Walk Difficulty"
};
walkDifficulty.SetBinding(EntryCell.TextProperty,
"Difficulty", BindingMode.TwoWay);

var walkImageUrl = new EntryCell
{
    Label = "ImageUrl:",
    Placeholder = "Image URL"
};
walkImageUrl.SetBinding(EntryCell.TextProperty,
"ImageUrl", BindingMode.TwoWay);

// Define our TableView
Content = new TableView
{
    Intent = TableIntent.Form,
    Root = new TableRoot
    {
        new TableSection()
        {
            walkTitle,
            walkNotes,
            walkLatitude,
            walkLongitude,
            walkKilometers,
            walkDifficulty,
            walkImageUrl
        }
    }
};

var saveWalkItem = new ToolbarItem
{
    Text = "Save"
};

saveWalkItem.SetBinding(MenuItem.CommandProperty,
```

```
                    "SaveCommand");

            ToolbarItems.Add(saveWalkItem);              }
       }
  }
```

In this section, we looked at the steps involved in modifying the `WalkEntryPage` so that it can take advantage of our updated `WalkEntryViewModel`. We looked at how to set the content page to an instance of the `WalkEntryViewModel` so that the `BindingContext` property for the `WalkEntryPage` will now point to an instance of the `IWalkNavService` interface.

Updating the walks trail page ViewModel and navigation service

Now that we have modified the MVVM ViewModel that will be used for our `WalkEntry` page, our next step is to begin modifying the `WalksTrailViewModel` to take advantage of the navigation service, so that it will be used to display the walk entry information that has been associated with the chosen walk.

Let's take a look at how we can achieve this, by performing the following the steps:

1. Ensure that the `WalksTrailViewModel.cs` file is displayed within the code editor, and enter in the following highlighted code sections:

```
//
//  WalksTrailViewModel.cs
//  TrackMyWalks ViewModels
//
//  Created by Steven F. Daniel on 22/08/2016.
//  Copyright © 2016 GENIESOFT STUDIOS. All rights reserved.
//
using System.Threading.Tasks;
using TrackMyWalks.Models;
using TrackMyWalks.Services;
using Xamarin.Forms;

namespace TrackMyWalks.ViewModels
{
    public class WalksTrailViewModel :
      WalkBaseViewModel<WalkEntries>
    {
        WalkEntries _walkEntry;
```

```
public WalkEntries WalkEntry
{
    get { return _walkEntry; }
    set
    {
        _walkEntry = value;
        OnPropertyChanged();
    }
}
```

2. Next, we need to create a `Command` property for our class. This will be used within our `WalkTrailPage` and will be used to handle when the user clicks on the **Begin This Trial** button. The `Command` property will run an action upon being pressed, and then execute a class instance method to determine whether the command can be executed or not, prior to navigating to the `DistTravelledViewModel`, and passing in the `trailDetails` for the chosen walk from the `WalksPage`. Proceed and enter in the following highlighted code sections:

```
Command<WalkEntries> _command;
public Command<WalkEntries> DistanceTravelled
{
    get
    {
        return _command
        ?? (_command =
        new Command<WalkEntries>(async (trailDetails) =>
        await NavService.NavigateToViewModel
        <DistTravelledViewModel, WalkEntries>(trailDetails)));
    }
}
```

3. Next, we need to declare and initialize our `WalksTrailViewModelBindingContext` to include the `IWalkNavService` constructor, which is used by the `WalkBaseViewModel` class, and is retrieved from the `Xamarin.FormsDependencyService` class. Proceed and enter in the following highlighted code sections:

```
public WalksTrailViewModel(IWalkNavService navService) :
  base(navService)
{
}
```

4. Finally, create the `Init` method within the `WalksTrailViewModel`. This will be used to initialize the `WalkTrailPage` when it is called. We use the `Task.Factory.StartNew` method to give the ViewModel enough time to display the page on screen, prior to initializing the `ContentPage` contents, using the passed in `walkDetails` for our model. Proceed and enter in the following highlighted code sections:

```
public override async Task Init(WalkEntries walkDetails)
{ await Task.Factory.StartNew(() =>
  {
      WalkEntry = walkDetails;
  });
  }
 }
}
```

In this section, we begin by ensuring that our ViewModel inherits from the `WalkBaseViewModel` class, and that it accepts the `WalkEntries` dictionary as its parameter. In our next step, we'll create a `DistanceTravelledCommand` method that will navigate to the `DistanceTravelledPage` content page within our `NavigationStack` that passes the `WalkEntry` dictionary to the `DistTravelledViewModel` ViewModel and pass a parameter containing the `trailDetails` of the chosen walk.

Updating the WalksTrailPage to use the updated ViewModel

In this section, we need to bind our model binding context, `BindingContext`, to the `WalksTrailViewModel` so that the walk information details will be displayed from the `WalkEntries` model when a walk has been clicked on within the main `WalksPage`. Let's take a look at how we can achieve this, by performing the following steps:

1. Ensure that the `WalkTrailPage.cs` file is displayed within the code editor, and enter in the following highlighted code sections:

```
//
//   WalkTrailPage.cs
//   TrackMyWalks
//
//   Created by Steven F. Daniel on 04/08/2016.
//   Copyright © 2016 GENIESOFT STUDIOS. All rights reserved.
//
using Xamarin.Forms;
```

```
using TrackMyWalks.Models;
using TrackMyWalks.ViewModels;
using TrackMyWalks.Services;

namespace TrackMyWalks
{
    public class WalkTrailPage : ContentPage
    {
        public WalkTrailPage(WalkEntries walkItem)
        {
            Title = "Walks Trail";
```

2. Next, we need to declare and initialize our
   WalkEntryViewModelBindingContext to include the IWalkNavService
   constructor, which is used by the WalkBaseViewModel class, and is retrieved
   from the Xamarin.FormsDependencyService class. Proceed and enter in the
   following highlighted code sections:

```
// Declare and initialize our Model Binding Context
BindingContext = new WalksTrailViewModel(DependencyService.
Get<IWalkNavService>());

var beginTrailWalk = new Button
{
    BackgroundColor = Color.FromHex("#008080"),
    TextColor = Color.White,
    Text = "Begin this Trail"
};
```

3. Next, we need to modify the beginTrailWalk.Clicked handler for our button,
   so that upon being clicked, it will navigate to the DistTravelledViewModel
   and pass in the WalkEntry dictionary for the chosen walk from the WalksPage.
   Proceed and enter in the following highlighted code sections:

```
// Declare and initialize our Event Handler
beginTrailWalk.Clicked += (sender, e) =>
{
    if (_viewModel.WalkEntry == null) return;
    _viewModel.DistanceTravelled.Execute(_viewModel.WalkEntry);
};

var walkTrailImage = new Image()
{
    Aspect = Aspect.AspectFill
};
walkTrailImage.SetBinding(Image.SourceProperty,
```

```
"WalkEntry.ImageUrl");

var trailNameLabel = new Label()
{
    FontSize = 28,
    FontAttributes = FontAttributes.Bold,
     TextColor = Color.Black
 };

    trailNameLabel.SetBinding(Label.TextProperty,
    "WalkEntry.Title");

    var trailKilometersLabel = new Label()
    {
        FontAttributes = FontAttributes.Bold,
        FontSize = 12,
        TextColor = Color.Black,
    };
    trailKilometersLabel.SetBinding(Label.TextProperty,
    "WalkEntry.Kilometers",
    stringFormat: "Length: {0} km");
    var trailDifficultyLabel = new Label()
    {
        FontAttributes = FontAttributes.Bold,
        FontSize = 12,
        TextColor = Color.Black
    };

    trailDifficultyLabel.SetBinding(Label.TextProperty,
    "WalkEntry.Difficulty", stringFormat: "Difficulty: {0}");

    var trailFullDescription = new Label()
    {
        FontSize = 11,
        TextColor = Color.Black,
        HorizontalOptions = LayoutOptions.FillAndExpand
    };
    trailFullDescription.SetBinding(Label.TextProperty,
    "WalkEntry.Notes");

    this.Content = new ScrollView
    {
        Padding = 10,
        Content = new StackLayout
        {
            Orientation = StackOrientation.Vertical,
            HorizontalOptions = LayoutOptions.FillAndExpand,
            Children =
```

```
        {
        walkTrailImage,
        trailNameLabel,
        trailKilometersLabel,
        trailDifficultyLabel,
        trailFullDescription,
        beginTrailWalk
        }
      }
    };
  }
 }
}
```

In this section, we looked at the steps involved in modifying the `WalksTrailPage` so that it can take advantage of the `WalksTrailViewModel`. We looked at how to set the content page to an instance of the `WalksTrailViewModel` so that the `BindingContext` property for the `WalkTrailPage` will now point to an instance of the `IWalkNavService` interface.

We also slightly modified our `Clicked` handler for the `beginTrailWalk` button so that it will now navigate to the `DistanceTravelledPage` content page within the `NavigationStack`, and pass in the `WalkEntry` dictionary object to the `DistTravelledViewModel` ViewModel.

Updating the distance travelled ViewModel and navigation service

Now that we have modified the MVVM ViewModel that will be used for our `WalkTrailPage`, our next step is to update the `DistTravelledViewModel` to take advantage of the navigation service, so that it can display the walk entry information that has been associated with the chosen walk.

Let's take a look at how we can achieve this, by performing the following steps:

1. Ensure that the `DistTravelledViewModel.cs` file is displayed within the code editor, and enter in the following highlighted code sections:

```
//
//  DistTravelledViewModel.cs
//  TrackMyWalks ViewModels
//
//  Created by Steven F. Daniel on 22/08/2016.
//  Copyright © 2016 GENIESOFT STUDIOS. All rights reserved.
```

```
//
using System;
using System.Threading.Tasks;
using TrackMyWalks.Models;
using TrackMyWalks.Services;
using TrackMyWalks.ViewModels;
using Xamarin.Forms;

namespace TrackMyWalks.ViewModels
{
    public class DistTravelledViewModel :
     WalkBaseViewModel<WalkEntries>
    {
        WalkEntries _walkEntry;

        public WalkEntries WalkEntry
        {
            get { return _walkEntry; }
            set
            {
                _walkEntry = value;
                OnPropertyChanged();
            }
        }

        double _travelled;
        public double Travelled
        {
            get { return _travelled; }
            set
            {
                _travelled = value;
                OnPropertyChanged();
            }
        }

        double _hours;
        public double Hours
        {
            get { return _hours; }
            set
            {
                _hours = value;
                OnPropertyChanged();
            }
        }

        double _minutes;
```

```
public double Minutes
{
    get { return _minutes; }
    set
    {
        _minutes = value;
        OnPropertyChanged();
    }
}

double _seconds;
public double Seconds
{
    get { return _seconds; }
    set
    {
        _seconds = value;
        OnPropertyChanged();
    }
}

public string TimeTaken
{
    get
    {
        return string.Format("{0:00}:{1:00}:{2:00}",
        this.Hours, this.Minutes, this.Seconds);
    }
}
```

2. Next, we need to modify the DistTravelledViewModel class constructor, which will now need to include a navService parameter that is included within the IWalkNavService interface class. We then set the ViewModel's class constructor to access all instance class members contained within the navService by using the base keyword and initialize the constructor with default values for the Hours, Minutes, Seconds, and Travelled properties.

3. Locate the DistTravelledViewModel class constructor, and enter the following highlighted code:

```
public DistTravelledViewModel(IWalkNavService navService) :
base(navService)
{
    this.Hours = 0;
    this.Minutes = 0;
    this.Seconds = 0;
    this.Travelled = 100;
```

```
}
```

4. Then, create the `Init` method within the `DistTravelledViewModel`, which will be used to initialize the `DistanceTravelledPage` content page when it is called. We need to specify and use the `Task.Factory.StartNew` method to give the ViewModel enough time to display the page on screen, prior to initializing the `ContentPage` contents, using the passed in `walkDetails` for our model. Proceed and enter in the following highlighted code sections:

```
public override async Task Init(WalkEntries walkDetails)
{
    await Task.Factory.StartNew(() =>
    {
        WalkEntry = walkDetails;
    });
}
```

5. Next, we need to create the `BackToMainPage` command property that will be used to bind to the **End This Trail** button that will run an action upon being pressed. This action will execute a class instance method, to determine whether the `Command` can be executed.

6. If the `Command` can be executed, a call will be made to the `BackToMainPage` method on the `NavService` navigation service class to take the user back to the `TrackMyWalks` main page, by removing all existing ViewModels within the `NavigationStack`, except the first page. Proceed and enter in the following highlighted code sections:

```
Command _mainPage;
public Command BackToMainPage
{
    get
    {
        return _mainPage  ?? (_mainPage = new
        Command(async () => await
        NavService.BackToMainPage()));
    }
}
```

In this section, we updated the `DistanceTravelledViewModel` to inherit from our `WalkBaseViewModel` Interface class and then modify the `DistTravelledViewModel` class constructor to point to an instance of the `IWalkNavService` interface class.

We then created the `Init` method that will initialize the `DistanceTravelledViewModel` when it is called and use the `Task.Factory.StartNew` method to give the ViewModel enough time to display the `DistanceTravelledPage` content page on screen, prior to initializing the `ContentPage` contents, using the passed in `walkDetails` for our model.

We also created the `BackToMainPage` command property that will be used to bind to the `End This Trail` button that will run an action to execute a class instance method, to determine whether the `Command` can be executed, and then a call will be made to `BackToMainPage` method on the `NavService` navigation service class to take the user back to the first page within the `NavigationStack`.

Updating the DistanceTravelledPage to use the updated ViewModel

Now that we have modified the MVVM ViewModel that will be used by our `DistanceTravelledPage` content page, our next step is to begin modifying the `DistanceTravelledPage` page to take advantage of our navigation service, and display walk information details. The calculations and distance travelled will be displayed from the `WalkEntries` model.

Let's take a look at how we can achieve this, by performing the following steps:

1. Ensure that the `DistanceTravelledPage.cs` file is displayed within the code editor, and enter in the following highlighted code sections:

```
//
//   DistanceTravelledPage.cs
//   TrackMyWalks
//
//   Created by Steven F. Daniel on 04/08/2016.
//   Copyright © 2016 GENIESOFT STUDIOS. All rights reserved.
//
using Xamarin.Forms;
using Xamarin.Forms.Maps;
using TrackMyWalks.Models;
using TrackMyWalks.Services;


namespace TrackMyWalks
{
    public class DistanceTravelledPage : ContentPage
    {
```

2. Next, we need to create a new private property named _viewModel within the DistanceTravelledPage class, which is of our DistTravelledViewModel type, and will essentially provide us with access to the ContentPage's BindingContext object. Proceed and enter in the following highlighted code sections:

```
DistTravelledViewModel _viewModel
{
    get { return BindingContext as DistTravelledViewModel; }
}
public DistanceTravelledPage()
{
    Title = "Distance Travelled";
```

3. Next, we need to declare and initialize the DistTravelledViewModelBindingContext to include our IWalkNavService constructor, which is used by the WalkBaseViewModel class, and is retrieved from the Xamarin.Forms DependencyService class. Proceed and enter in the following highlighted code sections:

```
// Declare and initialize our Model Binding Context
 BindingContext = new DistTravelledViewModel
(DependencyService.Get<IWalkNavService>());
```

4. Then, we need to create a new method called LoadDetails which will be used to grab the name of the chosen walk and the Latitude and Longitude values from the DistTravelledViewModel as well as zoom into the user entry location, using the MoveToRegion method. Proceed and enter in the following highlighted code sections:

```
public void LoadDetails()
{
    // Instantiate our map object
    var trailMap = new Map();

    // Place a pin on the map for the chosen
    // walk type
    trailMap.Pins.Add(new Pin
    {
        Type = PinType.Place,
        Label = _viewModel.WalkEntry.Title,
        Position = new Position(_viewModel.WalkEntry.Latitude,
         _viewModel.WalkEntry.Longitude)
    });
```

```
// Center the map around the list of
// walks entry's location
trailMap.MoveToRegion(MapSpan.FromCenterAndRadius(
 new Position(_viewModel.WalkEntry.Latitude,
   _viewModel.WalkEntry.Longitude),
   Distance.FromKilometers(1.0)));

var trailNameLabel = new Label()
{
    FontSize = 18,
    FontAttributes = FontAttributes.Bold,
    TextColor = Color.Black,
    HorizontalTextAlignment = TextAlignment.Center
};

trailNameLabel.SetBinding(Label.TextProperty,
"WalkEntry.Title");

var trailDistanceTravelledLabel = new Label()
{
    FontAttributes = FontAttributes.Bold,
    FontSize = 20,
    TextColor = Color.Black,
    HorizontalTextAlignment = TextAlignment.Center
};

trailDistanceTravelledLabel.SetBinding(Label.TextProperty,
"Travelled", stringFormat: "Distance Travelled: {0} km");

var totalTimeTakenLabel = new Label()
{
    FontAttributes = FontAttributes.Bold,
    FontSize = 20,
    TextColor = Color.Black,
    HorizontalTextAlignment = TextAlignment.Center
};

totalTimeTakenLabel.SetBinding(Label.TextProperty,
"TimeTaken", stringFormat: "Time Taken: {0}");

var walksHomeButton = new Button
{
    BackgroundColor = Color.FromHex("#008080"),
    TextColor = Color.White,
    Text = "End this Trail"
};
```

5. Next, we need to modify the `walksHomeButton.Clicked` handler for our button

so that, upon being clicked, it will allow the `DistanceTravelledPage` to navigate back to the first page within the `NavigationStack`. Proceed and enter in the following highlighted code sections:

```
// Set up our event handler
walksHomeButton.Clicked += (sender, e) =>
{
    if (_viewModel.WalkEntry == null) return;
    _viewModel.BackToMainPage.Execute(0);
};

this.Content = new ScrollView
{
    Padding = 10,
    Content = new StackLayout
    {
        Orientation = StackOrientation.Vertical,
        HorizontalOptions = LayoutOptions.FillAndExpand,
        Children = {
        trailMap,
        trailNameLabel,
        trailDistanceTravelledLabel,
        totalTimeTakenLabel,
        walksHomeButton
        }
    }
};
}
```

6. Finally, we need to create an `OnAppearing` instance method of the navigation hierarchy that will be used to correctly plot the walk's `Longitude` and `Latitude` coordinates within the map, along with the walk information, prior to the ViewModel appearing on screen. We need to ensure that the ViewModel has properly been initialized by checking to see that it isn't `null`, prior to calling the `Init` method of the `DistTravelledViewModel`. Proceed and enter in the following highlighted code sections:

```
protected override async void OnAppearing()
{
    base.OnAppearing();
    // Initialize our DistanceTravelledViewModel
    if (_viewModel != null)
    {
        await _viewModel.Init();
        LoadDetails();
    }
```

```
        }
      }
    }
```

In this section, we looked at the steps involved in modifying the `DistanceTraveledPage` so that it can take advantage of the `DistTravelledViewModel`. We looked at how to set the content page to an instance of the `DistTravelledViewModel` so that the `BindingContext` property for the `DistanceTravelledPage` will now point to an instance of the `IWalkNavService` interface.

We also slightly modified our `Clicked` handler for the `WalksHomeButton` button, so that it will now navigate to the `NavService.BackToMainPage` method, which is declared within the `IWalkNavService` interface class to allow the `DistanceTravelledPage` to navigate back to the first page within the `NavigationStack`.

Updating the Xamarin.Forms.App class to use the navigation service

In this section, we need to update our `Xamarin.Forms.App` class, by modifying the constructor in the main `App` class to create a new instance of the navigation service and register the application's `ContentPage` to ViewModel mappings.

Let's take a look at how we can achieve this, by performing the following steps:

1. Open the `TrackMyWalks.cs` file and ensure that it is displayed within the code editor.

2. Next, locate the `App` method and enter in the following highlighted code sections:

```
//
//   TrackMyWalks.cs
//   TrackMyWalks
//
//   Created by Steven F. Daniel on 04/08/2016.
//   Copyright © 2016 GENIESOFT STUDIOS. All rights reserved.
//using TrackMyWalks.Services;
using TrackMyWalks.ViewModels;
using Xamarin.Forms;

namespace TrackMyWalks
{
    public class App : Application
    {
```

```csharp
public App()
{
    // Check the Target OS Platform
    if (Device.OS == TargetPlatform.Android)
    {
        MainPage = new SplashPage();
    }
    else
    {
        // The root page of your application
        var walksPage = new NavigationPage(new WalksPage()
        {
            Title = "Track My Walks"
        });
        var navService = DependencyService.
        Get<IWalkNavService>() as WalkNavService;
        navService.navigation = walksPage.Navigation;
        navService.RegisterViewMapping(typeof
        (WalksPageViewModel), typeof(WalksPage));
        navService.RegisterViewMapping(
        typeof(WalkEntryViewModel),
        typeof(WalkEntryPage));
        navService.RegisterViewMapping(
        typeof(WalksTrailViewModel),
        typeof(WalkTrailPage));
        navService.RegisterViewMapping(
        typeof(DistTravelledViewModel),
        typeof(DistanceTravelledPage));
        MainPage = walksPage;
    }
}

protected override void OnStart()
{
    // Handle when your app starts
}

protected override void OnSleep()
{
    // Handle when your app sleeps
}

protected override void OnResume()
{
    // Handle when your app resumes
}
}
```

In the preceding code snippet, we begin by declaring a `navService` variable that points to an instance of the navigation service as defined by our assembly attribute for the `Xamarin.FormsDependencyService`, as declared in the `WalkNavService` class.

In our next step, we set the `navService.navigation` property to point to an instance of the `NavigationPage` class that the `walksPage.navigation` property currently points to, and will be used as the main root page.

Finally, we call the `RegisterViewMapping` instance method for each of the ViewModels and specify the associated `ContentPage` for each.

Summary

In this chapter, we updated our `TrackMyWalks` application and created a navigation service class that extends the default `Xamarin.Forms.Navigation` API, which provides us with a better method of performing ViewModel navigation. This separates the presentation aspects and business logic that are contained within the ViewModels.

In the next chapter, you'll learn how to create a location services class that will allow our `TrackMyWalks` app to retrieve location-based information, and determine the user's current location. You'll also learn how to set up our app to handle background location updates. You will also learn how to incorporate platform-specific features within your app, depending on the platform that is being run.

4
Adding Location-Based Features within Your App

In our previous chapter, we looked at how we can apply what we already know about the MVVM design pattern, and how we can navigate between our ViewModels, by creating a navigation service C# class that acts as the navigation service for our app, using the `Xamarin.FormsDependencyService` class.

In this chapter, you'll learn how to go about incorporating platform-specific features within the `TrackMyWalks` app, depending on the mobile platform. You'll learn how to create a C# class, which will act as the Location Service for our app, as well as creating a `IWalkLocationService` interface class file, which will include a number of class methods that both our iOS and Android platforms will inherit, and, in turn, update the content pages to bind with the ViewModels to allow location-based information between these Views to happen.

We will also be covering how to properly perform location updates while the application is either in the foreground or background, and we will also be touching on some key background concepts, which include registering an app as a background-necessary application.

This chapter will cover the following topics:

- Creating a location-based class that utilizes the native platform capabilities that come as part of the iOS and Android platforms
- Enabling background location updates as well as getting the user's current location
- Updating the `TrackMyWalks` application to use the `Location Service`
- Updating the `WalkEntryViewModel` to use the `Location Service Interface`

- Updating the `DistanceTravelledViewModel` to use the `Location Service Interface`

Creating and using platform-specific services

As mentioned in the introduction to this chapter, we created a customized navigation service, which provided an `IWalkNavService` Interface class for which our `WalkBaseViewModel` contained a property of that interface type, so that any implementations of the `IWalkNavService` can be provided to each of the ViewModels, as required.

The benefit of using an Interface to define platform-specific services is that it can be used within the `ViewModels` and the implementations of the service can be provided via dependency injection, using the `DependencyService`, with those implementations being actual services, or even mocked-up services for unit testing the ViewModels, which we will be covering in `Chapter 9`, *Unit Testing Your Xamarin.Forms Apps Using the NUnit and UITest Frameworks*.

In addition to the navigation service, we can use a couple of other platform-specific feature services within our `TrackMyWalks` app to enrich its data and user experience. In this section, we will be taking a look at how to create a `Location Service` class that allows us to get the specific geolocation coordinates from the actual device for both our iOS and Android platforms.

Creating the Location Service Interface for the TrackMyWalks app

Before we can begin allowing our `TrackMyWalks` app to take advantage of the device's geolocation capabilities for both our iOS and Android platforms, we will need to create an Interface within the `TrackMyWalks` Portable Class Library, which can then be used by the ViewModels for each platform.

We will need to define the interface for our location service, as this will contain method implementations, as well as a data structure that will be used to represent our `latitude` and `longitude` coordinates.

Let's take a look at how we can achieve this through the following steps:

1. Launch the Xamarin Studio application, and ensure that the `TrackMyWalks` solution is loaded within the Xamarin Studio IDE.

2. Next, create a new empty interface within the `TrackMyWalks` PCL project solution, under the `Services` folder.

3. Then, choose the **Empty Interface** option located within the **General** section and enter `IWalkLocationService` for the name of the new interface file to be created, as shown in the following screenshot:

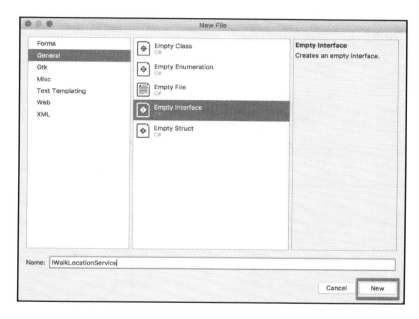

4. Next, click on the **New** button to allow the wizard to proceed and create the new **Empty Interface** class file, as shown in the preceding screenshot.

5. Our wizard has created our `IWalkLocationService` class file, which will be used by our ViewModels and content page Views to display geolocation coordinates. As we start to build the `Location Service Interface` class, you will see that it contains a couple of class members that will allow us to get the user's location as well as determining the distance that the user has travelled from point A to point B.

5. It also contains a data structure IWalkLocationCoords that will be used to hold our latitude and longitude geolocation coordinates. To proceed with creating the base IWalkLocationService Interface, perform the following steps:

6. Ensure that the IWalkLocationService.cs file is displayed within the code editor and enter the following code snippet:

```
//
//   IWalkLocationService.cs
//   TrackMyWalks Location Service Interface
//
//   Created by Steven F. Daniel on 16/09/2016.
//   Copyright © 2016 GENIESOFT STUDIOS. All rights reserved.
//
using System;

namespace TrackMyWalks.Services
{
    // Define our Walk Location Service Interface
    public interface IWalkLocationService
    {
        // Define our Location Service Instance Methods
        void GetMyLocation();

        double GetDistanceTravelled(double lat, double lon);
        event EventHandler<IWalkLocationCoords> MyLocation;
    }

    // Walk Location Coordinates Obtained
    public interface IWalkLocationCoords
    {
        double latitude { get; set; }
        double longitude { get; set; }
    }
}
```

In the preceding code snippet, we start by defining the implementation for our IWalkLocationService, which will provide our TrackMyWalks app with the ability to get the user's current location, calculating the distance travelled from the user's current location to the trail goal. We also define an EventHandlermyLocation, which will be called whenever the platform obtains a new location.

The IWalkLocationCoords interface defines a class that contains two properties that will be used by our EventHandler to return the latitude and longitude values.

An **Interface** contains only the methods, properties, and events signature definitions. Any class that implements the interface must implement all members of the interface that are specified in the interface definition.

Now that we have defined the property and method implementations that will be used by our `IWalkLocationService`, our next step will be to create the required `Location Service` class implementations for each of our platforms, as they are defined quite differently.

Creating the Location Service class for the Android platform

In this section, we will begin by setting up the basic structure for our `TrackMyWalks.Droid` solution to include the folder that will be used to represent our `Services`. Let's take a look at how we can achieve this through the following steps:

1. Launch the Xamarin Studio application, and ensure that the `TrackMyWalks` solution is loaded within the Xamarin Studio IDE.
2. Next, create a new folder within the `TrackMyWalks.Droid` project, called `Services`, as shown in the following screenshot:

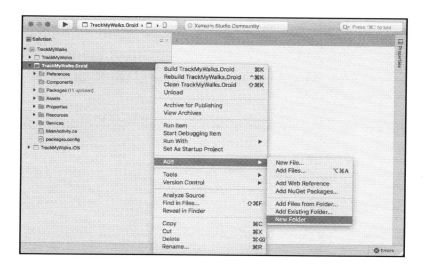

3. Next, create an empty class within the `Services` folder. If you can't remember how to do this, you can refer to the section entitled *Creating the Navigation Service Interface for the TrackMyWalks app*, within `Chapter 3`, *Navigating within the MVVM Model – The Xamarin.Forms Way*.

4. Then, choose the **Empty Class** option located within the **General** section and enter `WalkLocationService` for the name of the new class file to be created, as shown in the following screenshot:

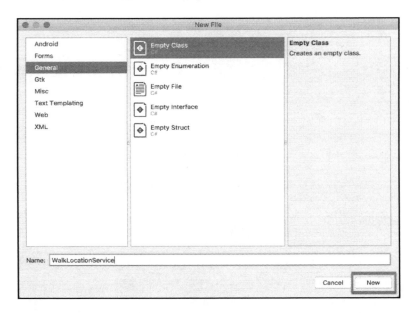

5. Next, click on the **New** button to allow the wizard to proceed and create the new empty class file, as shown in the preceding screenshot.

Up until this point, all we have done is create our `WalkLocationService` class file. This class will be used and will act as the base `Location Service` class that will contain the functionality required by our ViewModels.

As we start to build our `Location` Class, you will see that it contains a number of method members that will be used to help us get the user's current geolocation coordinates from their device, so that we can display this within each of our ViewModels, and it will implement the `IWalkLocationService` Interface.

To proceed with creating and implementing the base `WalkLocationService` class, perform the following steps:

1. Ensure that the `WalkLocationService.cs` file is displayed within the code editor, and enter the highlighted code sections shown in the following code snippet:

```
//
//   WalkLocationService.cs
//   TrackMyWalks Location Service Class (Android)
//
//   Created by Steven F. Daniel on 16/09/2016.
//   Copyright © 2016 GENIESOFT STUDIOS. All rights reserved.
//
using System;
using Android.Content;

using Android.Locations;
using TrackMyWalks.Droid;
using TrackMyWalks.Services;

using Xamarin.Forms;
```

2. First, we initialize our `WalkLocationService` class, which is to be marked as a dependency, by adding the `Dependency` metadata attribute just as we did for our navigation service. This is so that it can be resolved by the `Xamarin.FormsDependencyService` to allow it to find and use our method implementations as defined within our Interface. We also need to implement the `IWalkCoordinates` interface using the `LocationEventArgs` class that contains our `latitude` and `longitude` properties, which will be populated whenever a new location is obtained:

```
[assembly: Xamarin.Forms.Dependency(
  typeof(WalkLocationService))]
namespace TrackMyWalks.Droid
{
    // Event arguments containing latitude and longitude
    public class Coordinates : EventArgs, IWalkCoordinates
    {
        public double latitude { get; set; }
        public double longitude { get; set; }
    }
```

3. Next, we need to modify our `WalkLocationService` class constructor signature, so that it inherits from the `IWalkLocationService` Interface class, as well as implementing an `ILocationListener` interface class, which will be used to indicate whenever the user's location changes, by implementing four methods—`OnLocationChanged`, `OnProviderDisabled`, `OnProviderEnabled`, and `OnStatusChanged`:

```
public class WalkLocationService : Java.Lang.Object,
   IWalkLocationService, ILocationListener {
       LocationManager locationManager;
       Location newLocation;

       // Create the four methods for our LocationListener
       // interface.
       public void OnProviderDisabled(string provider) { }
       public void OnProviderEnabled(string provider) { }
       public void OnStatusChanged(string provider,
       Availability status, Android.OS.Bundle extras) { }
```

 We need to ensure that our `WalkLocationService` class inherits from the Android-specific `Java.Lang.Object` class, so that we can provide access to the system location services, in order to obtain periodic updates on the device's geographical location.

Whenever your classes inherit from the `ILocationListener` API, the `ILocationListener` Interface supports several different method types, which are explained in the following table:

Method name	Description
OnProviderDisabled	This method is fired up whenever the location service provider has been disabled by the user.
OnProviderEnabled	This method is fired up whenever the location service provider has been enabled by the user.
OnStatusChanged	This method is fired up whenever the location service provider status has been changed, that is, the location services have been disabled by the user.
OnLocationChanged	This method is fired up whenever a change in location has been detected.

4. Then, we need to set up an `EventHandler` delegate object that will be called whenever the location has been obtained or changed:

```
// Set up our EventHandler delegate that is called
// whenever a location has been obtained
public event EventHandler<IWalkCoordinates> MyLocation;
```

5. Next, we create the OnLocationChanged method that will be fired up whenever the user's location has been changed since the last time. This method accepts the user's current location, and we need to add a check to ensure that our location is not empty prior to creating an instance of our Coordinates class data structure, and then assigning the new location details for our latitude and longitude, before finally passing a copy of the Coordinates to the MyLocationEventHandler:

```
// Fired whenever there is a change in location
public void OnLocationChanged(Location location)
{
    if (location != null)

    {
        // Create an instance of our Coordinates
        var coords = new Coordinates();
        // Assign our user's Latitude and Longitude
        // values
        coords.latitude = location.Latitude;
        coords.longitude = location.Longitude;

        // Update our new location to store the
        // new details.
        newLocation = new Location("Point A");
        newLocation.Latitude = coords.latitude;
        newLocation.Longitude = coords.longitude;

        // Pass the new location details to our
        // Location Service EventHandler.
        MyLocation(this, coords);
    };
}
```

6. Then, we create the GetMyLocation method that will be used to start getting the user's location. We then set up our locationManager to request location updates. This is because, when dealing with Android, these services require a Context object in order for them to work. Xamarin.Forms comes with the Forms.Context object, and we use the NetworkProvider method to obtain the location using the cellular network and Wi-Fi. Consider the following code:

```
// Method to call to start getting location
public void GetMyLocation()
{
    locationManager = (LocationManager)

    long minTime = 0;      // Time in milliseconds
    float minDistance = 0; // Distance in metres
```

```
Forms.Context.GetSystemService(Context.LocationService);
locationManager.RequestLocationUpdates(
        LocationManager.NetworkProvider,
        minTime,
        minDistance,
        this);
}
```

7. Next, create the `GetDistanceTravelled` method, which accepts two parameters containing our `latitude` and `longitude` values. We create a new location, and set the `Latitude` and `Longitude` values that contain the ending coordinates for our trail. We then declare a variable `distance`, which calls the `DistanceTo` method on our `newLocation` object, to determine our current distance from the end goal. We divide the distance by `1000` to convert the distance travelled to meters:

```
// Calculates the distance between two points
public double GetDistanceTravelled(double lat, double lon)
{
    Location locationB = new Location("Trail Finish");
    locationB.Latitude = lat;
    locationB.Longitude = lon;

    float distance = newLocation.DistanceTo(locationB) / 1000;
    return distance;
}
```

8. Finally, create the `WalkLocationService` class finalizer; this will be used to stop all update listener events when our class has been set to `null`.

```
// Stop the location update when the object is set to null
 ~WalkLocationService()
 {
     locationManager.RemoveUpdates(this);
 }
 }
}
```

Now that we have created the `WalkLocationService` class for the Android portion of our `TrackMyWalks` app, our next step is to create the same class for the iOS portion, which will be covered in the next section.

Creating the Location Service class for the iOS platform

In the previous section, we created the class for our `WalkLocationService`. We also defined a number of different methods that will be used to provide location-based information within our MVVM ViewModel.

In this section, we will build the **iOS** portion for our `WalkLocationService`, just like we did for our **Android** portion. You will notice that the implementations for both of these classes are quite similar; however, these implement different methods, as you will see once we start implementing them.

Let's take a look at how we can achieve this through the following steps:

1. Create an empty class within the `Services` folder for our `TrackMyWalks.iOS` project, and enter `WalkLocationService` for the name of the new class file to create.

2. Once you have created the `WalkLocationService` class file, ensure that the `WalkLocationService.cs` file is displayed within the code editor and enter the highlighted code sections shown in the following code snippet:

```
//
//    WalkLocationService.cs
//    TrackMyWalks Location Service Class (iOS)
//
//    Created by Steven F. Daniel on 16/09/2016.
//    Copyright © 2016 GENIESOFT STUDIOS. All rights reserved.
//
using System;
using CoreLocation;
using TrackMyWalks.iOS;
using TrackMyWalks.Services;
using UIKit;
```

3. Next, we initialize our WalkLocationService class, which is to be marked as a dependency, by adding the Dependency metadata attribute just as we did for our navigation service. This is so that it can be resolved by the Xamarin.FormsDependencyService to allow it to find and use our method implementations as defined within our Interface. We also need to implement the IWalkCoordinates interface using the Coordinates class, which contains the latitude and longitude properties that will be populated whenever a new location is obtained:

```
[assembly: Xamarin.Forms.Dependency(typeof(WalkLocationService))]
namespace TrackMyWalks.iOS
{
    // Event arguments containing latitude and longitude
    public class Coordinates : EventArgs, IWalkCoordinates
    {
        public double latitude { get; set; }
        public double longitude { get; set; }
    }
}
```

4. Then, we need to modify our WalkLocationService class constructor signature, so that it inherits from the IWalkLocationService Interface class. We also need to declare our locationManager object, which will be used to obtain the user's location. We also create a newLocation object of type CLLocation, which will be used to convert the latitude and longitude coordinates from the locationManager object into a CLLocation object:

```
// Walk Location Service class that inherits from our
// IWalkLocationService interface
public class WalkLocationService : IWalkLocationService
{
    // Declare our Location Manager
    CLLocationManager locationManager;
    CLLocation newLocation;
```

5. Next, we need to set up an EventHandler delegate object that will be called whenever the location has been obtained or changed:

```
// Set up our EventHandler delegate that is called
// whenever a location has been obtained
public event EventHandler<IWalkCoordinates> MyLocation;
```

6. Then, we create the `GetMyLocation` method that will be used to start getting the user's location. Next, we set up our `locationManager` using the iOS `CLLocationManager` class to allow our class to request location updates. We then perform a check, using the `LocationServicesEnabled` property of the `CLLocationManager` class, to ensure that location services have been enabled on the user's device.

7. This is a good check to enforce prior to requesting the getting of the user's location, and if our `CLLocationManager` class determines that location services have been disabled, we display a message to the user, using the `UIAlertView` class:

```
// Method to call to start getting location
public void GetMyLocation()
{
    locationManager = new CLLocationManager();

    // Check to see if we have location services
    // enabled
    if (CLLocationManager.LocationServicesEnabled)
    {
        // Set the desired accuracy, in meters
        locationManager.DesiredAccuracy = 1;

        // CLLocationManagerDelegate Methods
```

8. Next, we set up an event handler, `LocationsUpdated`, that will start firing up whenever there is a change in the user's current location, and we call the `locationUpdated` instance method, passing in the location geo-coordinates:

```
// Fired whenever there is a change in
// location
locationManager.LocationsUpdated += (object sender,
CLLocationsUpdatedEventArgs e) =>
{
    locationUpdated(e);
};
```

9. Then, we set up an event handler, `AuthorizationChanged`, which will be called whenever it detects a change made to the authorization of location-based services. For example, this will be called if, for some reason, the user decides to turn off location-based services:

```
// This event gets fired whenever it
// detects a change, i.e., if the user
// has turned off or disabled location
```

```
// based services.
  locationManager.AuthorizationChanged += (object
  sender, CLAuthorizationChangedEventArgs e) =>
  {
      didAuthorizationChange(e);

      // Perform location changes within the
      // foreground.
      locationManager.RequestWhenInUseAuthorization();
  };
  }
}
```

10. Next, we create the `locationUpdated` method that will be fired up whenever the user's location has been changed since the last time. This method accepts the user's current location, which is defined by the `CLLocationsUpdatedEventArgs` in a variable called `e`. Next, we create an instance of our `Coordinates` class data structure, and then assign the new location details for the latitude and longitude, before finally passing a copy of the `Coordinates` to the `MyLocationEventHandler`:

```
// Method is called whenever there is a change in
// location
public void locationUpdated(CLLocationsUpdatedEventArgs e)
{
    // Create our Location Coordinates
    var coords = new Coordinates();

    // Get a list of our locations found
    var locations = e.Locations;

    // Extract our Latitude and Longitude values
    // from our locations array.
    coords.latitude = locations[locations.Length - 1].
      Coordinate.Latitude;
    coords.longitude = locations[locations.Length - 1].
      Coordinate.Longitude;

    // Then, convert both our Latitude and Longitude
    // values to a CLLocation object.
    newLocation = new CLLocation(coords.latitude,
      coords.longitude);
    MyLocation(this, coords);
}
```

11. Then, we create the `didAuthorizationChange` method, which will be called whenever the `CLLocationManager` delegate detects a change in the authorization status; you will be notified about those changes. To handle any changes in the authorization status while your app is running, and to prevent your application from crashing unexpectedly, you will need to ensure that the proper authorization is handled accordingly.

12. If we detect that the user has restricted or denied access to location services on the device, we will need to alert the user to this, and display an alert dialog popup:

```
public void didAuthorizationChange(
        CLAuthorizationChangedEventArgs authStatus)
{
    switch (authStatus.Status) {
        case CLAuthorizationStatus.AuthorizedAlways:
            locationManager.RequestAlwaysAuthorization();
            break;
        case CLAuthorizationStatus.AuthorizedWhenInUse:
            locationManager.StartUpdatingLocation();
            break;
        case CLAuthorizationStatus.Denied:
            UIAlertView alert = new UIAlertView();

            alert.Title = "Location Services Disabled";
            alert.AddButton("OK");
            alert.AddButton("Cancel");
            alert.Message = "Enable locations for this app
            via\nthe Settings app on your iPhone";
            alert.AlertViewStyle = UIAlertViewStyle.Default;

            alert.Show();

            alert.Clicked += (object s,
                              UIButtonEventArgs ev) =>
            {
                var Button = ev.ButtonIndex;
            };
            break;
        default:
            break;
    }
}
```

13. The `didAuthorizationChange` method contains a number of authorization status codes, and these are explained, along with their descriptions, in the following table:

Authorization status	Description
`.AuthorizedAlways` or `.AuthorizedWhenInUse`	Either of these cases can occur whenever the user has granted access for your app to use location services. These statuses are both mutually exclusive, as you can only receive one type of authorization at a time.
`.NotDetermined`	This generally happens whenever the user hasn't made a choice regarding whether your iOS app can begin accepting location updates, and can be caused if the user has installed your app for the first time and has not run it yet.
`.Restricted` or `.Denied`	You will generally receive this type of authorization status state whenever the user has explicitly denied access to your app for the use of location services, or when location services are currently unavailable.

If you are interested in finding out more information on the `CLLocationManager` class, please refer to the Xamarin developer documentation located at https://developer.xamarin.com/api/type/CoreLocation.CLLocationMa nager/.

14. Next, create the `GetDistanceTravelled` method, which accepts two parameters containing our `lat` and `lon` values, and declares a variable `distance`, which calls the `DistanceFrom` method on our `newLocation` object, to determine our current distance from the end goal. We divide the distance by `1000` to convert the distance travelled to meters:

```
// Calculates the distance between two points
public double GetDistanceTravelled(double lat, double lon)
{
    // Get the distance travelled from
    // current location to the previous location.
    var distance = newLocation.DistanceFrom(new
                CLLocation(lat, lon)) / 1000;
    return distance;
}
```

15. Finally, create the `WalkLocationService` class finalizer, which will be used to stop all update listener events and free the memory used when our class has been set to `null`:

```
// Stops performing location updates when the
// object has been set to null.
  ~WalkLocationService()
  {
      locationManager.StopUpdatingLocation();
  }
 }
}
```

Now that we have created the `WalkLocationService` class for the iOS portion of our `TrackMyWalks` app, our next step is to learn how to provide our iOS app with the functionality to perform continuous location updates in the background.

Enabling background updates and getting the user's current location

This relates to working with background location updates to continuously monitor changes to the user location in the background.

Let's take a look at how we can achieve this through the following steps:

1. Double-click on the `Info.plist` file, which is contained within the `TrackMyWalks.iOS` project, and ensure that the **Application** tab is showing.

2. Next, scroll down to the bottom of the page and select **Enable Background Modes** from under the **Background Modes** section to enable background updates.

2. Then, ensure that the **Location Updates** option has been selected, so that Xcode can provision your app to monitor location-based updates in the background:

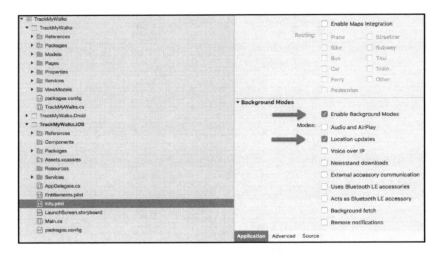

4. Now that we have modified our `TrackMyWalks.iOS` project to monitor location updates in the background, we need to do one more thing and tell Xcode to handle **Location updates**. So let's do that now.

5. Ensure that the `Info.plist` file is displayed within the Xamarin IDE, and that the **Source** tab is showing.

6. Next, create the keys `NSLocationAlwaysUsageDescription` and `NSLocationWhenInUseUsageDescription` by clicking within the **Add new entry** section of the `Info.plist`.

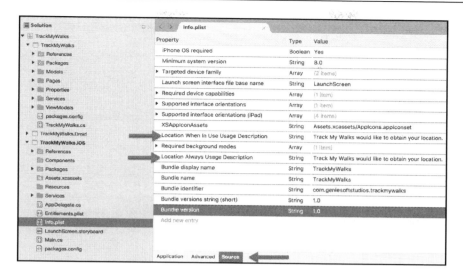

7. Then, add **Track My Walks would like to obtain your location** as the string description for the **Value** field, as shown in the preceding screenshot.

Next, we need to provide our app with the ability to monitor location updates in the background for our `TrackMyWalks.iOS` project. Let's take a look at how we can achieve this through the following steps:

1. Ensure that the `WalkLocationService.cs` file is displayed within the code editor.

2. Next, locate the `GetMyLocation` method and enter the following code snippet:

```
// Method to call to start getting location
public void GetMyLocation()
{
    locationManager = new CLLocationManager();

    // Check to see if we have location services
    // enabled
    if (CLLocationManager.LocationServicesEnabled)
    {
        // Set the desired accuracy, in meters
        locationManager.DesiredAccuracy = 1;

        // iOS 8 has additional permission
        // requirements
        if (UIDevice.CurrentDevice.CheckSystemVersion(8, 0))
        {
            // Perform location changes within the
```

```
    // background
        locationManager.RequestAlwaysAuthorization();
    }

    // iOS 9, comes with a new method that
    // allows us to receive location updates
    // within the back, when the app has
    // suspended.
    if (UIDevice.CurrentDevice.CheckSystemVersion(9, 0))
    {
        locationManager.AllowsBackgroundLocationUpdates = true;
    }

    // CLLocationManagerDelegate Methods
    // Fired whenever there is a change in
    // location
    locationManager.LocationsUpdated += (object sender,
    CLLocationsUpdatedEventArgs e) =>
    {
        locationUpdated(e);
    };

    // This event gets fired whenever it
    // detects a change, i.e., if the user has
    // turned off or disabled Location Based
    // Services.
    locationManager.AuthorizationChanged += (object
    sender, CLAuthorizationChangedEventArgs e) =>
    {
        didAuthorizationChange(e);

        // Perform location changes within
    // the foreground.
        locationManager.RequestWhenInUseAuthorization();
    };
    }
}
```

In the preceding code snippet, we check the iOS version currently running on the user's device, and use the `RequestAlwaysAuthorization` method call on the `locationManager` class to request the user's permission to obtain their current location. In iOS 9, Apple decided to add a new method called `AllowsBackgroundLocationUpdates`, which allows the handling of background location updates. Next, we also need to configure our Android portion of our `TrackMyWalks.Droid` project by modifying the `AndroidManifest.xml` file.

Let's take a look at how we can achieve this through the following steps:

1. Double-click on the `AndroidManifest.xml` file, which is contained within the `TrackMyWalks.Droid` project, and ensure that the **Source** tab is selected, as shown in the following screenshot:

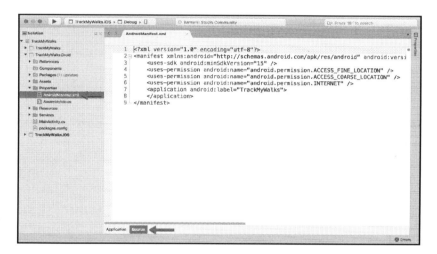

2. Ensure that the `AndroidManifest.xml` file is displayed within the code editor, and enter the following highlighted code sections:

```xml
<?xml version="1.0" encoding="utf-8"?>
<manifest xmlns:android="http://schemas.
  android.com/apk/res/android"
  android:versionCode="1" android:versionName="1.0"
  package="com.geniesoftstudios.trackmywalks">
<uses-sdk android:minSdkVersion="15" />
<uses-permission android:name="android.
  permission.ACCESS_FINE_LOCATION" />
<uses-permission android:name="android.
  permission.ACCESS_COARSE_LOCATION" />
```

```
<uses-permission android:name="android.
   permission.INTERNET" />
<application android:label="TrackMyWalks">
</application>
</manifest>
```

In the preceding code snippet, we begin by adding permissions that will allow our `TrackMyWalks` Android app to access location information for location updates, as well as the Internet. Google is pretty strict about which permissions are allowed, and these must be approved prior to your app being accepted into the Google Play Store.

Updating the WalkEntryViewModel to use the location service

Now that we have created our `WalkLocationService` for both our **Android** and **iOS** implementations, we need to begin modifying our **ViewModel**, which will be used by our `WalkEntry` page, to take advantage of our `Location Service`.

Let's take a look at how we can achieve this through the following steps:

1. Ensure that the `WalkEntryViewModel.cs` file is displayed within the code editor, and enter in the following highlighted code sections:

```
//
//  WalkEntryViewModel.cs
//  TrackMyWalks ViewModels
//
//  Created by Steven F. Daniel on 22/08/2016.
//  Copyright © 2016 GENIESOFT STUDIOS. All rights reserved.
//
    using System;
    using System.Diagnostics.Contracts;
    using System.Threading.Tasks;
    using TrackMyWalks.Models;
    using TrackMyWalks.Services;
    using TrackMyWalks.ViewModels;
    using Xamarin.Forms;

    namespace TrackMyWalks.ViewModels
    {
        public class WalkEntryViewModel : WalkBaseViewModel
        {
```

2. Next, we declare a `locationService` variable that will be used to provide a

reference to our IWalkLocationService and provide our class with a reference to the EventHandler, which is contained within our IWalkLocationService interface class; this will contain our location coordinate information whenever the location changes. To proceed, enter the following highlighted code sections:

```
IWalkLocationService locationService;

string _title;
public string Title
{
    get { return _title; }
    set
    {
        _title = value;
        OnPropertyChanged();
        SaveCommand.ChangeCanExecute();
    }
}

string _notes;
public string Notes
{
    get { return _notes; }
    set
    {
        _notes = value;
        OnPropertyChanged();
    }
}

double _latitude;
public double Latitude
{
    get { return _latitude; }
    set
    {
        _latitude = value;
        OnPropertyChanged();
    }
}

double _longitude;
public double Longitude
{
    get { return _longitude; }
    set
    {
```

```
            _longitude = value;
            OnPropertyChanged();
        }
    }

    double _kilometers;
    public double Kilometers
    {
        get { return _kilometers; }
        set
        {
            _kilometers = value;
            OnPropertyChanged();
        }
    }
    string _difficulty;
    public string Difficulty
    {
        get { return _difficulty; }
        set
        {
            _difficulty = value;
            OnPropertyChanged();
        }
    }

    double _distance;
    public double Distance
    {
        get { return _distance; }
        set
        {
            _distance = value;
            OnPropertyChanged();
        }
    }

    string _imageUrl;
    public string ImageUrl
    {
        get { return _imageUrl; }
        set
        {
            _imageUrl = value;
            OnPropertyChanged();
        }
    }
```

3. In our next step, we will need to modify the contents of our WalksEntryViewModel class constructor to declare and initialize our locationService variable, which will include our IWalkLocationService constructor that is retrieved from the Xamarin.FormsDependencyService class. We then proceed to call the MyLocation method on our EventHandler, which is defined within the IWalkLocationService interface; this will return the geographical location coordinates defined by their Latitude and Longitude values.

4. Locate the WalksEntryViewModel class constructor and enter the following highlighted code sections:

```
public WalkEntryViewModel(IWalkNavService navService) :
  base(navService)
{
    Title = "New Walk";
    Difficulty = "Easy";
    Distance = 1.0;

    // Get our Location Service
   locationService= DependencyService.Get<IWalkLocationService>();
    // Check to ensure that we have a value
     // for our object
    if (locationService != null)
    {
        locationService.MyLocation += (object sender,
          IWalkCoordinates e) =>
        {
            // Obtain our Latitude and Longitude
             // coordinates
            Latitude = e.latitude;
            Longitude = e.longitude;
        };
    }
    // Call our Service to get our GPS location
    locationService.GetMyLocation();
}

Command _saveCommand;
public Command SaveCommand
{
    get
    {
        return _saveCommand ?? (
        _saveCommand = new Command(async () =>
        await ExecuteSaveCommand(), ValidateFormDetails));
    }
```

```
}

async Task ExecuteSaveCommand()
{
    var newWalkItem = new WalkEntries
    {
        Title = this.Title,
        Notes = this.Notes,
        Latitude = this.Latitude,
        Longitude = this.Longitude,
        Kilometers = this.Kilometers,
        Difficulty = this.Difficulty,
        Distance = this.Distance,
        ImageUrl = this.ImageUrl
    };
```

5. Then, we locate and modify the `ExecuteSaveCommand` instance method to free the memory used by our `locationService` variable when the **Save** button is pressed. This is achieved by setting `this` to null, which in turn will call the `~GetMyLocation()` within the **iOS** and **Android** class de-constructor. Proceed to enter the following highlighted code sections:

```
        // Upon exiting our New Walk Entry Page,
         // we need to stop checking for location
         // updates
        locationService = null;

        // Here, we will save the details entered
        // in a later chapter.
        await NavService.PreviousPage();
    }

    // method to check for any form errors
    bool ValidateFormDetails()
    {
        return !string.IsNullOrWhiteSpace(Title);
    }

    public override async Task Init()
    {
        await Task.Factory.StartNew(() =>
        {
            Title = "New Walk";
            Difficulty = "Easy";
            Distance = 1.0;
        });
    }
```

```
        }
    }
```

In this section, we looked at the steps involved in modifying our `WalkEntryViewModel` so that it can take advantage of our `WalkLocationService`.

We then declared a `locationService` variable that will be used to provide a reference to our `IWalkLocationService` and provide our class with a reference to the `EventHandler`, which is contained within our `IWalkLocationService` interface class; this will contain our location coordinate information whenever the location changes.

We also modified our `WalkEntryViewModel` class constructor to initialize our `locationService` variable, to point to the `IWalkLocationService` constructor that is retrieved from the `Xamarin.FormsDependencyService` class, which needs to be done prior to calling the `MyLocation` method on our `EventHandler`, so that it can return the geographical location coordinates, defined by their `Latitude` and `Longitude` values.

Finally, we set our `locationService` object to null to stop checking for location updates.

Updating the DistanceTravelledViewModel to use the location service

Now that we have modified our MVVM ViewModel for our `WalkEntryViewModel`, our next step is to begin modifying our `DistTravelledViewModel` to take advantage of our `WalkLocationService` class, that will be used to calculate the distance travelled, and save this information back to our `DistTravelledViewModel`.

Let's take a look at how we can achieve this through the following steps:

1. Ensure that the `DistTravelledViewModel.cs` file is displayed within the code editor.

```
//
//   DistTravelledViewModel.cs
//   TrackMyWalks ViewModels
//
//   Created by Steven F. Daniel on 22/08/2016.
//   Copyright © 2016 GENIESOFT STUDIOS. All rights reserved.
//
using System;
using System.Threading.Tasks;
using TrackMyWalks.Models;
```

```
using TrackMyWalks.Services;
using TrackMyWalks.ViewModels;
using Xamarin.Forms;

namespace TrackMyWalks.ViewModels
{
    public class DistTravelledViewModel :
      WalkBaseViewModel<WalkEntries>
    {
        WalkEntries _walkEntry;
```

2. Next, we declared a `locationService` variable that will be used to provide a reference to our `IWalkLocationService` and provide our class with a reference to the `EventHandler`, which is contained within our `IWalkLocationService` interface class; this will contain our location coordinate information whenever the location changes. To proceed, enter the following highlighted code sections:

```
IWalkLocationService locationService;

public WalkEntries WalkEntry
{
    get { return _walkEntry; }
    set
    {
        _walkEntry = value;
        OnPropertyChanged();
    }
}

double _travelled;
public double Travelled
{
    get { return _travelled; }
    set
    {
        _travelled = value;
        OnPropertyChanged();
    }

}

double _hours;
public double Hours
{
    get { return _hours; }
    set
    {
```

```
            _hours = value;
            OnPropertyChanged();
        }
    }

    double _minutes;
    public double Minutes
    {
        get { return _minutes; }
        set
        {
            _minutes = value;
            OnPropertyChanged();
        }
    }

    double _seconds;
    public double Seconds
    {
        get { return _seconds; }
        set
        {
            _seconds = value;
            OnPropertyChanged();
        }
    }

    public string TimeTaken
    {
        get
        {
            return string.Format("{0:00}:{1:00}:{2:00}",
            this.Hours, this.Minutes, this.Seconds);
        }
    }
```

3. Next, we need to modify the `DistTravelledViewModel` class constructor to declare and initialize our `locationService` variable; this will include our `IWalkLocationService` constructor, which is retrieved from the `Xamarin.FormsDependencyService` class. We then proceed to call the `MyLocation` method on our `EventHandler`, which is defined within the `IWalkLocationService` interface; this will return the geographical location coordinates, defined by their `Latitude` and `Longitude` values.

4. Locate the `DistTravelledViewModel` class constructor and enter the following highlighted code:

```
public DistTravelledViewModel(IWalkNavService navService) :
base(navService)
{
    this.Hours = 0;
    this.Minutes = 0;
    this.Seconds = 0;
    this.Travelled = 100;

    locationService = DependencyService.Get
      <IWalkLocationService>();
    locationService.MyLocation += (object sender,
      IWalkCoordinates e) =>
    {
        // Determine Distance Travelled
        if (_walkEntry != null)
        {
            var distance = locationService.GetDistanceTravelled(
              _walkEntry.Latitude, _walkEntry.Longitude);
            this.Travelled = distance;
        }
    };
    locationService.GetMyLocation();
}
```

5. Then, we create the `Init` method within our `DistTravelledViewModel`, which will be used to initialize the `DistanceTravelled` when it is called. We need to specify and use the `Task.Factory.StartNew` method to give the ViewModel enough time to display the page on screen, prior to initializing the `ContentPage` contents and using the passed-in `walkDetails` for our model:

```
public override async Task Init(WalkEntries walkDetails)
{
    await Task.Factory.StartNew(() =>
    {
        WalkEntry = walkDetails;
    });
}
```

6. Next, we need to create the `BackToMainPage` command property that will be used to bind to the **End This Trail** button, which will run an action upon being pressed. This action will execute a class instance method to determine whether the command can be executed.

7. If the command can be executed, a call will be made to the `BackToMainPage` method on the `NavService` navigation service class to take the user back to the `TrackMyWalks` main page; this is done by removing all existing ViewModels within the `NavigationStack`, except the first page:

```
Command _mainPage;
public Command BackToMainPage
{
    get
    {
        return _mainPage ?? (_mainPage = new Command(
            async () => await
        NavService.BackToMainPage()));
    }
}
}
```

In this section, we looked at the steps involved in modifying our `DistanceTravelledViewModel` so that it can take advantage of our `WalkLocationService`. We then declared a `locationService` variable that will be used to provide a reference to our `IWalkLocationService` and provide our class with a reference to the `EventHandler`, which is contained within our `IWalkLocationService` interface class; this will contain our location coordinate information whenever the location changes.

We also modified our `DistTravelledViewModel` class constructor to initialize our `locationService` variable to point to the `IWalkLocationService` constructor that is retrieved from the `Xamarin.Forms DependencyService` class; this needs to be done prior to calling the `MyLocation` method on our `EventHandler`, so that it can return the geographical location coordinates, defined by their `Latitude` and `Longitude` values.

Updating the SplashPage to register our ViewModels

In this section, we need to update our `SplashPage` to register our ViewModels for our Android platform; this will involve creating a new instance of the navigation service, and registering the application `ContentPage` and ViewModel mappings:

1. Ensure that the `SplashPage.cs` file is displayed within the code editor, and enter in the following highlighted code sections:

```
//
//  SplashPage.cs
//  TrackMyWalks
//
//  Created by Steven F. Daniel on 04/08/2016.
//  Copyright © 2016 GENIESOFT STUDIOS. All rights reserved.
//
using System;
using System.Threading.Tasks;
using TrackMyWalks.Services;
using TrackMyWalks.ViewModels;
using Xamarin.Forms;

namespace TrackMyWalks
{
    public class SplashPage : ContentPage
    {
        public SplashPage()
        {
            AbsoluteLayout splashLayout = new AbsoluteLayout
            {
                HeightRequest = 600
            };

            var image = new Image()
            {
                Source = ImageSource.FromFile("icon.png"),
                Aspect = Aspect.AspectFill,
            };
            AbsoluteLayout.SetLayoutFlags(image,
                AbsoluteLayoutFlags.All);
            AbsoluteLayout.SetLayoutBounds(image,
                new Rectangle(0f, 0f, 1f, 1f));

            splashLayout.Children.Add(image);
```

```
            Content = new StackLayout()
            {
                Children = { splashLayout }
            };
    }
```

2. Next, locate the `OnAppearing` method and enter the following highlighted code sections:

```
protected override async void OnAppearing()
{
    base.OnAppearing();

    // Delay for a few seconds on the splash screen
    await Task.Delay(3000);

    // Instantiate a NavigationPage with the
    // MainPage
    var navPage = new NavigationPage(new WalksPage()
    {
        Title = "Track My Walks - Android"
    });

    navPage.BarBackgroundColor = Color.FromHex("#4C5678");
    navPage.BarTextColor = Color.White;
    // Declare our DependencyService Interface
    var navService = DependencyService.Get<IWalkNavService>()
        as WalkNavService;
    navService.navigation = navPage.Navigation;
    // Register our View Model Mappings between
        // our ViewModels and Views (Pages).navService.
        RegisterViewMapping(typeof(WalksPageViewModel),
            typeof(WalksPage));
        navService.RegisterViewMapping(
        typeof(WalkEntryViewModel),typeof(WalkEntryPage));
        navService.RegisterViewMapping(
        typeof(WalksTrailViewModel), typeof(WalkTrailPage));
        navService.RegisterViewMapping(
          typeof(DistTravelledViewModel),
            typeof(DistanceTravelledPage));
        // Set the MainPage to be our Walks Navigation Page
        Application.Current.MainPage = navPage;
    }
  }
}
```

In the preceding code snippet, we begin by customizing our `NavigationBar`, by setting the `Background` and `TextColor` attributes, and then declaring a variable `navService` that points to an instance of our navigation service as defined by our assembly attribute for our `Xamarin.FormsDependencyService`, which is declared in our `WalkNavService` class.

In our next step, we set the `navService.navigation` property to point to an instance of the `NavigationPage` class that our `walksPage.navigation` property currently points to, and this will be used as the main root page.

Finally, we call the `RegisterViewMapping` instance method for each of our ViewModels and specify the associated `ContentPage` for each.

Updating the MainActivity class to use Xamarin.Forms.Maps

In this section, we need to update our `MainActivity` Class to integrate with the `Xamarin.Forms.Maps` package for our **Android** platform, so that our ViewModels can use this to display mapping capabilities:

1. Open the `MainActivity.cs` file and ensure that it is displayed within the code editor.
2. Next, locate the `OnCreate` method and enter the following highlighted code sections:

```
//
//   MainActivity.cs
//   TrackMyWalks
//
//   Created by Steven F. Daniel on 04/08/2016.
//   Copyright © 2016 GENIESOFT STUDIOS. All rights reserved.
//
using Android.App;
using Android.Content.PM;
using Android.OS;

namespace TrackMyWalks.Droid
{
    [Activity(Label = "TrackMyWalks.Droid",
    Icon = "@drawable/icon", Theme = "@style/MyTheme",
    MainLauncher = true, ConfigurationChanges =
      ConfigChanges.ScreenSize |
      ConfigChanges.Orientation)]
```

```
public class MainActivity :
 global::Xamarin.Forms.Platform.Android.FormsAppCompatActivity
{
    protected override void OnCreate(Bundle savedInstanceState)
    {
        TabLayoutResource = Resource.Layout.Tabbar;
        ToolbarResource = Resource.Layout.Toolbar;

        base.OnCreate(savedInstanceState);

        global::Xamarin.Forms.Forms.Init(this,
          savedInstanceState);

        // Integrate Xamarin Forms Maps
        Xamarin.FormsMaps.Init(this, savedInstanceState);
        LoadApplication(new App());
    }
}
}
```

In the preceding code snippet, we begin by initializing our `MainActivity` class to use the `Xamarin.Forms.Maps` library, so that our `TrackMyWalks` solution can use the maps. If this is omitted from the class, the `DistanceTravelledPage` content page will not display the map, and therefore will not work as expected.

Updating the Xamarin.Forms App class to use platform specifics

In this section, we need to update our `Xamarin.Forms.App` class by modifying the constructor in the main `App` class to set the `MainPage` instance, depending on the `TargetPlatform` that our device is running. This is extremely easy when using `Xamarin.Forms`.

Let's take a look at how we can achieve this by following these steps:

1. Open the `TrackMyWalks.cs` file and ensure that it is displayed within the code editor.

2. Next, locate the `App` method and enter the following highlighted code sections:

```
//
//   TrackMyWalks.cs
//   TrackMyWalks
//
```

```
//   Created by Steven F. Daniel on 04/08/2016.
//   Copyright © 2016 GENIESOFT STUDIOS. All rights reserved.
//
using TrackMyWalks.Services;
using TrackMyWalks.ViewModels;
using Xamarin.Forms;

namespace TrackMyWalks
{
    public class App : Application
    {
        public App()
        {
            // Check the Device Target OS Platform
            if (Device.OS == TargetPlatform.Android)
            {
                // The root page of your application
                MainPage = new SplashPage();
            }
            else if (Device.OS == TargetPlatform.iOS)
            {
                // The root page of your application
                 var walksPage = new NavigationPage(new WalksPage()
                {
                    Title = "Track My Walks - iOS"
                });

                // Set the NavigationBar TextColor and
                // Background Color
                 walksPage.BarBackgroundColor =
                   Color.FromHex("#440099");
                 walksPage.BarTextColor = Color.White;
                // Declare our DependencyService Interface
                var navService = DependencyService.
                  Get<IWalkNavService>() as WalkNavService;
                navService.navigation = walksPage.Navigation;

                // Register our View Model Mappings
                // between our ViewModels and Views (Pages)
                navService.RegisterViewMapping(
                typeof(WalksPageViewModel), typeof(WalksPage));
                navService.RegisterViewMapping(
                typeof(WalkEntryViewModel), typeof(WalkEntryPage));
                navService.RegisterViewMapping(
                typeof(WalksTrailViewModel),
                  typeof(WalkTrailPage));
                navService.RegisterViewMapping(typeof(
                DistTravelledViewModel),
```

```
                    typeof(DistanceTravelledPage));

                // Set the MainPage to be our
                // Walks Navigation Page
                MainPage = walksPage;
            }
        }
        protected override void OnStart()
        {
            // Handle when your app starts
        }

        protected override void OnSleep()
        {
            // Handle when your app sleeps
        }

        protected override void OnResume()
        {
            // Handle when your app resumes
        }
    }
}
```

In the preceding code snippet, we use the TargetPlatform class that comes as part of the Xamarin.Forms.Core library, and we check this against the Device.OS class and handle it accordingly.

The TargetPlatform method contains a number platform codes, which are explained along with their descriptions in the following table:

Platform name	Description
Android	This indicates that the Xamarin.Forms platform is running on a device that is running the Android operating system.
iOS	This indicates that the Xamarin.Forms platform is running on a device that is running the Apple iOS operating system.
Windows	This indicates that the Xamarin.Forms platform is running on a device that is running the Windows platform.
WinPhone	This indicates that the Xamarin.Forms platform is running on a device that is running the Microsoft WinPhone OS.

For more information on the `Device` class, refer to the Xamarin documentation at
`https://developer.xamarin.com/guides/xamarin-forms/platform-feat`
`ures/device/`.

Now that we have updated the necessary MVVM ViewModels to take advantage of our `WalkLocationService`, our next step is to finally build and run the `TrackMyWalks` application within the iOS simulator. When compilation completes, the iOS simulator will appear automatically and the `TrackMyWalks` application will be displayed, as shown in the following screenshot:

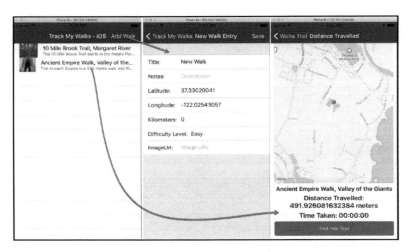

As you can see from the preceding screenshot, this displays our current list of walk trail entries, which are displayed within our `ListView`. When the user clicks on the **Add Walk** button link, this will display the **New Walk Entry** content page, and will display the current user's geolocation coordinates for the **Latitude** and **Longitude** `EntryCell` properties contained within our `WalkEntryViewModel`. The preceding screenshot, this shows the distance travelled page along with the placeholder pin marker showing the trail location within the map View. You will notice that the **Distance Travelled** section has been updated and shows the distance travelled by the user that is calculated by the `GetDistanceTravelled` method contained within our `IWalkLocationService` interface.

Summary

In this chapter, we updated our `TrackMyWalks` application, and created a `Location Service` class that extended the default native core Location Services classes for iOS and Android, which provides us with a better method of capturing geolocation coordinates within the ViewModel.

In the next chapter, you'll learn about custom renderers and how you can use them to change the appearance of the control elements within the user interface that target a specific platform.

You will learn how to work with `DataTemplates` by creating a C# class to layout your views beautifully throughout your application, and work with the *platform-specific* APIs to extend the default behavior of `Xamarin.Forms` controls through the use of custom renderers, by creating a custom picker control for iOS.

We will also be covering how you can use the Xamarin.Forms `EffectsAPI` to customize the appearance and styling of native control elements for each platform, by implementing a custom renderer class, and manipulate the visual appearance of data that is bound, through the use of Value and Image Converters.

5
Customizing the User Interface

In our previous chapter, we looked at how we can incorporate platform-specific features within the `TrackMyWalks` app, which is dependent on the mobile platform. You learned how to create a C# class, which acted as a location service that included a number of class methods for both iOS and Android platforms.

We also covered how to properly perform location updates whether the application's state is in the foreground or background by registering the app as a background-necessary application.

In this chapter, you'll learn how to work with the `DataTemplateCustomRenderer` by creating a C# class to lay out your views beautifully within your applications, and you will also get accustomed to working with platform-specific APIs to extend the default behavior of Xamarin.Forms' controls through the use of custom renderers, by creating a custom picker.

We will also be covering how to use the Xamarin.Forms `Effects` API to customize the appearance and styling of native control elements for each platform, by implementing a `CustomRenderer` class. We'll look at how to manipulate the visual appearance of data that is bound, through the use of value and image converters.

This chapter will cover the following points:

- Creating a custom `DataTemplate` class which utilizes native platform capabilities, that come as part of the iOS and Android platforms
- Working with custom renderers to change the appearance of control elements
- Using the platform `Effects` API to change the appearance of control elements
- Working with Boolean and string to image value converters
- Updating the walks content page application to use the data template
- Updating the `WalkEntry` content page to use the `CustomRenderer`

- Updating the `DistanceTravelled` content page to use the `Effects` API

Creating the DataTemplate class for the TrackMyWalks app

One of the features of the `Xamarin.Forms` toolkit is the ability to manipulate the user interface by leveraging the various platform-specific APIs that are available, whether it be manipulating the appearance of controls and their elements using custom renderers, or changing the appearance and styling of native control elements.

In this section, we will be working with the `Xamarin.Forms` data templates, which will provide the ability to define the presentation of data. Let's begin by creating a new folder called `Data Templates`, within our `TrackMyWalks` solution, which will be used to represent our `Data Templates`, by following these steps:

1. Launch the Xamarin Studio application, and ensure that the `TrackMyWalks` solution is loaded within the Xamarin Studio IDE.

2. Next, create a new folder, within the `TrackMyWalks` Portable Class Library project, called `Data Templates` as shown in the following screenshot:

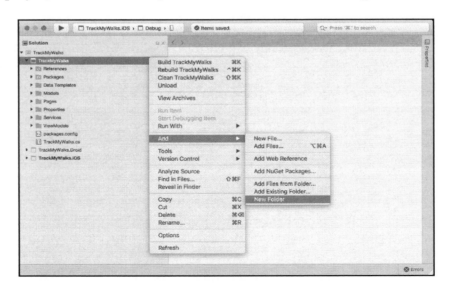

3. Next, create an empty class within the `Data Templates` folder. If you can't remember how to do this, you can refer to the section entitled *Creating the*

Navigation Service Interface for the TrackMyWalks app, within `Chapter 3`, *Navigating within the MVVM model – The Xamarin.Forms Way.*

4. Then, choose the **Empty Class** option located within the **General** section, and enter `WalkCellDataTemplate` as the name of the new class file, as shown in the following screenshot:

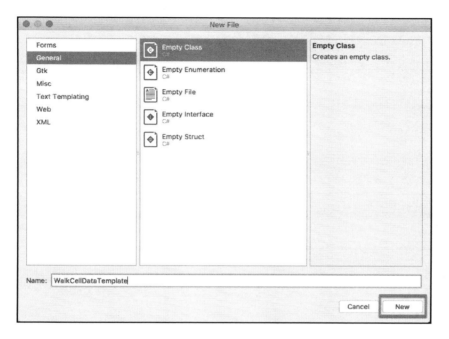

5. Next, click on the **New** button to allow the wizard to create the new empty class file, as shown in the preceding screenshot.

6. Our next step is to begin creating and implementing the code for our `WalkCellDataTemplate` class; perform the following steps.

7. Ensure that the `WalkCellDataTemplate.cs` file is displayed within the code editor, and enter the following code snippet:

```
//
//   WalkCellDataTemplate.cs
//   TrackMyWalks DataTemplate for Cells
//
//   Created by Steven F. Daniel on 01/10/2016.
//   Copyright © 2016 GENIESOFT STUDIOS. All rights reserved.
//
using TrackMyWalks.Converters;
using Xamarin.Forms;
```

```
namespace TrackMyWalks.Controls
{
    public class WalkCellDataTemplate : ViewCell
    {
        public WalkCellDataTemplate()
        {
            var walkTrailImage = new Image
            {
                WidthRequest = 140,
                HeightRequest = 140,
                HorizontalOptions = LayoutOptions.FillAndExpand,
                VerticalOptions = LayoutOptions.FillAndExpand,
                Aspect = Aspect.Fill
            };
            walkTrailImage.SetBinding(Image.SourceProperty,
              "ImageUrl");

            var TrailNameLabel = new Label()
            {
                FontAttributes = FontAttributes.Bold,
                FontSize = 16,
                TextColor = Color.Black
            };

            TrailNameLabel.SetBinding(Label.TextProperty,
              "Title");

            var totalKilometersLabel = new Label()
            {
                FontAttributes = FontAttributes.Bold,
                  FontSize = 12,
                TextColor = Color.FromHex("#666")
            };
            totalKilometersLabel.SetBinding(Label.TextProperty,
              "Kilometers", stringFormat: "Kilometers: {0}");

            var trailDifficultyLabel = new Label()
            {
                FontAttributes = FontAttributes.Bold,
                  FontSize = 12,
                TextColor = Color.Black
            };

            trailDifficultyLabel.SetBinding(Label.TextProperty,
              "Difficulty", stringFormat: "Difficulty: {0}");

            var trailDifficultyImage = new Image
            {
```

[172]

```
        HeightRequest = 50,
        WidthRequest = 50,
        Aspect = Aspect.AspectFill,
        HorizontalOptions = LayoutOptions.Start
    };

    trailDifficultyImage.SetBinding(Image.SourceProperty,
        "Difficulty", converter: new TrailImageConverter());

    var notesLabel = new Label()
    {
        FontSize = 12,
        TextColor = Color.Black
    };
    notesLabel.SetBinding(Label.TextProperty, "Notes");

    var notesStack = new StackLayout()
    {
        Spacing = 3,
        Orientation = StackOrientation.Vertical,
          VerticalOptions = LayoutOptions.FillAndExpand,
            Children = { notesLabel }
    };

    var statusLayout = new StackLayout
    {
        Orientation = StackOrientation.Vertical,
        Children = { totalKilometersLabel,
                     trailDifficultyLabel,
                     trailDifficultyImage
                   }
    };

    var DetailsLayout = new StackLayout
    {
        Padding = new Thickness(10, 0, 0, 0),
        Spacing = 0,
        HorizontalOptions = LayoutOptions.FillAndExpand,
          Children = { TrailNameLabel, statusLayout,
                       notesStack
                     }
    };

 var cellLayout = new StackLayout
 {
        Spacing = 0,
        Padding = new Thickness(10, 5, 10, 5),
        Orientation = StackOrientation.Horizontal,
```

```
                        HorizontalOptions = LayoutOptions.FillAndExpand,
                        Children = { walkTrailImage, DetailsLayout }
                };

                this.View = cellLayout;
            }
        }
    }
```

In the preceding code snippet, we began by ensuring that our class inherits from the `Xamarin.FormsViewCell` class renderer, and is essentially a cell that can be added to any `ListView` or `TableView` control that contains a defined view. When working with `Xamarin.Forms`, and the `ViewCell` class, every cell has an accompanying renderer that is associated with each platform that creates an instance of a native control. Whenever a `ViewCell` class is rendered under the iOS platform, the `ViewCellRenderer` class will instantiate the native `UITableViewCell` control. Alternatively, under the Android platform, the `ViewCellRenderer` class instantiates a native `View` control.

Finally, on the Windows Phone platform, the `ViewCellRenderer` class instantiates a native `DataTemplate` control. Next, we create the cell layout information using the `StackLayout` control, and then use the `SetBinding` property to create and bind each of our model values to a specific property. Finally, we define a `cellLayout` variable that uses the `StackLayout` control, to add each of our child elements and then assign the resulting `cellLayout` to the class `View`.

 If you are interested in finding out more information about `DataTemplates`, please refer to the Xamarin developer documentation located at `https://developer.xamarin.com/guides/xamarin-forms/te mplates/data-templates/`.

Now that we have created our `WalkCellDataTemplate`, the next step is to modify the walks main page so that it can make use of this class.

Updating the walks main page to use the data template

In the previous section, we created the class for our `WalkCellDataTemplate`, as well as defining the layout information for each of the control elements that we would like to have displayed within our `View`.

In this section, we will take a look at how to implement the necessary code changes so that the `WalksPageContentPage` can take advantage of our `WalkCellDataTemplate` class.

Let's take a look at how we can achieve this, by following the steps:

1. Ensure that the `WalksPage.cs` file is displayed within the code editor, and enter in the following highlighted code sections as shown in the following code snippet:

```
//
//  WalksPage.cs
//  TrackMyWalks
//
//  Created by Steven F. Daniel on 04/08/2016.
//  Copyright © 2016 GENIESOFT STUDIOS. All rights reserved.
//
using Xamarin.Forms;
using TrackMyWalks.Models;
using TrackMyWalks.ViewModels;
using TrackMyWalks.Services;
using TrackMyWalks.DataTemplates;

namespace TrackMyWalks
{
    public class WalksPage : ContentPage
    {
        WalksPageViewModel _viewModel
        {
            get { return BindingContext as WalksPageViewModel; }
        }

        public WalksPage()
        {
            var newWalkItem = new ToolbarItem
            {
                Text = "Add Walk"
            };
            ...
            ...
            ...

            // Define our Data Template Class
            var walksList = new ListView
            {
                HasUnevenRows = true,
                ItemTemplate = new DataTemplate(typeof(
                    WalkCellDataTemplate)),
```

```
                         SeparatorColor = (Device.OS
                             == TargetPlatform.iOS) ?
                         Color.Default : Color.Black
              };
              ...
              ...
              ...
          }
      }
```

In the preceding code snippet, we began by including a reference to our `DataTemplates` class, via the `using` statement. Then we passed in the `WalkCellDataTemplate` data template to the `DataTemplate` class object, which will be assigned to the `ItemTemplate` property of the `ListView` class. Next, depending on the operating system we are running on, we'll set the separator color for our `TableView`.

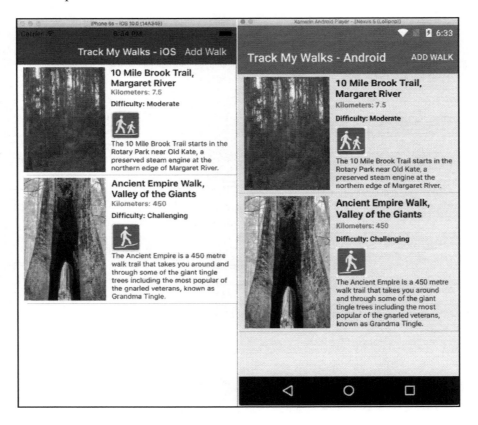

As you can see from the preceding screenshot, this will show you a list of our current walks trail entries, which are nicely rendered using the `DataTemplate`, and displayed within the `ListView` control.

In our next section, you will see how we can go about creating a custom picker for our `WalkEntry` content page, so that we can display a list of difficulty choices for the user to choose from.

Creating a TableView EntryCell custom picker for the iOS platform

Our `TrackMyWalks` app uses a `TableView` with `EntryCells` to present a form to the user to add new walk entries within the `WalkEntryPage`. Currently, the difficulty field within the form is using the regular `EntryCell` control, which presents the user with an editable text field using the default keyboard.

As you can imagine, this is not the ideal user experience that we are after, as this can cause issues when it comes to validating the information entered. Our goal is to present the user with a standard, custom platform-specific picker that contains a number of choices the user can choose from.

In this section, we will be creating a custom renderer that will extend the `EntryCellRenderer` to display an `EntryCell` that will behave much like the standard picker control. Since we don't want our picker to render all of the `EntryCells` within the `WalkEntryPage`, we will need to create a custom `EntryCell` control that the custom renderer will associated with.

Let's take a look at how we can achieve this, by following the steps:

1. Create a new folder within the `TrackMyWalks` Portable Class Library project, called `Controls` and then create an empty class within the `Controls` folder.
2. Next, choose the **Empty Class** option located within the **General** section, and enter `DifficultyPickerEntryCell` as the name of the new class file to create.
3. Next, once you have created the `DifficultyPickerEntryCell` class file, ensure that the `DifficultyPickerEntryCell.cs` file is displayed within the code editor, and enter in the following code snippet:

```
//
//  DifficultyPickerEntryCell.cs
//  TrackMyWalks CustomRenderer for Difficulty Entry Cells
//
//  Created by Steven F. Daniel on 01/10/2016.
```

[177]

```
//  Copyright © 2016 GENIESOFT STUDIOS. All rights reserved.
//
using System;
using Xamarin.Forms;

namespace TrackMyWalks.Controls
{
```

4. Then, we need to modify the `DifficultyPickerEntryCell` class constructor signature, so that it inherits from the `Xamarin.Forms.Entry` `EntryCell` class, since the `WalkEntryPage` contains a number of `EntryCell` controls:

```
public class DifficultyPickerEntryCell : EntryCell  {
```

5. Next, we need to create a string `BindableProperty` so that the custom control can be data-bound just like our other controls:

```
public static readonly BindableProperty DifficultyProperty =
BindableProperty.Create<DifficultyPickerEntryCell,
String>(p => p.Difficulty, "Easy", propertyChanged:
new BindableProperty.BindingPropertyChangedDelegate<String>
(DifficultyPropertyChanged));
```

6. Then, we create a `Difficulty` property so that, when the values changes within the custom control, it can return the value back to our `EntryCell`:

```
public String Difficulty
{
    get { return (String)GetValue(DifficultyProperty); }
    set { SetValue(DifficultyProperty, value); }
}
```

7. Next, we create a `CompletedEventHandler` that will be used in relation to the `DifficultyPropertyChanged` event, so we can respond to the `Completed` events on our `DifficultyPickerEntryCell`:

```
public new event EventHandler Completed;

static void DifficultyPropertyChanged(BindableObject bindable,
  String oldValue, String newValue)
{
    var @this = (DifficultyPickerEntryCell)bindable;

    if (@this.Completed != null)
        @this.Completed(bindable, new EventArgs());
}
```

```
        }
    }
```

Now that we have created the `DifficultyPickerEntryCell` class for the iOS portion of our `TrackMyWalks` app, our next step is to create the custom picker renderer for the iOS platform, which we will be covering in the next section.

Creating the custom picker renderer class for the iOS platform

In the previous section, we created a class for the `DifficultyPickerEntryCell`, as well as defining a number of different data-bindable property methods that will be used to handle the user choosing an item within our custom picker.

In this section, we will build the custom picker renderer model that will be used by the iOS portion of the `DifficultyPickerEntryCell`. Let's take a look at how we can achieve this, by following these steps:

1. Create a new folder within the `TrackMyWalks.iOS` project, called `Renderers`.

2. Next, create an empty class within the `Renderers` folder for our `TrackMyWalks.iOS` project, and enter `DifficultyPickerModel` as the name of the new class file to create.

3. Then, ensure that the `DifficultyPickerModel.cs` file is displayed within the code editor, and enter in the following code snippet:

```
//
//  DifficultyPickerModel.cs
//  TrackMyWalks Level Model for UIPickerViewModel (iOS)
//
//  Created by Steven F. Daniel on 01/10/2016.
//  Copyright © 2016 GENIESOFT STUDIOS. All rights reserved.
//
using System;
using UIKit;

namespace TrackMyWalks.iOS.Renderers
{
```

4. Next, we need to modify the `DifficultyPickerModel` class constructor signature, so that it inherits from the `UIPickerViewModel` interface class, as well as declaring our `difficultyString` object which contains a valid list of choices for the user to choose from:

```
// Declare our Difficulty Picker Model Class
public class DifficultyPickerModel : UIPickerViewModel
{
// Define our list of difficulty levels
static public string[] difficulty = new string[]
{
    "Easy",
    "Moderate",
    "Challenging",
    "Difficult",
    "Very Difficult",
    "Extreme"
};
```

5. Then, we need to create the `GetComponentCount` method, which accepts a `pickerView` object that tells the `UIPickerView` how many components we are expecting our custom picker to contain:

```
public override nint GetComponentCount(UIPickerView pickerView)
{
    return 1;
}
```

6. Next, we need to create the `GetRowsInComponent` method that accepts a `pickerView` object and a `component` value. This method works out how many rows to display within our `UIPickerView` custom control, which is derived from the `difficulty` string array. The component parameter determines which section to display those values in:

```
public override nint GetRowsInComponent(UIPickerView pickerView,
  nint component)
{
    return difficulty.Length;
}
```

7. Finally, we need to create the `GetTitle` method, which accepts a `pickerView` object, a `row` parameter, and a `component` value. This method is used to display the title information for each `row` contained within our `difficulty` array:

```
public override string GetTitle(UIPickerView pickerView,
```

```
    nint row, nint component)
  {
      return difficulty[row];
  }
 }
}
```

Up until this point, all we have done is create our model for our
`DifficultyPicker`, which acts as the base model needed by our
`DifficultyPickerCellRenderer` class. Our next step is to create the
`DifficultyPickerCellRenderer` that will use the model for the iOS platform
to display a custom list of entries for the user to choose from.

1. Create an empty class within the `Renderers` folder for the `TrackMyWalks.iOS`
   project, and enter in `DifficultyPickerCellRenderer` as the name of the new
   class file to create.

2. Next, ensure that the `DifficultyPickerCellRenderer.cs` file is displayed
   within the code editor, and enter the following code snippet:

```
//
//   DifficultyPickerCellRenderer.cs
//   TrackMyWalks CustomRenderer for UIPickerView Entry Cells (iOS)
//
//   Created by Steven F. Daniel on 01/10/2016.
//   Copyright © 2016 GENIESOFT STUDIOS. All rights reserved.
//
using Xamarin.Forms.Platform.iOS;
using UIKit;
using TrackMyWalks.Controls;
using Xamarin.Forms;
using TrackMyWalks.iOS.Renderers;
```

3. Then, we need to initialize our `DifficultyCellRenderer` class to be marked as
   an `ExportRenderer` by including the `ExportRenderer` assembly attribute at
   the top of our class definition. This lets our class know that it inherits from the
   `ViewRenderer` class:

```
[assembly: ExportRenderer(typeof(DifficultyPickerEntryCell),
typeof(DifficultyPickerCellRenderer))]
namespace TrackMyWalks.iOS.Renderers
{
```

4. Next, we need to modify the `DifficultyCellRenderer` class constructor
   signature, so that it can inherit from the `EntryCellRenderer` class:

```
public class DifficultyPickerCellRenderer : EntryCellRenderer
{
```

5. Then, we need to override the `EntryCellRendererGetCell` method so that it can override the default behavior of the `EntryCell` for iOS by setting the `InputView` of the `UITextField` to a `UIPickerView` class instance:

```
public override UITableViewCell GetCell(Cell item,
  UITableViewCell reusableCell, UITableView tv)
{
    var cell = base.GetCell(item, reusableCell, tv);
    var entryPickerCell = (EntryCell)item;

    UITextField textField = null;

    if (cell != null)
        textField = (UITextField)cell.ContentView.Subviews[0];
```

6. Next, we create an instance to our iOS `UIPickerView` native control, that points to the `DifficultyPickerModel`; and then we create a toolbar that will contain a `Done` button and will provide us with a mechanism to update the `EntryCellUITextField` with the chosen value from the `difficultyPicker` object. Then dismiss the custom picker control:

```
// Create our iOS UIPickerView Native Control
  var difficultyPicker = new UIPickerView
  {
      AutoresizingMask = UIViewAutoresizing.FlexibleWidth,
      ShowSelectionIndicator = true,
      Model = new DifficultyPickerModel(),
      BackgroundColor = UIColor.White,
  };

// Create a toolbar with a done button that will
// set the selected value when closed.
var done = new UIBarButtonItem("Done",
  UIBarButtonItemStyle.Done, (s, e) =>
  {
      // Update the value of the UITextField within
      // the Cell.
      if (textField != null)
      {
          textField.Text = DifficultyPickerModel.difficulty
          [difficultyPicker.SelectedRowInComponent(0)];
          textField.ResignFirstResponder();
      }
  });
```

```
var toolbar = new UIToolbar
{
    BarStyle = UIBarStyle.BlackTranslucent,
    Translucent = true
};

toolbar.SizeToFit();
toolbar.SetItems(new[] { done }, true);
```

7. Then, we set the input view and toolbar and an initial default value for the EntryCell's `TextField` if nothing has been chosen. This is done by setting the `InputView` of the `UITextField` to a `UIPickerView` class instance:

```
// Set the input view, toolbar and initial value
// for the Cell's UITextField.
if (textField != null)
{
    textField.InputView = difficultyPicker;
    textField.InputAccessoryView = toolbar;
    textField.Font = UIFont.FromName("Courier", 16);
    textField.BorderStyle = UITextBorderStyle.Bezel;
    textField.TextColor = UIColor.Red;
```

8. Finally, if we have selected a difficulty value from our `UIPickerView` control, we first need to ensure that we have chosen a value, and then assign this value to the `DifficultyEntryCell` field within the entry form:

```
    if (entryPickerCell != null)
    {
        textField.Text = DifficultyPickerModel.difficulty
        [difficultyPicker.SelectedRowInComponent(0)];
    }
    }
    return cell;
    }
  }
}
```

 If you are interested in finding out more information about the `UIPickerView` class, please refer to the Xamarin developer documentation at `https://developer.xamarin.com/api/type/MonoTouch.UIKit.UIPickerView/`.

Now that we have created the `DifficultyPickerCellRenderer` class for the iOS portion of our `TrackMyWalks` app, our next step is to implement this within the `WalkEntry` content page.

Updating the WalksEntryPage to use the custom picker renderer

In the previous section, we created the class for our `DifficultyPickerCellRenderer`, as well as defining the various methods that will handle the display of the `UIPickerView` control when an `EntryCell` within the ViewModel has been tapped.

In this section, we will take a look at how to implement the code changes required so that the `WalkEntryPage` content page can take advantage of the `DifficultyPickerCellRenderer` class.

Let's take a look at how we can achieve this, by following these steps:

Ensure that the `WalkEntryPage.cs` file is displayed within the code editor, and enter the following highlighted code sections as shown in the following code snippet:

```
//
//   WalkEntryPage.cs
//   TrackMyWalks
//
//   Created by Steven F. Daniel on 04/08/2016.
//   Copyright © 2016 GENIESOFT STUDIOS. All rights reserved.
//
using Xamarin.Forms;
using TrackMyWalks.Services;
using TrackMyWalks.Controls;
namespace TrackMyWalks
{

    public class WalkEntryPage : ContentPage
    {
        WalkEntryViewModel _viewModel
        {
            get { return BindingContext as WalkEntryViewModel; }
        }

        public WalkEntryPage()
        {
            // Set the Content Page Title
            Title = "New Walk Entry";

            // Declare and initialize our Model Binding Context
            BindingContext = new WalkEntryViewModel
              (DependencyService
            .Get<IWalkNavService>());
            ...
```

```
. . .
. . .
var walkDifficulty = new DifficultyPickerEntryCell
{
    Label = "Difficulty Level:",
    Placeholder = "Walk Difficulty"
};
walkDifficulty.SetBinding(
  DifficultyPickerEntryCell.DifficultyProperty,
    "Difficulty", BindingMode.TwoWay);
. . .
. . .
. . .
            }
        }
    }
```

In this section, we looked at the steps involved in modifying our `WalkEntryPage` to take advantage of the `DifficultyPickerEntryCell` class custom renderer. We looked at updating the `walkDifficulty` object variable, to reference the `DifficultyPickerEntryCell` class, and updated the `setBinding` to return the value from the `DifficultyProperty` that is implemented within the `DifficultyPickerEntryCell` class.

As you can see from the preceding screenshot, this shows our custom UIPickerView control, populated with the entries from the DifficultyPickerModel, as well as the **Done** button displayed as the header. Scrolling through the list of choices operates in the same way as you would expect under iOS; clicking on the **Done** button will populate the **Difficulty Level** UITextField with the highlighted choice within the UIPickerView control.

In our next section, we will focus on how we can use the Xamarin.Forms Effects API to customize the appearance and styling of native control elements for both the iOS and Android platforms by implementing a custom renderer class. You will notice that the implementations for both of these classes are quite similar. However, these implement different methods, as you will see once we start implementing them.

Creating PlatformEffects using the Effects API for the iOS platform

In this section, we will build the iOS portion of our PlatformEffects, which will allow us to customize the appearance of the Xamarin.Forms control elements. We will be creating two completely different platform effects—LabelShadow and ButtonShadow, for both the iOS and Android platforms.

Let's take a look at how we can achieve this, by following these steps:

1. Create a new folder within the TrackMyWalks.iOS project, called PlatformEffects.
2. Next, create an empty class within the PlatformEffects folder for our TrackMyWalks.iOS project.
3. Then, enter ButtonShadowEffect as the name of the new class file to create, ensure that the ButtonShadowEffect.cs file is displayed within the code editor, and enter the following code snippet:

```
//
// ButtonShadowEffect.cs
// TrackMyWalks Button Shadow Effect (iOS)
//
// Created by Steven F. Daniel on 02/10/2016.
// Copyright © 2016 GENIESOFT STUDIOS. All rights reserved.
//
using TrackMyWalks.iOS.PlatformEffects;
using UIKit;
```

```
using Xamarin.Forms;
using Xamarin.Forms.Platform.iOS;
```

4. Next, we initialize the `ButtonShadowEffect` class assembly to be marked with two important attributes for our class so that it can be used as an effect within the `TrackMyWalks` application:

```
[assembly: ResolutionGroupName("com.geniesoftstudios")]
[assembly: ExportEffect(typeof(ButtonShadowEffect),
  "ButtonShadowEffect")]
namespace TrackMyWalks.iOS.PlatformEffects
{
```

5. Then, we need to modify our `ButtonShadowEffect` class constructor so that it can inherit from the `PlatformEffect` class and access each of the platform-specific implementations of the `PlatformEffect` class:

```
public class ButtonShadowEffect : PlatformEffect
{
```

6. Next, we create the `OnAttached` method that will be called whenever an affect is attached to a `Xamarin.Forms` control and then use the `Container` property to reference the platform-specific control that is used to implement the layout:

```
protected override void OnAttached()
{
    Container.Layer.ShadowOpacity = 0.5f;
    Container.Layer.ShadowColor = UIColor.Black.CGColor;
    Container.Layer.ShadowRadius = 2;
}
```

7. Then, we create the `OnDetached` method, which will be called whenever an effect is detached from a `Xamarin.Forms` control to perform any effect clean-up. Here, in this method, we set the `ShadowOpacity` of the `Container` property to zero:

```
protected override void OnDetached()
{
    Container.Layer.ShadowOpacity = 0;
}
  }
}
```

Each platform-specific `PlatformEffect` class exposes a number of properties and these are explained in the following table:

Platform effect	Description
Container	This particular type references the platform-specific control that is being used to implement the layout.
Control	This type references the platform-specific control that is being used to implement the Xamarin.Forms control.
Element	This type references the Xamarin.Forms control that is currently being rendered.

Whenever you create your own PlatformEffects, these inherit from the PlatformEffect class, which is dependent on the platform that is being run. However, the API for an effect is pretty much identical across each of the platforms as they derive from the PlatformEffect<T, T> and contain different generic parameters. There are also two very important attributes that you need to set for each class that subclasses from the PlatformEffect class, and these are explained in the following table:

Attribute type	Description
ResolutionGroupName	This attribute sets a company-wide namespace for effects, preventing collisions with other effects with the same name. It is worth mentioning that, if you create multiple PlatformEffects, you can only apply this attribute once per project.
ExportEffect	This attribute registers the effect using a unique ID and is used by the Xamarin.Forms platform along with the group name. The attribute takes two parameters: the type name of the effect, and a unique string that will be used to locate the effect prior to applying it to a control.

 If you are interested in finding out more information about the PlatFormEffect class, please refer to the Xamarin developer documentation at https://developer.xamarin.com/guides/xamarin-forms/effects/.

Now that we have created the ButtonShadowEffect class, our next step is to create the LabelShadowEffect for the iOS portion of our TrackMyWalks app:

1. Next, create an empty class within the PlatformEffects folder for the TrackMyWalks.iOS project and enter LabelShadowEffect as the name of the new class file to create.

2. Then, ensure that the LabelShadowEffect.cs file is displayed within the code editor, and enter the following code snippet:

```
//
//   LabelShadowEffect.cs
//   TrackMyWalks Label Shadow Effect (iOS)
//
//   Created by Steven F. Daniel on 02/10/2016.
//   Copyright © 2016 GENIESOFT STUDIOS. All rights reserved.
//
using System;
using CoreGraphics;
using TrackMyWalks.iOS.PlatformEffects;
using Xamarin.Forms;
using Xamarin.Forms.Platform.iOS;
```

3. Next, we initialize the `LabelShadowEffect` class assembly to be marked with the `ExportEffect` attribute so that it can be used as an effect within the `TrackMyWalks` application:

```
[assembly: ExportEffect(typeof(LabelShadowEffect),
  "LabelShadowEffect")]
namespace TrackMyWalks.iOS.PlatformEffects
{
```

4. Then, we need to modify the `LabelShadowEffect` class constructor so that it can inherit from the `PlatformEffect` class, and access each of the platform-specific implementations of the `PlatformEffect` class:

```
public class LabelShadowEffect : PlatformEffect  {
```

5. Next, we create the `OnAttached` method that will be called whenever an affect is attached to a `Xamarin.Forms` control and then use the `Control` property to reference the platform-specific control that will be used to change the appearance of the control.

```
protected override void OnAttached()
{
    try
    {
        Control.Layer.CornerRadius = 5;
        Control.Layer.ShadowColor = Device.OnPlatform(
        Color.Black, Color.White, Color.Black).ToCGColor();
        Control.Layer.ShadowOffset = new CGSize(4, 4);
        Control.Layer.ShadowOpacity = 0.5f;
    }
    catch (Exception ex)
    {
        Console.WriteLine("Cannot set property on attached
```

```
        control.Error: ", ex.Message);
    }
}
```

6. Then, we create the OnDetached method, which will be called whenever an effect
   is detached from a Xamarin.Forms control to perform any effect cleanup. Here,
   in this method, we don't need to do anything, but we still need to implement this
   to conform with the PlatformEffect class protocol implementations:

```
protected override void OnDetached()
{
}
}
}
```

Now that we have created the PlatformEffects for the iOS platform, we need to
implement the same PlatformEffects for the Android platform, which we will be
covering in the next section.

Creating PlatformEffects using the Effects API for the Android platform

In this section, we will build the Android portion of our PlatformEffects that will allow
us to customize the appearance of Xamarin.Forms control elements just like we did for the
iOS portion, and we will be implementing the same PlatformEffects—LabelShadow
and ButtonShadow to show you how these implementations differ on each platform, even
though the resulting rendering is the same.

Let's take a look at how we can achieve this, by following the steps:

1. Create a new folder within the TrackMyWalks.Droid project, called
   PlatformEffects.
2. Next, create an empty class within the PlatformEffects folder for our
   TrackMyWalks.Droid project.
3. Then, enter ButtonShadowEffect as the name of the new class file to create,
   ensure that the ButtonShadowEffect.cs file is displayed within the code
   editor, and enter the following code snippet:

```
//
//   ButtonShadowEffect.cs
//   TrackMyWalks Button Shadow Effect (Droid)
```

```
//
//    Created by Steven F. Daniel on 02/10/2016.
//    Copyright © 2016 GENIESOFT STUDIOS. All rights reserved.
//
using TrackMyWalks.Droid.PlatformEffects;
using Xamarin.Forms;
using Xamarin.Forms.Platform.Android;
using System;
```

4. Next, we initialize the `ButtonShadowEffect` class assembly to be marked with the same two attributes for our class, just like we did for the iOS portion, so that it can be used as an effect within the `TrackMyWalks` application:

```
[assembly: ResolutionGroupName("com.geniesoftstudios")]
[assembly: ExportEffect(typeof(ButtonShadowEffect),
   "ButtonShadowEffect")]
namespace TrackMyWalks.Droid.PlatformEffects
{
```

5. Then, we need to modify the `ButtonShadowEffect` class constructor so that it can inherit from the `PlatformEffect` class, and access each of the platform-specific implementations of the `PlatformEffect` class:

```
public class ButtonShadowEffect : PlatformEffect
{
```

6. Next, we create the `OnAttached` method that will be called whenever an affect is attached to a `Xamarin.Forms` control and then use the `Control` property to reference the platform-specific control that will be used to change the appearance of the control. Under Android we need to create a `control` object and convert the `Button` into a `Control` object, and then apply the customizations to the `Control`. We wrap this within a `try...catch()` block, to catch any errors that may occur if, for some reason, we can't apply the `color` or `shadowLayer` for our control:

```
protected override void OnAttached()
{
    try
    {
        var control = Control as Android.Widget.Button;
        Android.Graphics.Color color =
        Android.Graphics.Color.Red;
        control.SetShadowLayer(12, 4, 4, color);
    }
    catch (Exception ex)
```

[191]

```
    {
        Console.WriteLine("Cannot set property on attached
        control. Error: ", ex.Message);
    }
}
```

7. Then, we create the `OnDetached` method, which will be called whenever an effect is detached from a `Xamarin.Forms` control to perform any effect cleanup. Here in this method, we don't need to do anything, but we still need to implement this to conform with the `PlatformEffect` class protocol implementations:

```
protected override void OnDetached()
{
    throw new NotImplementedException();
}
    }
}
```

Now that we have created the `ButtonShadowEffect` class, our next step is to create the `LabelShadowEffect` for the Android portion of our `TrackMyWalks` app:

1. Next, create an empty class within the `PlatformEffects` folder for the `TrackMyWalks.Droid` project and enter `LabelShadowEffect` as the name of the new class file to create.

2. Then, ensure that the `LabelShadowEffect.cs` file is displayed within the code editor, and enter the following code snippet:

```
//
//  LabelShadowEffect.cs
//  TrackMyWalks Label Shadow Effect (Droid)
//
//  Created by Steven F. Daniel on 02/10/2016.
//  Copyright © 2016 GENIESOFT STUDIOS. All rights reserved.
//
using System;
using TrackMyWalks.Droid.PlatformEffects;
using Xamarin.Forms;
using Xamarin.Forms.Platform.Android;
```

3. Next, we initialize our `LabelShadowEffect` class assembly to be marked with the `ExportEffect` attribute so that it can be used as an effect within the `TrackMyWalks` application:

```
[assembly: ExportEffect(typeof(LabelShadowEffect),
  "LabelShadowEffect")]
```

[192]

```
namespace TrackMyWalks.Droid.PlatformEffects
{
```

4. Then, we need to modify the `LabelShadowEffect` class constructor so that it can inherit from the `PlatformEffect` class, and access each of the platform-specific implementations of the `PlatformEffect` class:

```
public class LabelShadowEffect : PlatformEffect
{
```

5. Next, we create the `OnAttached` method that will be called whenever an affect is attached to a `Xamarin.Forms` control and then use the `Control` property to reference the platform-specific control that will be used to change the appearance of the control. In Android we need to create a `control` object, convert the `TextView` into a `Control` object, and then apply the customizations to the `Control`. We wrap this within a `try...catch()` block, to catch any errors that may occur if, for some reason, we can't apply the `color` or `shadowLayer` for our control:

```
protected override void OnAttached()
{
    try
    {
        var control = Control as Android.Widget.TextView;
        float radius = 5;
        float distanceX = 4;
        float distanceY = 4;
        Android.Graphics.Color color = Device.OnPlatform(
        Color.Black, Color.White, Color.Black).ToAndroid();
        control.SetShadowLayer(
           radius, distanceX, distanceY, color);
    }
    catch (Exception ex)
    {
        Console.WriteLine("Cannot set property on attached control.
          Error: ", ex.Message);
    }
}
```

6. Then, we create the `OnDetached` method that will be called whenever an effect is detached from a `Xamarin.Forms` control to perform any effect cleanup in this method. As what we did in the iOS implementation, we don't need to do anything, but we still need to implement this to conform with the `PlatformEffect` class protocol implementations:

```
protected override void OnDetached()
    {
    }
  }
}
```

Now that we have created `PlatformEffects` for both the iOS and Android implementations, our next step is to begin creating two value converters that will be used by our application, before we can start modifying the content pages, and this will be covered in the next section.

Implementing value converters within the TrackMyWalks app

As mentioned in the previous section, value converters form an important concept in data binding as they allow you to customize the appearance of a data property at the time it is bound. This process is quite similar to **WPF (Windows Presentation Foundation)** on the Windows application development platform. `Xamarin.Forms` provides you with a number of **value converter** interfaces as part of its API.

Value converters are extremely helpful when working with the `Xamarin.Forms` platform, as they allow you to toggle the visibility of elements, based on a Boolean property.

In this section, we will create a `BooleanConverter` that we will use to hide controls until the ViewModel has completely finished loading. We will also create a converter that converts a string value into a URL property that will be used to display an image for our difficulty rating.

Let's take a look at how we can achieve this, by following the steps:

1. Create a new folder, within the `TrackMyWalks` Portable Class Library project, called `ValueConverters` and then create an empty class within the `ValueConverters` folder.
2. Next, choose the **Empty Class** option located within the **General** section, and enter `BooleanConverter` as the name of the new class file to create.
3. Next, ensure that the `BooleanConverter.cs` file is displayed within the code editor, and enter the following code snippet:

```
//
//  BooleanConverter.cs
//  TrackMyWalks ValueConverter for converting Boolean values
```

```
//
//    Created by Steven F. Daniel on 02/10/2016.
//    Copyright © 2016 GENIESOFT STUDIOS. All rights reserved.
//
using System;
using Xamarin.Forms;

namespace TrackMyWalks.ValueConverters
{
```

4. Then, we need to modify the `BooleanConverter` class constructor so that it can inherit from the `IValueConverter` class:

```
public class BooleanConverter : IValueConverter
{
```

5. Next, create the `Convert` and `ConvertBack` methods of the `IValueConverter` class, so that the converter will return the opposite of a given `Boolean` value:

```
public object Convert(object value, Type targetType,
  object parameter, System.Globalization.CultureInfo culture)
{
    if (!(value is Boolean))
        return value;
    return !((Boolean)value);
}

public object ConvertBack(object value, Type targetType,
  object parameter, System.Globalization.CultureInfo culture)
{
    if (!(value is Boolean))
      return value;

    return !((Boolean)value);
  }
 }
}
```

In the preceding code snippet, we began by modifying the `BooleanConverter` class constructor so that it can inherit from the `IValueConverter` class. Then we proceeded to create the `Convert` and `ConvertBack` methods of the `IValueConverter` class. This is so that the converter will return the opposite of a given `Boolean` value; for example, if the value is `True`, it will return `False`, and convert it from `False` back to `True`.

Now that we have created the `BooleanConverter` class, our next step is to begin creating the `TrailImageConverter` that will be used by the `TrackMyWalks` app. This class will be used to convert a string value into a URL property that will be used to display an image for our difficulty rating:

1. Create an empty class within the `ValueConverters` folder, which is located within the `TrackMyWalks` Portable Class Library project.

2. Next, choose the **Empty Class** option located within the **General** section, and enter `TrailImageConverter` as the name of the new class file to create.

3. Next, ensure that the `TrailImageConverter.cs` file is displayed within the code editor, and enter the following code snippet:

```
//
//  TrailImageConverter.cs
//  TrackMyWalks ValueConverter for converting difficulty value
//  to an image.
//
//  Created by Steven F. Daniel on 02/10/2016.
//  Copyright © 2016 GENIESOFT STUDIOS. All rights reserved.
//
using System;
using Xamarin.Forms;

namespace TrackMyWalks.ValueConverters
{
```

4. Then, we need to modify our `TrailImageConverter` class constructor so that it can inherit from the `IValueConverter` class:

```
public class TrailImageConverter : IValueConverter
{
```

5. Next, create the `Convert` and `ConvertBack` methods of the `IValueConverter` class, so that the converter will return back an image URL based on the difficulty level:

```
public object Convert(object value, Type targetType,
   object parameter, System.Globalization.CultureInfo culture)
{
    // Return back the relevant image based on the
    // difficulty level.
    switch ((string)value)
    {
        case "Easy":
            return "http://www.yourdomain.com/g1.jpeg";
```

```
        case "Moderate":
            return "http://www.yourdomain.com/g2.jpeg";
        case "Challenging":
        case "Difficult":
            return "http://www.yourdomain.com/g3.jpeg";
        case "Very Difficult":
        case "Extreme":
            return "http://www.yourdomain.com/g5.jpeg";
        default:
            return "http://www.yourdomain.com/g1.jpeg";
    }
}

public object ConvertBack(object value, Type targetType,
object parameter, System.Globalization.CultureInfo culture)
{
    throw new NotImplementedException();
}
}
}
```

In the preceding code snippet, we began by modifying our `TrailImageConverter` class constructor so that it can inherit from the `IValueConverter` class. In our next step, we'll proceed to create the `Convert` and `ConvertBack` protocol methods of the `IValueConverter` class. This is so that the converter will return back an image URL based on the difficulty level and will be displayed within our `TrackMyWalks` app.

Updating the WalkBaseViewModel to use our Boolean converter

In this section, we will proceed to update our `WalkBaseViewModel` class to include references to our `Boolean` value converter. Since the `WalkBaseViewModel` already inherits and is used by each of the `ViewModels`, it makes sense to place it within this class. That way, if we need to add additional methods, we can just add them within this class. To proceed, perform the following steps, as shown here.

Ensure that the `WalkBaseViewModel.cs` file is displayed within the code editor, and enter the following highlighted code sections, as shown in the following code snippet:

```
//
//  WalkBaseViewModel.cs
//  TrackMyWalks Base ViewModel
//
```

```
//  Created by Steven F. Daniel on 22/08/2016.
//  Copyright © 2016 GENIESOFT STUDIOS. All rights reserved.
//
using System.ComponentModel;
using System.Runtime.CompilerServices;
using System.Threading.Tasks;
using TrackMyWalks.Services;

namespace TrackMyWalks.ViewModels
{
    public abstract class WalkBaseViewModel :
      INotifyPropertyChanged
    {
        protected IWalkNavService NavService
        { get; private set; }

        bool _isProcessBusy;
        public bool IsProcessBusy
        {
            get { return _isProcessBusy; }
            set
            {
                _isProcessBusy = value;
                OnPropertyChanged();
                OnIsBusyChanged();
            }
        }
        ...
        ...
        ...
        protected virtual void OnIsBusyChanged()
        {
           // We are processing our Walks Trail Information
        }
    }

    public abstract class WalkBaseViewModel<WalkParam> :
    WalkBaseViewModel
    {
        protected WalkBaseViewModel(
          IWalkNavService navService) :
        base(navService)
        {
        }

        public override async Task Init()
        {
            await Init(default(WalkParam));
```

```
            }

        public abstract Task Init(WalkParam walkDetails);
        }
    }
```

In the preceding code snippet, we began by creating a `Boolean` property, called `isProcessBusy`, which we will only set to `True` while we are in the process of actually loading data within our `ListView`, or doing some other process that takes quite a long time. The `IsProcessBusy` property contains both the getter (`get`) and setter (`set`) implementations. When we set the `IsProcessBusy` property, we assign this value to our `_isProcessBusy` variable, and then call the `OnPropertyChanged` and `OnIsBusyChanged` instance methods to tell the `ViewModels` that a change has been made.

Updating the WalksPageViewModel to use our Boolean converter

In this section, we will proceed to update the `WalksPageViewModel` ViewModel to reference our `Boolean` value converter. Since the `WalksPageViewModel` is used to display information from the `WalkEntries` model, we will need to update the `LoadWalks` instance method to toggle between the `IsProcessBusy` value while it is loading data within the `ListView`. To proceed, perform the following steps, as shown here:

Ensure that the `WalksPageViewModel.cs` file is displayed within the code editor, and enter the following highlighted code sections, as shown in the following code snippet:

```
//
//    WalksPageViewModel.cs
//    TrackMyWalks ViewModels
//
//    Created by Steven F. Daniel on 22/08/2016.
//    Copyright © 2016 GENIESOFT STUDIOS. All rights reserved.
//
using System.Collections.ObjectModel;
using System.Threading.Tasks;
using TrackMyWalks.Models;
using TrackMyWalks.Services;
using Xamarin.Forms;

namespace TrackMyWalks.ViewModels
{
    public class WalksPageViewModel : WalkBaseViewModel
    {
```

```csharp
ObservableCollection<WalkEntries> _walkEntries;

public ObservableCollection<WalkEntries> walkEntries
{
    get { return _walkEntries; }
    set
    {
        _walkEntries = value;
        OnPropertyChanged();
    }
}

public WalksPageViewModel(IWalkNavService navService) :
  base(navService)
{
    walkEntries = new ObservableCollection<WalkEntries>();
}

public override async Task Init()
{
    await LoadWalkDetails();
}

public async Task LoadWalkDetails()
{
    // Check to see if we are already processing our
    // Walk Trail Items
    if (IsProcessBusy) {
        return;
    }
    // If we aren't currently processing, we need to
    // initialise our variable to true.
    IsProcessBusy = true;
    // Add a temporary timer, so that we can see
    // our progress indicator working
    await Task.Delay(1000);
    ...
    ...
    ...
    // Re-initialise our process busy value back to false
    IsProcessBusy = false;
}
...
...
...
}
}
```

In the preceding code snippet, we began by updating the `LoadWalks` method to toggle between the `Boolean` property called `IsProcessBusy`. We set this to `True` while we are in the process of actually loading data within the `ListView`. We then added a temporary timer so we can see this process in action, but we will be removing this in Chapter 7, *Incorporating API Data Access*, when we load the Trail information from an API. Finally, we re-initialized our `IsProcessBusy` state value by setting this to `False` to tell the `WalkBaseViewModel` that we have completed processing of the walk trail items.

Now that the ViewModel is aware of when it is busily processing items within the `ListView`, our next step is to modify the user interface for the walks page to include an activity indicator that inherits from the `Xamarin.Forms.Core` platform. We will also be modifying our `DistanceTravelled` and `WalksTrailPage` to include the `PlatFormEffects` classes.

Updating the walks main page to use the updated ViewModel

In this section, we will proceed to update the `WalksPage` content page, which will include an activity process indicator that will display a text string to the user, letting them know that the trail walks are being populated within the `ListView` control. We will also be making use of our `PlatformEffects` classes for the `LabelShadow`. To proceed, perform the following steps:

1. Ensure that the `WalksPage.cs` file is displayed within the code editor, and enter in the following highlighted code sections, as shown in the following code snippet:

```
//
//  WalksPage.cs
//  TrackMyWalks
//
//  Created by Steven F. Daniel on 04/08/2016.
//  Copyright © 2016 GENIESOFT STUDIOS. All rights reserved.
//
using Xamarin.Forms;
using TrackMyWalks.Models;
using TrackMyWalks.ViewModels;
using TrackMyWalks.Services;
using TrackMyWalks.DataTemplates;
using TrackMyWalks.ValueConverters;

namespace TrackMyWalks
{
    public class WalksPage : ContentPage    {
```

```
    WalksPageViewModel _viewModel
{
    get {
        return BindingContext as WalksPageViewModel; }
}

public WalksPage()
{
    var newWalkItem = new ToolbarItem
    {
        Text = "Add Walk"
    };

    . . .
    . . .
    . . .
    // Declare and initialize our Model Binding Context
    BindingContext = new WalksPageViewModel(DependencyService
    .Get<IWalkNavService>());

    // Define our Item Template
    var walksList = new ListView
    {
        HasUnevenRows = true,
        ItemTemplate = new DataTemplate(typeof(
        WalkCellDataTemplate)),
        SeparatorColor = (Device.OS == TargetPlatform.iOS) ?
        Color.Default : Color.Black
    };

    // Set the Binding property for our walks Entries
    walksList.SetBinding(ItemsView<Cell>.ItemsSourceProperty,
    "walkEntries");
```

2. Next, we need to set up the Binding to the IsVisibleProperty that we defined within the WalkBaseViewModel class. This will be called when this property has been set True to display our WalkEntries within the ListView and is handled by the IsProcessBusy property. Proceed and enter the following highlighted code sections, as shown in the code snippet:

```
walksList.SetBinding(ItemsView<Cell>.IsVisibleProperty,
    "IsProcessBusy", converter: new BooleanConverter());

    // Initialize our event Handler to use when the item
    // is tapped
    walksList.ItemTapped += (object sender,
    ItemTappedEventArgs e) =>
```

```
    {
        var item = (WalkEntries)e.Item;
        if (item == null) return;
        _viewModel.WalkTrailDetails.Execute(item);
        item = null;
    };
```

3. Then, we declare and initialize a new `progressLabel` control, which will be used to display instructive information to the user when the `ListView` is being populated. Proceed and enter in the following highlighted code sections, as shown in the code snippet:

```
// Declare our Progress Label
var progressLabel = new Label()
{
    FontSize = 14,
    FontAttributes = FontAttributes.Bold,
    TextColor = Color.Black,
    HorizontalTextAlignment = TextAlignment.Center,
    Text = "Loading Trail Walks..."
};
```

4. Next, we apply the `PlatformEffectLabelShadowEffect` class to our `progressLabel` control, instantiate and initialize the `ActivityIndicator` class, and set the `IsRunning` property to `True`, before creating a `StackLayout` variable `progressIndicator` and adding both the `activityIndicator` and `progressLabel` items. Finally, we set up the `Binding` for our `ProgressIndicator` using the `isVisibleProperty` of the `StackLayout` control. This will use the `IsProcessBusy` property to determine whether or not to show the `ActivityIndicator`. Proceed and enter in the following highlighted code sections, as shown in the code snippet:

```
// Apply PlatformEffects to our Progress Label
progressLabel.Effects.Add(Effect.Resolve("com.geniesoftst
udios.LabelShadowEffect"));
// Instantiate and initialise our Activity Indicator.
var activityIndicator = new ActivityIndicator()
{
    IsRunning = true
};
var progressIndicator = new StackLayout
{
    Orientation = StackOrientation.Vertical,
    HorizontalOptions = LayoutOptions.CenterAndExpand,
    VerticalOptions = LayoutOptions.CenterAndExpand,
```

```
        Children = {
            activityIndicator,
            progressLabel
        }
    };
    progressIndicator.SetBinding(StackLayout.IsVisibleProperty,
     "IsProcessBusy");

    var mainLayout = new StackLayout
    {
        Children =
        {
            walksList,
            progressIndicator
        }
    };

    Content = mainLayout;
}

protected override async void OnAppearing()
{
    base.OnAppearing();

    // Initialize our WalksPageViewModel
    if (_viewModel != null)
    await _viewModel.Init();
  }
 }
}
```

In the preceding code snippet, we began by setting up the `Binding` to our `IsVisibleProperty`, which we defined within the `WalkBaseViewModel` class; this will be called when the property has been set to `True` to display the `WalkEntries` within the `ListView`, and is handled by the `IsProcessBusy` property. In our next step, we declared and initialized a new `progressLabel` control, which will be used to display instructive information to the user when the `ListView` is being populated.

Then we applied the `LabelShadowEffect` class to the `progressLabel` control, instantiated and initialized the `ActivityIndicator` class, and set the `IsRunning` property to `True`, before creating a `StackLayout` variable `progressIndicator` and adding both the `activityIndicator` and `progressLabel` items.

Next, we set up the `Binding` for the `ProgressIndicator` using the `isVisibleProperty` of our `StackLayout` control, which will use the `IsProcessBusy` property to determine whether or not to show the `ActivityIndicator`. Finally, we added the `ProgressIndicator` to our `mainLayout` as part of the `Children` property, so that this can be displayed as part of the main content page.

If you don't export an `Effect` for a particular platform, the `Effect.Resolve` will return a non-null value that effectively doesn't do anything, and you won't see any rendering happen on your controls. You will need to ensure that, within your `PlatformEffect` classes, you include the `ExportEffect` assembly attribute at the top of your class implementations.

Updating the WalksTrailPage to use the updated ViewModel

In this section, we will proceed to update our `WalksTrailPage` content page will make use of the `PlatformEffects` classes for the `ButtonShadow`. To proceed, perform the following steps:

Ensure that the `WalksTrailPage.cs` file is displayed within the code editor, and enter the following highlighted code sections, as shown in the code snippet:

```
//
//  WalkTrailPage.cs
//  TrackMyWalks
//
//  Created by Steven F. Daniel on 04/08/2016.
//  Copyright © 2016 GENIESOFT STUDIOS. All rights reserved.
//
using Xamarin.Forms;
using TrackMyWalks.ViewModels;
using TrackMyWalks.Services;
using TrackMyWalks.ValueConverters;

namespace TrackMyWalks
{
    public class WalkTrailPage : ContentPage
    {
        WalksTrailViewModel _viewModel
        {
            get { return BindingContext
                as WalksTrailViewModel; }
```

```
        }

        public WalkTrailPage()
        {
            Title = "Walks Trail";
            ...
            ...
            ...
    beginTrailWalk.Effects.Add(Effect.Resolve
    ("com.geniesoftstudios.ButtonShadowEffect"));
    ...
    ...
    ...
    trailDifficultyLabel.SetBinding(Label.TextProperty,
    "WalkEntry.Difficulty", stringFormat: "Difficulty: {0}");

    var trailDifficultyImage = new Image
    {
        HeightRequest = 50,
        WidthRequest = 50,
        Aspect = Aspect.AspectFill,
        HorizontalOptions = LayoutOptions.Start
    };
    trailDifficultyImage.SetBinding(Image.SourceProperty,
     "WalkEntry.Difficulty",
     converter: new TrailImageConverter());
    ...
    ...
    ...
    }
   }
  }
```

In the preceding code snippet, we began by applying the ButtonShadowEffect class to our beginTrailWalk button, and then updated the binding of thetrailDifficultyImage to use the TrailImageConverter value converter. This will convert the string representation for the chosen difficulty, and return back an image URL that will be displayed within the content page.

Updating the DistanceTravelledPage to use the updated ViewModel

In this section, we will proceed to update an other `DistanceTravelledPage` content page that will make use of the `PlatformEffects` classes for our `ButtonShadow`. To proceed, perform the following steps:

Ensure that the `DistanceTravelledPage.cs` file is displayed within the code editor, and enter the following highlighted code sections, as shown in the code snippet:

```
//
//   DistanceTravelledPage.cs
//   TrackMyWalks
//
//   Created by Steven F. Daniel on 04/08/2016.
//   Copyright © 2016 GENIESOFT STUDIOS. All rights reserved.
//
using Xamarin.Forms;
using Xamarin.Forms.Maps;
using TrackMyWalks.Services;

namespace TrackMyWalks
{
    public class DistanceTravelledPage : ContentPage
    {
        DistTravelledViewModel _viewModel
        {
            get { return BindingContext as
                DistTravelledViewModel; }
        }

        public DistanceTravelledPage()
        {
            Title = "Distance Travelled";

            ...
            ...
            ...
    var walksHomeButton = new Button
    {
        BackgroundColor = Color.FromHex("#008080"),
        TextColor = Color.White,
        Text = "End this Trail"
    };
    walksHomeButton.Effects.Add(Effect.Resolve
      ("com.geniesoftstudios.ButtonShadowEffect"));
```

```
        . . .
        . . .
        . . .
        }
    }
```

In the preceding code snippet, we begin by applying the ButtonShadowEffect class to our walksHomeButton control so that it can take advantage of the nice platform-specific rendering effects to visual control elements.

Updating the WalkCellDataTemplate class to use PlatformEffects

In this section, we will proceed to update the WalkCellDataTemplate class, which will make use of the PlatformEffects classes for our LabelShadow, so that the DataTemplate will inherit some of the nice visual representations that your users will love. To proceed, perform the following steps, as shown here:

Ensure that the WalkCellDataTemplate.cs file is displayed within the code editor, and enter the following highlighted code sections, as shown in the code snippet:

```
//
//  WalkCellDataTemplate.cs
//  TrackMyWalks DataTemplate for Cells
//
//  Created by Steven F. Daniel on 01/10/2016.
//  Copyright © 2016 GENIESOFT STUDIOS. All rights reserved.
//
using TrackMyWalks.ValueConverters;
using Xamarin.Forms;

namespace TrackMyWalks.DataTemplates
{
    public class WalkCellDataTemplate : ViewCell
    {
        public WalkCellDataTemplate()
        {
            . . .
            . . .
            . . .
            // Apply PlatformEffects to our TrailNameLabel Control
            TrailNameLabel.Effects.Add(Effect.Resolve
            ("com.geniesoftstudios.LabelShadowEffect"));
            TrailNameLabel.SetBinding(Label.TextProperty, "Title");
```

[208]

```
    ...
    ...
    ...
trailDifficultyImage.SetBinding(Image.SourceProperty,
 "Difficulty", converter: new TrailImageConverter());
    ...
    ...
    ...
this.View = cellLayout;
  }
 }
}
```

In the preceding code snippet, we began by applying the `LabelShadowEffect` class to our `TrailNameLabel` control, and then updated the binding of the `trailDifficultyImage` to use the `TrailImageConverter` value converter. This will convert the string representation for our chosen difficulty, and return back an image URL that will be displayed within the content page.

Now that you have updated the necessary `ViewModels` and `ContentPages` to take advantage of our `PlatFormEffects` and `ValueConverters`, our next step is to finally build and run the `TrackMyWalks` application within the iOS simulator.

When the compilation is complete, the iOS simulator will appear automatically, and the `TrackMyWalks` application will be displayed, as shown in the following screenshot:

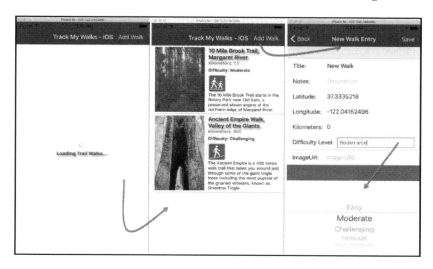

As you can see from the preceding screenshot, this currently displays our `ActivityIndicator` spinner control, with the associated **Loading Trail Walks...** text.

After this the `ListView` containing the list of trail walks from the `DataTemplate` control will display. You will notice that it displays a nice image associated with the difficulty for the trail walk, which is pulled directly from the `TrailImageValueConverter` class.

When the **Add Walk** button is pressed from the main **Track My Walks** content page, this displays the **New Walk Entry** screen, with the **Difficulty Level** custom picker showing the list of choices as defined within our `DifficultyPickerModel`:

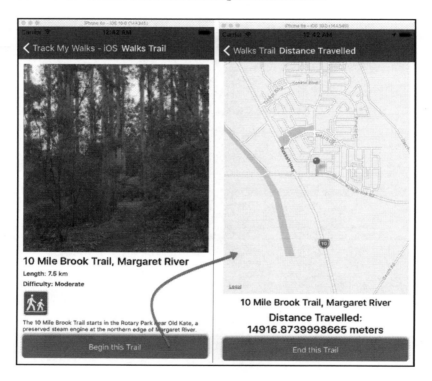

The preceding screenshot shows the updated ViewModel and `ContentPages` that make use of the `PlatformEffects` classes for the `ButtonShadow` effects, as well as the `ValueConverters` for the `TrailImageValueConverter`. As you can see, by using the power of `Xamarin.FormsPlatformEffects` and `ValueConverters` within your own applications, you can really create some stunning user interfaces that will show off your apps and that your users will love.

Summary

In this chapter, we updated the `TrackMyWalks` application to use `CustomRenderers` to change the appearance of control elements that are displayed within the user interface for each specific platform. Next, you learned how to work with `DataTemplates`, by creating a custom class to represent the information that is presented within the `ListView` class, as well as creating two `ValueConverter` classes `BooleanValueConverter` that are used to determine when information is currently being displayed within the user interface. You also created a `TrailImageValueConverter` that returns an image URL based on the string passed into it. Finally, you learned how to work with the `PlatformEffects` class, to create a `LabelShadow` and `ButtonShadow`, and updated the ViewModel and `ContentPages` to apply those effects to control elements.

In the next chapter, you'll learn about the **Razor Templating Engine** and how you can use it to create a hybrid mobile solution. You'll learn how to create, and use models within your application, as well as calling JavaScript code using C# to execute method calls.

6
Working with Razor Templates

In our previous chapter, we looked at how to work with the `DataTemplateCustomRenderer` by creating a C# class to layout your views beautifully within your applications, and how you will also get accustomed to working with the platform-specific APIs to extend the default behavior of `Xamarin.Forms` controls using custom renderers, by creating a custom picker.

You also learned how to use the Xamarin.Forms `Effects` API to customize the appearance and styling of native control elements for each platform, by implementing a custom renderer class, and looked at how to manipulate the visual appearance of data that is bound, using value and image converters.

In this chapter, you'll learn about the Razor HTML template engine and how you can use it to create a hybrid mobile solution. You'll learn how to build a book library mobile solution using the power of Razor templates, and learn how to create, and use models within your application and connect this up to an SQLite database to store, retrieve, update, and delete book details.

This chapter will cover the following topics:

- Introduction to the Razor HTML template engine
- How to build a hybrid mobile solution using Xamarin Studio
- Incorporating `SQLite.Net` and creating a SQLite database wrapper
- Creating the book database model
- Creating the book listing main page
- Creating the book listing add page
- Creating the book listing edit page

Understanding the Razor template engine

The Razor templating engine was first introduced as part of the ASP.Net MVC architecture, and was originally designed to run on a web server to generate HTML files to be served to web browsers.

Since Razor made its first appearance on the development scene, the Razor templating engine has come a long way and now extends the standard HTML syntax, so that you can use C# to express the layout of your HTML files, and incorporate CSS style sheets and JavaScript easily.

Each Razor template has the ability to reference a Model class which can be of any custom type, and properties can be accessed directly from the template, by having the ability to mix HTML and C# syntax easily.

As you work through this chapter, you will see how, by working with Xamarin Studio, you can utilize the Razor HTML templating engine and be equipped with the flexibility of building cross-platform templated HTML views that use both JavaScript and CSS, as well as having access to the underlying platform APIs using the power of C#.

 For more information on using Razor syntax (C#) with ASP.NET web programming refer to the following URL: `https://www.asp.net/web-pag es/overview/getting-started/introducing-razor-syntax-c`.

Creating and implementing Razor templates within Xamarin Studio

In this section, we will look at how to go about creating a new Razor template solution using Xamarin Studio. We will begin by developing the basic structure for our application, as well as adding all the necessary database models and user interface files.

Before we can proceed, we need to create the `BookLibrary` project. It is very simple to create this using Xamarin Studio. Simply follow the given steps:

1. Launch the Xamarin Studio application, and choose the **New Solution...** option, or alternatively choose **File | New | Solution...** or simply press *Shift + Command + N*.

2. Next, choose the **WebView App** option which is located under the **iOS | App** section, ensure that you have selected **C#** as the programming language to use, and click **Next**:

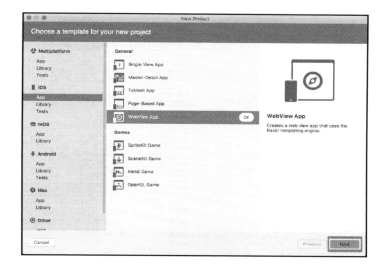

3. Then, enter in `BookLibrary` as the name for your app in the **App Name** field as well as specifying a name for the **Organization Identifier** field.

4. Next, ensure that both the **iPad** and **iPhone** checkboxes have been selected for the **Devices** field, as well as ensuring that you have chosen **iOS 10.0** for the **Target** field to support the minimum iOS version that we want our app to support:

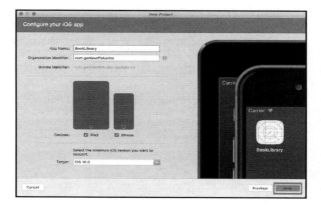

5. Click on the **Next** button to proceed to the next step in the wizard:

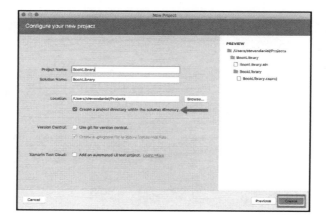

6. Next, ensure that the **Create a project directory within the solution directory.** checkbox has been selected and click on the **Create** button to save your project at the specified location.

Once your project has been created, you will be presented with the Xamarin Studio development environment, along with several project files that the template created for your Razor template Solution, as shown in the following screenshot:

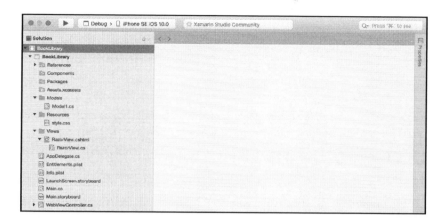

As you can see from the preceding screenshot, the `BookLibrary` solution has been divided into three separate folders. The following table provides a brief description of what each area is used for:

Folder type	Description
Models	This section is responsible for representing the model that our views will use, and contains a structure of fields that will be displayed and/or written to by our Razor templates.
Resources	This section contains a place for you to add the images and CSS, or JavaScript files that your application will use.
Views	This section is responsible for containing all of the HTML5 Razor templates that your application will be referencing, and they need to contain and be prefixed with the `.cshtml` extension.

One thing you will notice is that our solution contains a file called `style.css`. This is because our application is essentially a hybrid mobile solution, and contains the files you might expect from a web solution, as can be seen in the following code snippet:

```
/* This is a minimal style sheet intended to demonstrate
   how to include static content in your hybrid app.
   Other static content, such as javascript files and images,
   can be included in this same folder(Resources on iOS or Assets
   on Android), with the same Build Action(BundleResource on iOS
   or AndroidAsset on Android), to be accessible from a path starting
```

```
at the root of your hybrid application. */

#page {
margin-top:10px;
}
```

As you can see, this file doesn't contain much information, but as we work our way through this chapter, we will be adding to this file, and building the Razor template user-interface files.

Adding the SQLite.Net package to the BookLibrary solution

Now that we have created our `BookLibrary` solution, the next step is to add the `SQLite.Net` NuGet package to our solution, since this doesn't get added automatically for us. The `SQLite.Net` package will essentially provide us with the ability to have our application write to an SQLite database, to store our book details.

 A NuGet package is essentially the package manager for the Microsoft development platform that contains the client tools that provide our solution with the ability to produce and consume .NET packages.

Let's look at how to add the `SQLite.NETNuGet` package within our `BookLibrary` solution, by performing the following steps:

1. Right-click on the `Packages` folder that is contained within the `BookLibrary` solution, and choose the **Add Packages...** menu option, as shown in the following screenshot.

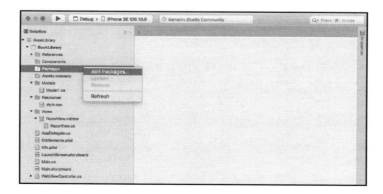

2. This will display the **Add Packages...** dialog. Enter in SQLite.Net within the search dialog, and then click on the **sqlite-net** option within the list, as shown in the following screenshot:

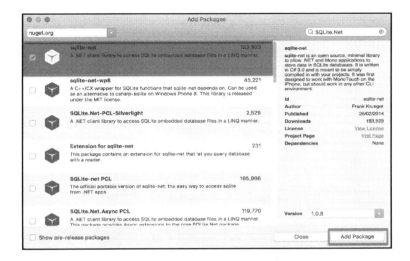

3. Finally, click on the **Add Package** button to add the **sqlite-netNuGet** package to the Packages folder, contained within the **BookLibrary** solution.

When you click on the **Add Package** button, you will notice that the package manager will create two new files for us within our solution. These are called SQLite.cs and SQLiteAsync.cs, and are basically wrapper convenience classes that allow .NET and Mono applications to store data within a SQLite 3 database.

Now that you have added the NuGet package for the sqlite-net library, we can begin to utilize this library within the BookLibrary solution that we will be covering in the next section.

Creating and implementing the book library database model

In this section, we will begin by building the database model that will be used by our BookLibrary project solution that will be used by our Razor templates when we create these, and then the WebViewController.cs file will communicate and interact with each of the Razor template views and handle the actions within them.

Let's look at how we can achieve this, by performing following steps:

1. Create an empty class within the `Models` folder, by choosing **Add** | **NewFile...**, as shown in the following screenshot:

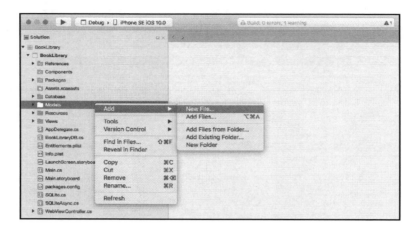

2. Next, choose the **Empty Class** option, located within the **General** section, and enter in `BookItem`, as shown in the following screenshot:

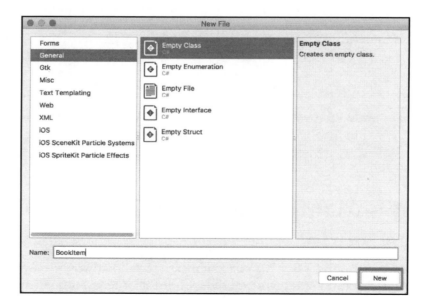

3. Next, click on the **New** button to allow the wizard to proceed and create the new empty class file.

Up until now, all we have done is create our `BookItem` class file. This class will be used by each of our Razor template views, as well as our `WebViewController.cs` file that will eventually allow communication to happen between each of the Razor template views, as well as being able to handle actions within them, whenever the user interacts with them.

Let's now start to implement the code required for our `BookItem` class model, by performing the following steps:

1. Ensure that the `BookItem.cs` file is displayed within the code editor, and enter the following code snippet:

```
//
//  BookItem.cs
//  BookLibrary Database Model
//
//  Created by Steven F. Daniel on 20/10/2016.
//  Copyright © 2016 GENIESOFT STUDIOS. All rights reserved.
//
using SQLite;

namespace BookLibrary {
    public class BookItem
    {
        public BookItem()
        {
        }
        [PrimaryKey, AutoIncrement]
        public int Id { get; set; }
        public string Title { get; set; }
        public string Author { get; set; }
        public string Isbn { get; set; }
        public string Synopsis { get; set; }
    }
}
```

In the preceding code snippet, we have successfully defined our database model that will be used to represent our book items. You will notice something that is different within our model to what you would have seen within our `TrackMyWalks` app: here we have defined a `[PrimaryKey, AutoIncrement]` item for our `id` field, this will tell our `BookLibrary` database to set the `id` property to automatically increment whenever we add a new item to our database.

If you have used relational databases in the past, such as Microsoft SQLServer, Oracle, or Microsoft Access, this should be quite familiar to you. In the next section, we will use this model to set up and initialize our database, by creating a database library wrapper to handle connections to our database, as well as **Creation, Retrieval, Updating,** and **Deletion (CRUD)**, of each of our book entries.

The Android version of the `BookItem` class model is available in the companion source code for this book.

Creating and implementing the book database wrapper

In the previous section, we successfully created and implemented our `BookItem` database model that will be used by our `BookLibrary` application. Our next step is to begin implementing the code required for our `BookItemDatabase` class model, by performing the following steps:

1. Create a new folder within the `BookLibrary` project solution, called `Database` as shown in the following screenshot:

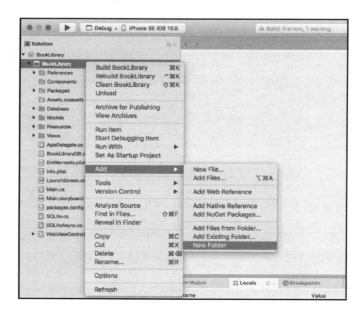

2. Next, create an empty class within the `Database` folder, by choosing **Add | New File...**, as you did when creating the model in the previous section entitled *Creating and implementing the book library database model,* located within this chapter.

3. Then, enter in `BookDatabase` for the name of the new class that you want to create, and click on the **New** button to allow the wizard to proceed and create the new file.

4. Next, ensure that the `BookDatabase.cs` file is displayed within the code editor window, and then enter in the following code snippet:

```
//
//   BookDatabase.cs
//   BookLibrary Database to handle performing database
//   Creation, Retrieval, Updating and Deletion of Book Items.
//
//   Created by Steven F. Daniel on 20/10/2016.
//   Copyright © 2016 GENIESOFT STUDIOS. All rights reserved.
//
using System.Collections.Generic;
using System.Linq;
using SQLite;

namespace BookLibrary
{
    public class BookDatabase
    {
```

5. Next, we need to create a `locker` variable that will be used to create a mutually-exclusive lock on the database while we are either creating, updating, retrieving, or deleting book items. We do this so that no other operation can interfere while we are processing, and this will prevent issues from arising. We also need to declare a `database` variable, that points to an instance of our `SQLiteConnection` located within our `SQLite` library, so that we can perform database operations:

```
static object locker = new object();
SQLiteConnection database;
```

6. Then, we need to create the `BookDatabase(SQLiteConnection conn)` method that accepts a `conn` object, which is an instance of our `SQLiteConnection` class, and this instance method will be used to create the necessary database table structure, based on our `BookItem` model:

```
/// <summary>
```

```
/// Initializes a new instance of the BookLibrary
/// Database class.
/// </summary>
/// <param name="conn">Conn.</param>
public BookDatabase(SQLiteConnection conn)
{
    database = conn;

    // Create the tables within our Book Library Database
    database.CreateTable<BookItem>();
}
```

7. Next, we need to create the `GetItems()` method that will be used to extract all of the existing book entries that have been saved to the database. We use the LINQ language syntax to iterate and retrieve all items from our `BookItem` table, and convert this collection to a list instance, as determined by the `.ToList()` method:

```
/// <summary>
/// Gets all of the book library items from our database.
/// </summary>
/// <returns>The items.</returns>
public IEnumerable<BookItem> GetItems()
{
    // Set a mutual-exclusive lock on our database, while
    // retrieving items.
    lock (locker)
    {
        return (from i in database.Table<BookItem>()
                select i).ToList();
    }
}
```

8. Then, we need to create the `GetItem()` method that will extract the selected book entry from the `BookItem` database table, using their `id` as the key. Again, we use the LINQ language syntax to retrieve the first item from the `BookItem` table that matches the `id` of the book item:

```
/// <summary>
/// Gets a specific book item from the database.
/// </summary>
/// <returns>The item.</returns>
/// <param name="id">Identifier.</param>
public BookItem GetItem(int id)
{
    // Set a mutual-exclusive lock on our database, while
    // retrieving the book item.
    lock (locker)
```

```
        {
            return database.Table<BookItem>().FirstOrDefault(x =>
                x.Id == id);
        }
    }
```

9. Next, we need to create the `SaveItem()` method that will save the book item to the `BookItem` database table. In this instance method, we are handling two case scenarios: one if the item we are saving is an existing item, we check the `id` of the book item, and if it is a non-zero value, we proceed to update the book item using the `Update` method on the `database` object, and return the book item `id` back.

10. However, if the item is a new book record, that is all new books that get created will have an `id` of 0, this will be directly inserted into the `BookItem` table, using the `Insert` method on the `database` object:

```
/// <summary>
/// Saves the book item currently being edited.
/// </summary>
/// <returns>The item.</returns>
/// <param name="item">Item.</param>
public int SaveItem(BookItem item)
{
    // Set a mutual-exclusive lock on our database, while
    // saving/updating our book item.
    lock (locker)
    {
        if (item.Id != 0)
        {
            database.Update(item);
            return item.Id;
        }
        else {
            return database.Insert(item);
        }
    }
}
```

11. Finally, we create the `DeleteItem()` method that will, as you might have guessed, delete a book item from the `BookItem` database table using the book's item `id` and then calling the `Delete` method on the `database` object:

```
/// <summary>
/// Deletes a specific book item from the database.
/// </summary>
/// <returns>The item.</returns>
/// <param name="id">Identifier.</param>
```

```
public int DeleteItem(int id)
{
    // Set a mutual-exclusive lock on our database, while
    // deleting our book item.
    lock (locker)
    {
      return database.Delete<BookItem>(id);
    }
  }
 }
}
```

Now that we have created our BookDatabase class, we can proceed and create our BookLibraryDB database wrapper that will use our BookDatabase class to handle all the operations for creating, retrieving, updating, and deletion of book items from our database. That will be used by our WebViewController.cs class to interact with our Razor template Views.

 The Android version of the BookDatabase class is available in the companion source code for this book.

Creating and implementing the BookLibrary database wrapper

In the previous section, we successfully created and implemented our BookDatabase database class that will be used by our BookLibrary application. Our next step is to begin implementing the code required for our BookLibraryDB class that will act as a wrapper for our BookDatabase class, to perform all database actions for our BookLibrary application.

Let's begin by performing the following steps:

1. Create an empty class within the BookLibrary solution, by choosing **Add | New File...**, as you did when creating the model in the previous section entitled *Creating and implementing the book library database model*, located within this chapter.

2. Then, enter in BookLibraryDB for the name of the new class that you want to create, and click on the **New** button to allow the wizard to proceed and create the new file.

2. Next, ensure that the `BookLibraryDB.cs` file is displayed within the code editor window, and then enter in the following code snippet:

```
//
//   BookLibraryDB.cs
//   BookLibrary Database Layer
//
//   Created by Steven F. Daniel on 20/10/2016.
//   Copyright © 2016 GENIESOFT STUDIOS. All rights reserved.
//
using SQLite;

namespace BookLibrary
{
    public class BookLibraryDB
    {
```

4. Next, we need to create a `conn` variable that will be used to set a connection to our `BookLibrary` database, and we also need to declare a `database` variable, that points to an instance of our `BookDatabase` that contains each of the operations for handling and performing the insertion, updating, and deletion of book entries:

```
static SQLiteConnection conn;
static BookDatabase database;
```

5. Then, we need to create the `SetDatabaseConnection()` method that will set a connection to our `BookDatabase` database class, so that it can access each of our instance methods for handling the creation, updating, retrieval, and deletion of our book entries, within our `BookItem` database table. Within this instance method, we set up and initialize the `conn` variable that contains the value of our `connection` parameter, and then instantiates a connection to our `BookDatabase` class, passing in the `conn` connection object so that the class can return our `database` object:

```
/// <summary>
/// Sets a connection to our BookDatabase database class.
/// </summary>
/// <param name="connection">Connection.</param>
public static void SetDatabaseConnection(SQLiteConnection
                    connection)
{
    conn = connection;
    database = new BookDatabase(conn);
}
```

6. Finally, we create the `Database` method that gets a reference to our `BookLibrary` database to use:

```
/// <summary>
/// Gets a reference to our BookLibrary database.
/// </summary>
/// <value>The database.</value>
    public static BookDatabase Database
    {
        get { return database; }
    }
  }
}
```

Now that we have created our `BookLibraryDB` class, we can create our Razor template user interface files that will connect to our `BookLibrary` database, and allow the user to interact with the database model to create, retrieve, update, and delete book items from the database.

 The Android version of the `BookLibraryDB` class is available in the companion source code for this book.

Creating and implementing the book listing main page

In the previous section, we created and implemented our `BookLibraryDB` database wrapper class that will be used by our `BookLibrary` application. The next step is to begin creating each of the Razor templates that will connect to our database model allowing the user to interact with the database visually by entering in book details, and having this information presented back to them, so they can make changes, or delete the book item altogether.

Let's begin by performing the following steps:

1. Create an empty class within the `Views` folder, by choosing **Add | NewFile...**, as you did when creating the model in the previous section entitled *Creating and implementing the book library database model,* located within this chapter.

2. Next, choose the **Preprocessed Razor Template** option, located within the **Text Templating** section, and enter in `BookLibraryListing`, as shown in the following screenshot:

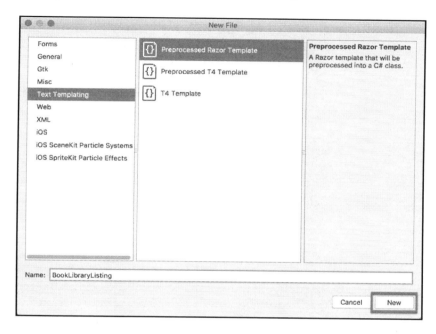

3. Next, click on the **New** button to allow the wizard to proceed and create the new empty Razor template file.

Congratulations, you have created your first Razor template! This file will be used to list all the book entries that are stored within our `BookItem` database table, contained within our `BookLibrary` database. The next step is to start to implement the code required for our `BookLibraryListing` Razor template, by performing the following step:

1. Ensure that the `BookLibraryListing.cshtml` file is displayed within the code editor, and enter in the following code snippet:

```
@using BookLibrary
@model List<BookItem>
<html>
<head><link rel="stylesheet" href="style.css" /></head>
<body>
<p></p>
<h1>Book Library Database Listing</h1>
```

```
<table border="1" cellpadding="8">
 @foreach (var book in @Model) {
   <tr>
   <td>@book.Id</td>
   <td>@book.Title</td>
   <td>@book.Author</td>
   <td>@book.Isbn</td>
   <td>
   <a href="hybrid:EditBookDetails?id=@book.Id">
   Edit</a>
   </td>
   </tr>
   }
   <tr>
   <td colspan="8">
    <a href="hybrid:CreateNewBook?">
    <input type="submit" name="Button"
    value="Add New Book"/></a>
   </td>
   </tr>
</table>
</body>
</html>
```

In the preceding code snippet, we define the HTML layout information that will be used by our `BookLibraryListing` Razor template. We firstly specify that we are using the `BookLibrary.iOS` namespace, so that we can have access to our database model as specified by the `@model` directive, and this must be the very first line preceding the `<html>` tag within a Razor template file. You will notice that the `@model` directive has the type of `List`. This is because we are iterating through each of our book items within our `Model`, and displaying the `id`, `title`, `author`, and `isbn` details for each book.

Next, we set up a `<a href` tag, that points to our `WebViewController.cs` class, and in-turn will call the `BookLibraryEdit.cshtml` Razor template to retrieve and display the book entry details for the associated identifier. The `hybrid` tag, used to identify if the URL is not our own custom scheme, and will just let the **WebView** load the URL as usual. Finally, we set up another `<a href` tag, that points to our `WebViewController.cs` class, and in-turn will call the `BookLibraryAdd.cshtml` Razor template to allow the user to create another book. You will notice that we don't need to pass in an `id` for the book, as this will be automatically assigned once the book has successfully been written to the database.

Creating and implementing the BookLibraryAdd Razor template

In the previous section, we created and implemented the `BookLibraryListing` Razor template that will be used to display a list of all books that have been previously added to the `BookLibrary` application. Our next step is to begin creating the Razor template that will allow the user to create a new book and save this to our database model.

Let's begin by performing the following steps:

1. Create an empty class within the `Views` folder, by choosing **Add | NewFile...**, as you did when creating the `BookLibraryListing` in the previous section entitled *Creating and implementing the book listing main page*, located within this chapter.
2. Next, choose the **Preprocessed Razor Template** option, located within the **Text Templating** section, and enter in `BookLibraryAdd`.
3. Next, click on the **New** button to allow the wizard to proceed and create the new empty Razor template file.

Our next step is to start to implement the code required for our `BookLibraryAdd` Razor template, by performing the following steps:

Ensure that the `BookLibraryAdd.cshtml` file is displayed within the code editor, and enter in the following code snippet:

```
@using BookLibrary
@model BookItem

<html>
<head>
    <link rel="stylesheet" href="style.css" />
</head>
<body>
    <h1>Add New Book Details</h1>
    <table border="1" cellpadding="8">
    <form action="hybrid:SaveBookDetails" method="GET">
    <input name="id" type="hidden" value="@Model.Id" />
    <tr>
    <td>Title:
      <input name="Title" value="@Model.Title" /></td>
    <tr>
    <td>Author:
      <input name="Author" value="@Model.Author" /></td>
    <tr>
```

```
      <td>Book ISBN:
        <input name="ISBN" value="@Model.Isbn" /></td>
      <tr>
      <td>Synopsis:
          <textarea name="Synopsis" rows="5" cols="40">
          @Model.Synopsis
          </textarea>
      </td>
      <tr>
      <td colspan="8">
          <input type="submit" name="Button" value="Save"/>
          <input type="submit" name="Button" value="Cancel"/>
      </td>
      </tr>
      </form>
  </table>
  </body>
  </html>
```

In the preceding code snippet, we defined the HTML layout information that will be used by our BookLibraryAdd Razor template. We firstly specified that we are using the BookLibrary.iOS namespace, so that we can have access to our database model as specified by the @model directive. We've already explained that this must be the very first line preceding the <html> tag within a Razor template file.

Next, we set up a <form action tag so that when the form gets submitted, the Save or Cancel buttons are pressed, our WebViewController.cs class will be called, and the appropriate action will take place. We specify the hybrid tag here again to identify if the URL is not our own custom scheme, and will just let the WebView load the URL as usual.

Creating and implementing the BookLibraryEdit Razor template

In the previous section, we created and implemented the BookLibraryAdd Razor template that will be used to allow the user to add new book entries to the BookLibrary application. Our next step is to begin creating the Razor template that will allow the user to edit an existing book and save this back to our database model.

Let's begin by performing the following steps:

1. Create an empty class within the `Views` folder, by choosing **Add | NewFile...**, as you did when creating the `BookLibraryListing` in the previous section entitled *Creating and implementing the book listing main page,* located within this chapter.
2. Next, choose the **Preprocessed Razor Template** option, located within the **Text Templating** section, and enter in `BookLibraryEdit`.
3. Next, click on the **New** button to allow the wizard to proceed and create the new empty Razor template file.

Our next step is to start to implement the code required for our `BookLibraryEdit` Razor template, by performing the following steps:

Ensure that the `BookLibraryEdit.cshtml` file is displayed within the code editor, and enter in the following code snippet:

```
@using BookLibrary
@model BookItem
<html>
<head>
    <link rel="stylesheet" href="style.css" />
</head>
<body>
    <h1>Edit Book Details</h1>
    <table border="1" cellpadding="8">
    <form action="hybrid:SaveBookDetails" method="GET">
    <input name="id" type="hidden" value="@Model.Id" />
        <tr>
        <td>Title:
        <input name="Title" value="@Model.Title" /></td>
        <tr>
        <td>Author:
        <input name="Author" value="@Model.Author" /></td>
        <tr>
        <td>Book ISBN:
        <input name="ISBN" value="@Model.Isbn" /></td>
        <tr>
        <td>Synopsis:
        <textarea name="Synopsis" rows="5" cols="40">
          @Model.Synopsis
          </textarea></td>
        <tr>
        <td colspan="8">
        <input type="submit" name="Button" value="Save"/>
        <input type="submit" name="Button" value="Cancel"/>
        @if (Model.Id > 0) {
```

```
            <input type="submit" name="Button" value="Delete"/>
            }
            </td>
            </tr>
        </form>
    </table>
    </body>
    </html>
```

In the preceding code snippet, we define the HTML layout information that will be used by our `BookLibraryEdit` Razor template. We firstly specify that we are using the `BookLibrary.iOS` namespace, so that we can have access to our database model as specified by the `@model` directive, which and we have said that this must be the very first line preceding the `<html>` tag within a Razor template file.

Next, we set up a `<form action` tag, so that when the form gets submitted the **Save** or **Cancel** buttons are pressed, our `WebViewController.cs` class will be called, and the appropriate action will take place. We specify the `hybrid` tag here again to identify if the URL is not our own custom scheme, and will just let the WebView load the URL as usual. You will notice that this implementation is quite similar to that of our `BookLibraryAdd`. The only thing that this Razor template does differently, is if we have a value for our book `id`, we display the **Delete** button so that the user can choose to delete the book entry.

 The Android version of the Razor templates are available in the companion source code for this book.

Creating and implementing the WebViewController class

In the previous section, we successfully created and implemented each of our Razor templates that will be used by our `BookLibrary` application. Our next step is to begin implementing the code for our application, that will be responsible for interacting with our Razor templates, and handling the actions associated with each model. It will use our `BookDatabase` class, to handle the performance of all the database actions for our `BookLibrary` application.

Let's begin by performing the following steps:

1. Ensure that the `WebViewController.cs` file is displayed within the code editor window, and then enter in the following highlighted code sections, as shown in the following code snippet:

```
//
//  WebViewController.cs
//  Web Container for representing Razor Templates
    within a Web View
//
//  Created by Steven F. Daniel on 20/10/2016.
//  Copyright © 2016 GENIESOFT STUDIOS. All rights reserved.
//
using System;
using System.Linq;
using Foundation;
using UIKit;
using System.Collections.Specialized;


namespace BookLibrary
{
    public partial class WebViewController :
      UIViewController
    {
        static bool UserInterfaceIdiomIsPhone
      {
          get { return UIDevice.CurrentDevice.UserInterfaceIdiom
            == UIUserInterfaceIdiom.Phone; }
      }
    }
```

2. Next, we declare a `webView` object that will point to our `UIWebView` instance, and then declare our `WebViewController()` class constructor method that will be instantiated from our `AppDelegate` class, as you will see once we begin implementing the necessary changes.

3. Enter in the following highlighted code sections, as shown in the following code snippet:

```
UIWebView webView;
public WebViewController()
  {
  }
protected WebViewController(IntPtr handle) : base(handle)
{
    // Note: this constructor should not contain any
```

```
        // initialization logic.
    }

    public override void ViewDidLoad()
    {
        base.ViewDidLoad();
```

4. Then, we define and specify the screen dimensions that we would like our `webView` to contain. In this case, we set this to take up the whole region of our screen and then add this to our existing view container. In the next step, we call the `GetItems` instance method on our `BookLibraryDB.Database` to return all existing book entries within the database, and assign this to our model.

5. In the next step, we specify the `BookLibraryListing` Razor template, and pass in the `model` that will be used to populate the ViewModel. Next, we call the `GenerateString()` method on our template, to execute the template within the main application bundle and return the output as a string, and then load this within our `webView`, using the `LoadHtmlString` method:

```
        webView = new UIWebView(UIScreen.MainScreen.Bounds);
        View.Add(webView);

        // Intercept URL loading to handle native calls from
        // browser
        webView.ShouldStartLoad += HandleShouldStartLoad;

        // Render the view to use our BookList.cshtml file
         var model = BookLibraryDB.Database.GetItems().ToList();
         var template = new BookLibraryListing()
           { Model = model };
         var page = template.GenerateString();

        // Load the rendered HTML into the view with a base URL
        // that points to the root of the bundled Resources
        // folder
        webView.LoadHtmlString(page, NSBundle.MainBundle.BundleUrl);

        // Perform any additional setup after loading the view,
        // typically from a nib.
    }

    public override void DidReceiveMemoryWarning()
    {
        base.DidReceiveMemoryWarning();
        // Release any cached data, images, etc that aren't
        // in use.
    }
```

```
bool HandleShouldStartLoad(UIWebView webView, NSUrlRequest
    request, UIWebViewNavigationType navigationType)
{
    // If the URL is not our own custom scheme, just
    // let the webView load the URL as usual
    const string scheme = "hybrid:";

    if (request.Url.Scheme != scheme.Replace(":", ""))
        return true;

    // This handler will treat everything between the
    // protocol and "?" as the method name. The querystring
    // has all of the parameters.
    var resources = request.Url.ResourceSpecifier.Split('?');
    var method = resources[0];
    var parameters = System.Web.HttpUtility.ParseQueryString(
        resources[1]);
```

6. Next, we create a `switch` statement to handle the type of `method` operation that we obtained from the Razor template directly after the `hybrid:` tag, and handle accordingly:

```
switch (method)
{
    case "CreateNewBook":
        CreateNewBook(webView);
        break;
    case "EditBookDetails":
        EditBookDetails(webView, parameters);
        break;
    case "SaveBookDetails":
        SaveBookDetails(webView, parameters);
        break;
    default:
        // Cases not covered are handled here.
        break;
}
return false;
}
```

7. Then, we need to create the `CreateNewBook()` instance method that will be responsible for handling the creation of our new book entry. This method accepts the name of the `webView` to display its content and we specify the `BookLibraryAdd` Razor template, and pass in the `model` that will be used to populate the ViewModel. Next, we call the `GenerateString()` method on our template, to execute the template within the main application bundle and return the output as a string, and then load this within our `webView`, using the `LoadHtmlString` method:

```
/// <summary>
/// Handles the creation of our new book entry.
/// </summary>
/// <param name="webView">Web view.</param>
void CreateNewBook(UIWebView webView,
    NameValueCollection parameters)
{
    var template = new BookLibraryAdd()
    {Model = new BookItem()};
    var page = template.GenerateString();
    webView.LoadHtmlString(page,
      NSBundle.MainBundle.BundleUrl);
}
```

8. Next, we need to create the `EditBookDetails()` instance method that will be responsible for handling the editing of our book entry. This method accepts the name of the `webView` to display its content as well as any parameters. Next, we specify the `BookLibraryEdit` Razor template, and pass in the `model` as well as the `id` value for the selected book entry to be used to populate the ViewModel. Next, we call the `GenerateString()` method on our template, to execute the template within the main application bundle and return the output as a string, and then load this within our `webView`, using the `LoadHtmlString` method:

```
/// <summary>
/// Handles the editing of our book details.
/// </summary>
/// <param name="webView">Web view.</param>
/// <param name="parameters">Parameters.</param>
void EditBookDetails(UIWebView webView,
System.Collections.Specialized.NameValueCollection parameters)
{
    var model = BookLibraryDB.Database.GetItem(
    Convert.ToInt32(parameters["Id"]));
    var template = new BookLibraryEdit() { Model = model };
    var page = template.GenerateString();
    webView.LoadHtmlString(page,
```

```
                        NSBundle.MainBundle.BundleUrl);
    }
```

9. Then, we need to create the SaveBookDetails() instance method that will be responsible for handling the saving of our book entry. This method accepts the name of the webView to display its content as well as any parameters. Next, we grab the name of the button that we pressed from the relevant Razor template and use a switch statement to handle the type of button operation and handle accordingly. Once the operation has completed successfully, we return, and load the BookLibraryListing page within the webView container:

```
/// <summary>
/// Saves the book details to the SQLite BookDetails Database.
/// </summary>
/// <param name="webView">Web view.</param>
/// <param name="parameters">Parameters.</param>
void SaveBookDetails(UIWebView webView,
System.Collections.Specialized.NameValueCollection parameters)
{
    // Points to our Edit Book Details HTML page.
    var button = parameters["Button"];
    switch (button)
    {
        case "Save":
            SaveDetailsToDatabase(parameters);
            break;
        case "Delete":
            DeleteBookDetails(parameters);
            break;
        case "Cancel":
            break;
        default:
            // Cases not covered are handled here.
            break;
    }
    var model = BookLibraryDB.Database.GetItems().ToList();
    var template = new BookLibraryListing() { Model = model };
    webView.LoadHtmlString(template.GenerateString(),
    NSBundle.MainBundle.BundleUrl);
}
```

10. Next, we need to create the `SaveDetailsToDatabase()` instance method that will be responsible for handling the saving of our book entry to the SQLite database. This method accepts a list of parameters that have been entered within the `BookLibraryAdd` or `BookLibraryEdit` Razor template screens, and creates a `BookItem` database model. This then gets passed to the `SaveItem` method that our `BookLibraryDB` wrapper class calls the `BookDatabase` class:

```
/// <summary>
/// Saves the book details to our SQLite database.
/// </summary>
/// <returns>The details to database.</returns>
/// <param name="parameters">Parameters.</param>
void SaveDetailsToDatabase(System.Collections.Specialized.NameV
alueCollection parameters)
{
    var book = new BookItem
    {
        id = Convert.ToInt32(parameters["Id"]),
        title = parameters["Title"],
        author = parameters["Author"],
        isbn = parameters["Isbn"],
        synopsis = parameters["Synopsis"]
    };
    BookLibraryDB.Database.SaveItem(book);
}
```

11. Then, we need to create the `DeleteBookDetails()` instance method that will be responsible for handling the saving of our book entry to the SQLite database. This method accepts a list of parameters that have been entered within the `BookLibraryEdit` Razor template screen, and passes the `id` of the book entry to the `DeleteItem` method that our `BookLibraryDB` wrapper class calls the `BookDatabase`:

```
/// <summary>
/// Handle when the Delete button has been pressed
/// </summary>
/// <returns>The book details.</returns>
/// <param name="parameters">Parameters.</param>
void DeleteBookDetails(System.Collections.Specialized.NameValue
Collection parameters)
{
    BookLibraryDB.Database.DeleteItem(Convert.ToInt32(
    parameters["Id"]));
}
}
```

Now we have successfully added the necessary code to our
WebViewController.cs class to allow it to communicate with our Razor
templates when book entries have been created, updated, retrieved, deleted, and
saved.

 The Android version of the WebViewController.cs class is available in
the companion source code for this book.

12. Next, we need to initialize our books library SQLite library database within each
    of our platform-specific start-up classes (for example, AppDelegate.cs for iOS and
    MainActivity.cs for Android).

13. Ensure that the AppDelegate.cs file is displayed within the code editor
    window, and then enter in the following highlighted code sections, as shown in
    the following code snippet:

```
using System;
using System.IO;
using Foundation;
using UIKit;
using SQLite;
namespace BookLibrary
{
    // The UIApplicationDelegate for the application.
       This class
    // is responsible for launching the User Interface of the
    // application, as well as listening
       (and optionally responding)
    // to application events from iOS.
     [Register("AppDelegate")]
    public class AppDelegate : UIApplicationDelegate
    {
        // class-level declarations
        public override UIWindow Window
        {
            get;
            set;
        }

    public override bool FinishedLaunching(UIApplication
            application, NSDictionary launchOptions)
    {
        // Override point for customization after application
         // launch. If not required for your application you can
        // safely delete this method
```

```
        // create a new window instance based on the screen size
        Window = new UIWindow(UIScreen.MainScreen.Bounds);
        // Declare the name to use for our database name
        var sqliteFilename = "BookLibrary.db";
        string documentsPath = Environment.GetFolderPath(
          Environment.SpecialFolder.Personal);
        string libraryPath = Path.Combine(documentsPath, "..",
          "Library");
        var databasePath = Path.Combine(libraryPath, sqliteFilename);
        // Set a connection to our database
         var databaseConn = new SQLiteConnection(databasePath);
        BookLibraryDB.SetDatabaseConnection(databaseConn);
        // Set our RootViewController to be the instance of
         // our BookViewController class and make it visible.
        Window.RootViewController = new WebViewController();
        Window.MakeKeyAndVisible();
        return true;
    }
    ...
    ...
    ...
}
```

In the preceding code snippet, we began by importing both the SQLite and System.IO classes, and then modified the FinishedLaunching method to create a new Window instance based on the screen size of the device. Since we have specified that we want our project to work on both iPad and iPhone devices, this will take up the full screen dimensions.

Next, we declared the name to use for our database name and specified the location of where to save the BookLibrary.db database to, as determined by the databasePath string. In our next step, we set up a connection to our database, and then set the RootViewController to be the instance of our BookViewController class, before finally making this become visible on screen.

 The Android version of the MainActivity.cs class is available in the companion source code for this book.

Updating the book library Cascading Style Sheet (CSS)

In this section, we need to make some final changes to the `styles.css` file. This file is essentially a CSS, and any Razor templates that utilize this style sheet will inherit everything that it contains. We will basically be making some minor changes to the body or our HTML pages, applying padding to margins, setting font sizes, and colors of web links when they are pressed.

Let's begin by performing the following step:

1. Ensure that the `Style.css` file is displayed within the code editor window, and then enter in the following highlighted code sections, as shown in the following code snippet:

```
/* This is a minimal style sheet intended to demonstrate
   how to include static content in your hybrid app.
   Other static content, such as javascript files and images,
   can be included in this same folder (Resources on iOS
   or Assets on Android), with the same Build Action
   (BundleResource on iOS or AndroidAsset on Android),
   to be accessible from a path starting at the root
   of your hybrid application.  */

#page {
     margin-top:10px;
}
html,
body {
  margin: 7px;
  padding: 0px;
  border: 0px;
  color: #000;
  background: #ffffe0;}html, body, p, th, td, li, dd, dt {
  font: 1em Arial, Helvetica, sans-serif;
}
h1 {
  font-family: Arial, Helvetica, sans-serif;
  font-size: 18;}a:link {
    color: #00f; }a:visited {
      color: #009; }a:hover {
        color: #06f; }a:active {
          color: #0cf;
  }
```

Now that we have finished building all the necessary components for our `BookLibrary` application, our next step is to finally build and run the `BookLibrary` application within the iOS simulator. When compilation completes, the iOS Simulator will appear automatically and the `BookLibrary` application will be displayed, as shown in the following screenshot:

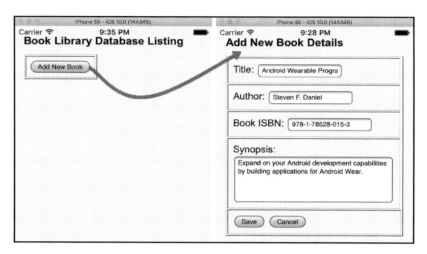

As you can see from the preceding screenshot, this currently displays our **Book Library Database Listing** page. Since we don't have any details added yet, this will show up as blank, and you must press the **Add New Book** button to display the **Add New Book Details** screen:

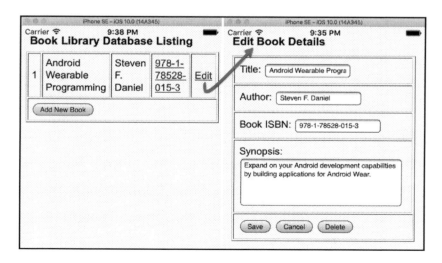

The preceding screenshot shows the updated **Book Library Database Listing** Razor template page ViewModel with the information saved from the previous screen. Clicking on the **Edit** link will display the **Edit Book Details** screen with all the previously entered book details populated.

Summary

In this chapter, you learned about the Razor templating engine and how you can use it to create a hybrid mobile solution. You also learned how to create and use models within your application, and have the information saved to an SQLite database, and retrieved later. Finally, you learned how you can use JavaScript code using C# to execute method calls.

In the next chapter, you'll learn how to create and consume a RESTful web service API, so that it can be used within the `TrackMyWalks` application to save and retrieve information entered within the ViewModels.

7
Incorporating API Data Access Using Microsoft Azure App Services

In the previous chapter, we learned about the Razor templating engine and how you can use it to create a hybrid mobile solution. You learned how to create and use models within your application, and how to save the information to a SQLite database and retrieve it later. Towards the end of the chapter, you learned how you can use JavaScript code using C# to execute method calls.

Up until this point, you have been building the `TrackMyWalks` app with static walk trail information that has been hard-coded within the `TrackMyWalks` app. However, in the real world, it is very rare that your app will depend purely on local static data, and you will need to source your information from a remote data source, typically using a RESTful API. In some cases, your app may even communicate with a third-party API, for example Facebook.

In this chapter, you'll learn how you can use **Microsoft Azure App** services to create your very first live, cloud-based backend HTTP web service to handle all the communication between the cloud and the app. You will also learn how to create a `DataService` API that will allow the app to consume the API so that we can retrieve, store, and delete walk trail information from the cloud all within the `TrackMyWalks` app.

This chapter will cover the following points:

- Gain an understanding of what Microsoft Azure App services are
- Setting up the `TrackMyWalks` app within the Microsoft Azure portal

- Adding the `HttpClient` and JSON.Net `NuGet` packages to the solution
- Creating the `TrackMyWalks` base HTTP service
- Creating the `TrackMyWalks` API data service
- Updating the `TrackMyWalksViewModels` to use the API data service
- Running the `TrackMyWalks` app within the simulator

Setting up our TrackMyWalks app using Microsoft Azure

In this section, we will look at the steps required to set up the `TrackMyWalks` application within Microsoft Azure. Nearly all mobile applications that you will develop will require the ability to communicate with an API to store, retrieve, update, and delete information. This API can be an existing one that someone within your organization has already created, but sometimes you will need to create your own API for your application.

Microsoft Azure, or ("Azure" as it's best known for), is essentially a cloud-based platform that was created by Microsoft back in February 2010. Azure was designed for building, deploying, and managing several applications and their associated services, such as **SaaS**, **PaaS**, and **IaaS**.

Each of the Microsoft Azure specific associated services are explained in the following table:

Azure service	Description
SaaS	**Software as a Service** provides software licensing and delivery models where software is licensed on a subscription basis and is centrally hosted.
PaaS	**Platform as a Service** provides customers with a platform to develop, run, and manage applications without the complexities of maintaining the infrastructure when developing and launching an app.
IaaS	**Infrastructure as a Service** provides virtualized computing resources over the Internet.

One of the main benefits of using Microsoft Azure Mobile Apps is that they provide you with a very quick and easy way to get a fully functional backend service up and running within a matter of minutes. Before we can proceed with setting up and creating our `TrackMyWalks` database within the cloud, you will need to have a Microsoft Azure account. If you don't already have one, you can create one for free at https://azure.microsoft.com/en-us/pricing/free-trial/.

Once you have created your Microsoft Azure account, you will need to log into the Microsoft Azure portal using your web browser. Let's look at how to do this, by performing the following steps:

1. Launch your web browser with the following URL `https://portal.azure.com/` and log in to the Microsoft Azure portal using your credentials.

2. Next, from the main Microsoft Azure portal dashboard, click the **+** button in the top-left hand corner from the **New** section, and select the **Web + Mobile** option, and then choose the **Mobile App** option as shown in the following screenshot:

3. Then, enter in `TrackMyWalks` to use as the name for our app for the **App name** field.

4. Next, either choose your **Subscription** type, or leave the default of **Free Trial**.

5. Then, provide a name for your **Resource Group**, either by creating a new one, or choosing from an existing one.

6. Next, ensure that the **Pin to dashboard** option has been selected, so that you can have your **Mobile App** displayed on the Microsoft Azure **Dashboard**. This is particularly useful, and provides easy access.

Now that we have successfully created our **Mobile App** within Microsoft Azure, our next step is to begin setting up the database that will allow our app to store walk entry information. Let's look at how we can achieve this with the following steps:

1. From the **Dashboard**, click on the **TrackMyWalks** service, as shown in the following screenshot:

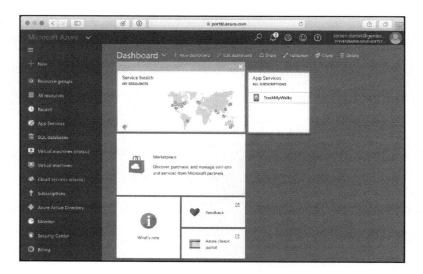

2. Next, choose the **Data connections** option from the **MOBILE** section under the **TrackMyWalks App Service** section, as shown in the following screenshot:

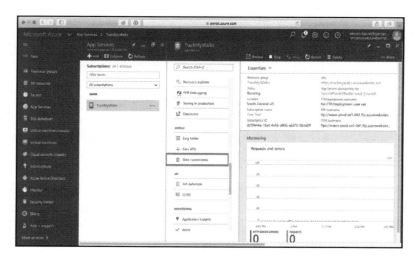

3. Then, within the **TrackMyWalks – Data connections** screen, click on the **+ Add** button, to display the **Add data connection** screen, as shown in the following screenshot:

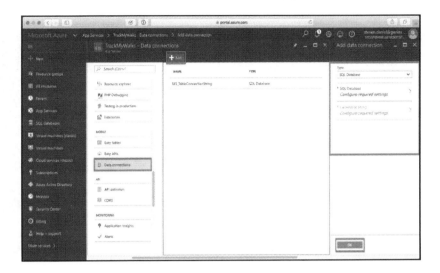

4. Next, ensure that you have selected **SQL Database** from the **Type** dropdown, and proceed to configure your **SQL Database**.

5. Then, click on the **OK** button to save your changes and create the new data connection for our `TrackMyWalks` SQL server database.

Once you have created your `TrackMyWalks` mobile app and SQL database within Microsoft Azure, by default, your database won't contain any database tables or data. Before we can start communicating with and consuming the API within our `TrackMyWalks` app, we need to create a new table that will store our walk trail entries.

Let's look at the following steps to achieve this:

1. From the **Dashboard**, click on the **TrackMyWalks** service, then choose the **Easy tables** option from the **MOBILE** section under the **TrackMyWalks App Service** section.

2. Next, within the **TrackMyWalks – Easy tables** screen, click on the **+ Add** button, to display the **Add a table** screen, as shown in the following screenshot:

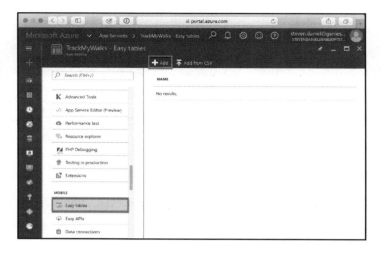

3. Then, enter in `WalkEntries` to use as the name for our table for the **Name** field.

4. Next, leave the default permissions that have been set for our **Insert permission**, **Update permission**, **Delete permission**, **Read permission**, and **Undelete permission** dropdown entries:

5. Then, click on the **OK** button to save your changes, and your new **WalkEntries** table will be added to the list of **Easy Tables** entries.

 Whenever you choose the **Allow anonymous access** permission during the creation of your table, you are essentially making the API available without providing any specific authentication headers as part of the HTTP request.

Before we can start making calls to our API and consuming this within our `TrackMyWalks` app, we'll run a quick check to see if our API endpoint is working correctly. This is achieved by issuing a GET HTTP request using the command line, or if you'd prefer, you can use a REST console client.

6. Open your terminal window, and type in the following statement from the command line as follows:

```
Last login: Sun Nov 6 10:48:41 on console
GENIESOFT-MAC-Mini:~ stevendaniel$ curl
https://trackmywalks.azurewebsites.net/tables/
walkentries --header "ZUMO-API-VERSION:2.0.0"
```

If you have set everything up correctly within the Microsoft Azure portal, you should receive back a 200 (Success) status code, along with an empty collection in the response body as follows:

```
Last login: Sun Nov 6 10:48:41 on console
GENIESOFT-MAC-Mini:~ stevendaniel$ curl
https://trackmywalks.azurewebsites.net/tables/
walkentries --header "ZUMO-API-VERSION:2.0.0"
[] GENIESOFT-MAC-Mini:~ stevendaniel$
```

 There are several REST console clients that exist for you to choose from, if you don't already have one installed. I tend to use `Postman` for handling REST APIs, which you can download from `http://www.getpostman.com/`.

Now that we have successfully created our `TrackMyWalks` API and `WalkEntries` data table within the service, we can begin making calls to our API and receiving those response messages directly back from the API. In the next section, we will begin to add the `Json.Net` and `HttpClient` .NET Framework libraries that will be responsible for handling the REST API requests to save and retrieve our walk entry details.

Adding the Json.Net NuGet package to the TrackMyWalks app

Now that you have set up and created the `TrackMyWalks` database within the Microsoft Azure platform, our next step is to add the Json.Net `NuGet` package to our `TrackMyWalks` Portable Class Library solution. The `Json.Net` package is a high-performance JSON framework for the .NET platform that allows you to serialize and deserialize any type of .NET object with help of the JSON serializer.

When we start to incorporate this framework within our `TrackMyWalks` solution, we will have the ability of performing LINQ to JSON capabilities that will enable us to create, parse, query, and modify the JSON structure that we receive back from our Microsoft Azure `TrackMyWalks` database table.

Let's look at how to add the Json.Net `NuGet` package to our `TrackMyWalks` Portable Class Library , by performing the following steps:

1. Right-click on the `Packages` folder that is contained within the `TrackMyWalks` Portable Class Library solution, and choose **Add Packages...** menu option, as shown in the following screenshot:

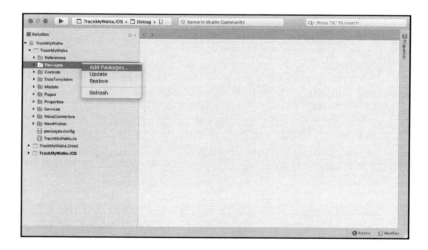

2. This will display the **Add Packages** dialog, enter in `Json.Net` within the search dialog, and select the **Json.Net** option within the list, as shown in the following screenshot:

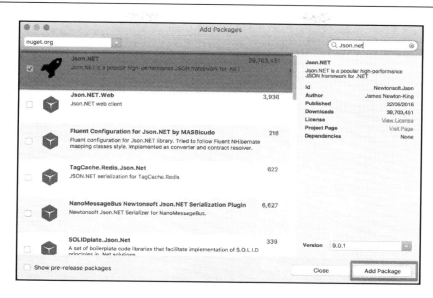

3. Finally, click on the **Add Package** button to add the NuGet package to the Packages folder, contained within the TrackMyWalks Portable Class Library solution.

Now that you have added the Json.Net NuGet package, our next step is to add the HttpClient framework to our TrackMyWalks Portable Class Library, which we will be covering in the next section.

Adding the HttpClient NuGet package to the TrackMyWalks app

In the previous section, we added the Json.Net NuGet package to our TrackMyWalks solution. Our next step is to add the HTTP library to our TrackMyWalks solution to enable it to communicate with an API over HTTP.

Since we are using both .NET and C# to build our Xamarin.Forms application, we can leverage a library within the .NET Framework called System.Net.Http.HttpClient. This HttpClient framework provides us with a mechanism of sending and receiving data using standard HTTP methods, such as GET and POST.

Let's look at how to add the HttpClient `NuGet` package to our `TrackMyWalks` Portable Class Library, by performing the following steps:

1. Right-click on the `Packages` folder that is contained within the `TrackMyWalks` Portable Class Library solution, and choose the **Add Packages...** menu option. If you can't remember how to do this, you can refer to the section entitled Adding the Json.Net `NuGet` package to the `TrackMyWalks` app located within this chapter.

2. This will display the **Add Packages** dialog. Here, enter in `Http` within the search dialog, and select the **System.Net.Http** option, as shown in the following screenshot:

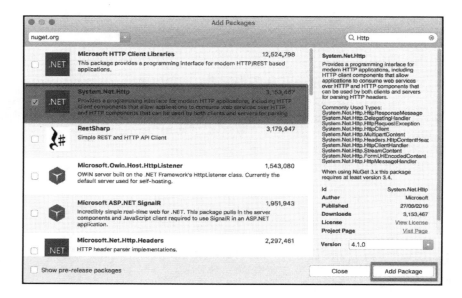

3. Finally, click on the **Add Package** button to add the `NuGet` package to the `Packages` folder, contained within the `TrackMyWalks` Portable Class Library solution.

Now that you have added both the `Json.Net` and `System.Net.HttpNuGet` packages to our solution, we can begin utilizing these framework libraries as we progress throughout this chapter.

Updating the WalkEntries model to use the Json.Net framework

In this section, we will begin by updating the `WalkEntries` data model to take advantage of our backend service calls, when we create these, and then the `WalkDataService.cs` and `WalkWebService.cs` files will communicate and interact with our Microsoft Azure `TrackMyWalks` database to store, delete, and retrieve walk entry information.

Let's now start to modify and implement the code required for our `WalkEntries` class model, by performing the following steps:

Ensure that the `WalkEntries.cs` file is displayed within the code editor, and enter in the following highlighted code sections:

```
//
//   WalkEntries.cs
//   TrackMyWalks
//
//   Created by Steven F. Daniel on 04/08/2016.
//   Copyright © 2016 GENIESOFT STUDIOS. All rights reserved.
//
 using System;
 using Newtonsoft.Json;
namespace TrackMyWalks.Models
{
    public class WalkEntries
   {
     [JsonProperty("id")]
     public string Id { get; set; }
     public string Title { get; set; }
     public string Notes { get; set; }
     public double Latitude { get; set; }
     public double Longitude { get; set; }
     public double Kilometers { get; set; }
     public string Difficulty { get; set; }
     public double Distance { get; set; }
     public Uri ImageUrl { get; set; }
   }
}
```

In the preceding code snippet, we have successfully modified the database model that will be used to store walk entry information within our Microsoft Azure database. You will notice that we have defined a [JsonProperty("id")] item, as well as a string property named Id that will serve as a unique primary key for each record that we store within the database. We have also updated our ImageUrl property to include the Uri type that will be used to convert the URL entered within the walk entry page, so that it is stored correctly within the database.

 If you are interested in finding out more information about the JsonProperty and the Newtonsoft.Json classes, please refer to the Json.NET documentation located at http://www.newtonsoft.com/json/help/html/T_Newtonsoft_Json_Seria lization_JsonProperty.htm.

Creating the HTTP web service class for the TrackMyWalks app

In the previous section, we successfully modified the WalkEntries database model that will be used by our TrackMyWalks application. This will allow us to have a live backend service that will enable our application to communicate over HTTP so that it can send requests to the API to retrieve, add, and delete trail walk entries. In this section, we will need a means for our app to communicate with our API over HTTP, and therefore it will require an HTTP library.

Since we are using .NET and C#, we can use a library within the .NET Framework, called System.Net.Http.HttpClient. This Framework provides a mechanism for allowing our app to send and receive data using standard HTTP methods such as GET and POST. We will begin by creating a base service class within our TrackMyWalks Portable Class Library that will be responsible for handling all the HTTP communications for us.

Let's now start to implement the code required for our WalkWebService base-class model, by performing the following steps:

1. Create an empty class within the Services folder, by choosing **Add** | **New File...**, as you did in the section entitled, *Creating the navigation service interface for the TrackMyWalks app* within Chapter 3, *Navigating within the MVVM Model – The Xamarin.Forms Way*.

2. Then, enter in `WalkWebService` for the name of the new class that you want to create, and click on the **New** button to allow the wizard to proceed and create the new file.

3. Next, ensure that the `WalkWebService.cs` file is displayed within the code editor, and enter in the following code snippet:

```
//
//   WalkWebService.cs
//   TrackMyWalks Http Web Service Class
//
//   Created by Steven F. Daniel on 30/10/2016.
//   Copyright © 2016 GENIESOFT STUDIOS. All rights reserved.
//
    using System;
    using System.Collections.Generic;
    using System.Net.Http;
    using System.Text;
    using System.Threading.Tasks;
    using Newtonsoft.Json;

    namespace TrackMyWalks.Services
    {
        public abstract class WalkWebService
        {
```

4. Then, we need to create a `protected async` method called `SendRequestAsync<T>` that accepts a `Uri` named `url` as well a `HttpMethod` named `httpMethod`, and finally a `Dictionary<string, string>` object named `headers`, as well as an object named `requestData`, that will be used to construct the HTTP request. Proceed and enter in the following code snippet:

```
protected async Task<T> SendRequestAsync<T>(
  Uri url, HttpMethod httpMethod = null,
  IDictionary<string, string> headers = null,
  object requestData = null)
{
```

5. Next, we'll set up the `result` to the `default(T)` type that will return a default value to a parameterized type since we don't know what our result will contain at this point. We'll then declare our `method` variable to contain the `GET` HttpMethod. This will be used to return the content and then create a `request` variable that will set up an instance of our `HttpRequestMessage` class and then serialize our requested data to our `request` object and return the information back in `Json` format as defined by the `application/json` type. Proceed and enter in the following code snippet:

```
var result = default(T);
var method = httpMethod ?? HttpMethod.Get;
var request = new HttpRequestMessage(method, url);

// Serialize our request data
var data = requestData == null ? null :
  JsonConvert.SerializeObject(requestData);
if (data != null)
{
   // Add the serialized request data to our request
   // object.
   request.Content = new StringContent(data,
     Encoding.UTF8, "application/json");
}
```

6. Then, we'll begin iterating through our headers collection to add each of our specific `headers` to the `request` object that will be sent along with the `HttpRequestMessage` class. Proceed and enter in the following code snippet:

```
// Add each of the specified headers to our request
if (headers != null)
{
   foreach (var h in headers)
   {
       request.Headers.Add(h.Key, h.Value);
   }
}
```

7. Next, we'll set up and declare a `handler` variable that instantiates an instance of the `HttpClientHandler` class which is essentially a `HttpMessageHandler` that contains a common set of properties that work across the `HttpWebRequest` API. In the next step, we'll declare a `client` variable that instantiates our `HttpClient` class that accepts our `handler` variable to begin sending our request over HTTP.

8. Next, we'll declare our `response` object that performs a `SendAsync` and accepts our `request` object, along with our `HttpCompletionOption.ResponseContentRead` that completes after reading the entire `response` content.

9. Finally, we'll perform a comparison check to see if we have successfully read our content and have a response code of `200` (Success) returned, before deserializing our content into `Json` format, using the `JsonConvert` method. Proceed and enter in the following code snippet:

```
// Get a response from our Web Service
var handler = new HttpClientHandler();
var client = new HttpClient(handler;
var response = await client.SendAsync(request,
  HttpCompletionOption.ResponseContentRead);

    if (response.IsSuccessStatusCode &&
    response.Content != null)
    {
        var content = await response.Content.
                    ReadAsStringAsync();
        result = JsonConvert.DeserializeObject<T>(content);
    }
    return result;
  }
 }
}
```

Now that we have successfully created our base HTTP service class, we can begin to use this within our `ViewModels` as well as our `WalkEntries` database model, by creating a base sub-class within our `DataService` API which we will be covering in the next section.

If you are interested in finding out more information about the `HttpClientHandler` and `HttpClient` classes, please refer to the Microsoft developer documentation located at `https://msdn.microsoft.com/en-us/library/system.net.http.httpclient(v=vs.118).aspx`.

Creating the DataService API for the TrackMyWalks app

In the previous section, we created a `WalkWebService` class that provides us with a means of sending HTTP requests to our `TrackMyWalks` Microsoft Azure database. In this section, we will begin by creating a data service class that will allow us to send and receive responses back from our API, in `Json` format which will update the `WalkEntries` database model so our application can use this.

We will begin by creating the interface for our data service that can be used to communicate with each of the `ViewModels` that our `TrackMyWalks` application utilizes. Let's now start to implement the code required for our `IWalkDataService` base-class model, by performing the following steps:

1. Create an empty interface within the `Services` folder. If you can't remember how to do this, you can refer to the section entitled *Creating the navigation service interface for the TrackMyWalks app* within `Chapter 3`, *Navigating within the MVVM Model – The Xamarin.Forms Way*.

2. Next, enter in `IWalkDataService` for the name of the new interface that you want to create, and click on the **New** button to allow the wizard to proceed and create the file.

3. Then, ensure that the `IWalkDataService.cs` file is displayed within the code editor, and enter in the following code snippet:

```
//
//  IWalkDataService.cs
//  TrackMyWalks Data Service Interface
//
//  Created by Steven F. Daniel on 30/10/2016.
//  Copyright © 2016 GENIESOFT STUDIOS. All rights reserved.
//
using System;
using System.Threading.Tasks;
using System.Collections.Generic;
using TrackMyWalks.Models;

namespace TrackMyWalks.Services
{
    public interface IWalkDataService
    {
     Task <IList<WalkEntries>> GetWalkEntriesAsync();
     Task AddWalkEntryAsync(WalkEntries entry);
     Task DeleteWalkEntryAsync(WalkEntries entry);
```

```
        }
    }
```

In the preceding code snippet, we begin by implementing the methods that will be required to retrieve, update, and delete our `WalkEntries` information. The `GetWalkEntriesAsync` instance method uses a generic type which is used to restrict the `WalkEntries` to use objects of the `IList` class.

The `AddWalkEntryAsync` instance method accepts an `entry` parameter that contains the walk entry details to be added of type `WalkEntries`, and our `DeleteWalkEntryAsync` instance method accepts an `entry` parameter that needs to be deleted from our database. We use the `Task` class to essentially handle all asynchronous operations, by ensuring that the asynchronous methods that we initiate will eventually finish, thus completing the task in hand.

Creating the DataService API class for the TrackMyWalks app

In the previous section, we created our data service base interface class for our data service, and we defined several different instance methods that our class will be utilizing. This will essentially be used by each of our `ViewModels` along with the Views (pages). Let's now start to implement the code required for our `WalkDataService` class, by performing the following steps:

1. Create an empty class within the `Services` folder, by choosing **Add | New File...**, as you did when creating the `DataService` interface in the previous section entitled *Creating the DataService API for the TrackMyWalks app* located within this chapter.

2. Then, enter in `WalkDataService` for the name of the new class that you want to create, and click on the **New** button to allow the wizard to proceed and create the new file.

3. Next, ensure that the `WalkDataService.cs` file is displayed within the code editor, and enter the following code snippet:

```
//
//  WalkDataService.cs
//  TrackMyWalks API Data Service Class
//
//  Created by Steven F. Daniel on 30/10/2016.
//  Copyright © 2016 GENIESOFT STUDIOS. All rights reserved.
```

```
//
using System;
using System.Collections.Generic;
using System.Threading.Tasks;
using System.Net.Http;
using TrackMyWalks.Models;
using Newtonsoft.Json;

namespace TrackMyWalks.Services
{
```

4. Next, we need to modify our `WalkDataService` class constructor, so that it can inherit from both our `WalkWebService` base-class as well as the `IWalkDataService` class:

```
public class WalkDataService : WalkWebService, IWalkDataService
{
```

5. Next, we'll declare two private class properties, `_baseUri` and `_headers`. The `_baseUri` property will be used to store the base URL and the `_headers` property of the `IDictionary<string, string>` type that will be used to store the header information that we want to pass to our `WalkWebService` class.

6. The `zumo-api-version` is basically a special header value that is used by the HTTP client when communicating with Microsoft Azure databases. Proceed and enter in the following code snippet.

```
readonly Uri _baseUri;
readonly IDictionary<string, string> _headers;

// Our Class Constructor that accepts the Azure Database
// Uri path
public WalkDataService(Uri baseUri)
{
    _baseUri = baseUri;
    _headers = new Dictionary<string, string>();
    _headers.Add("zumo-api-version", "2.0.0");
}
```

7. Next, we'll implement the `GetWalkEntriesAsync` instance method that will retrieve all `WalkEntries` that are contained within our database. We'll define a `url` variable that constructs a new `Uri` object using our `_baseUri` URL and combining this with our `walkEntries` database table within the `tables` section of our `TrackMyWalks` Azure database and call the `SendRequestAsyncWalkWebService` base-class instance method.

8. We'll pass in the `HttpMethod.Get` method type to tell our base class that we are ready to retrieve our `WalkEntries`. Proceed and enter in the following code snippet:

```
// API to retrieve our Walk Entries from our database
public async Task<IList<WalkEntries>> GetWalkEntriesAsync()
{
    var url = new Uri(_baseUri, "/tables/walkentries");
    return await SendRequestAsync<WalkEntries[]>
    (url, HttpMethod.Get, _headers);
}
```

9. Next, we'll implement the `AddWalkEntryAsync` instance method that will add walk entry information to the `walkEntries` table contained within our database. We define a `url` variable that constructs a new `Uri` object using our _baseUri URL and combining this with the `walkEntries` database table within the `tables` section of our `TrackMyWalks` Azure database and call the `SendRequestAsyncWalkWebService` base-class instance method.

10. We'll pass in the `HttpMethod.Post` method type that will tell our base class that we are ready to submit information to our `walkEntries` database table. Proceed and enter in the following code snippet:

```
// API to add our Walk Entry information to the database
public async Task<WalkEntries> AddWalkEntryAsync(
  WalkEntries entry)
{
    var url = new Uri(_baseUri, "/tables/walkentries");
    await SendRequestAsync<WalkEntries>(url,HttpMethod.Post,
    _headers, entry);
}
```

11. Next, we'll implement the `DeleteWalkEntryAsync` instance method that will permanently delete associated walk entry information from our `walkEntries` table contained within our database. We'll define a `url` variable that constructs a new `Uri` object using our _baseUri URL and combining this with our `walkEntries` database table, and pass in the `Id` value of our selected walk entry within the `WalksPageListView`.

12. We'll then call the `SendRequestAsyncWalkWebService` base class instance method. We'll pass in the `HttpMethod.Delete` method type that will tell our base class that we are ready to permanently delete the walk entry within our `walkEntries` database table. Proceed and enter in the following code snippet:

```
// API to delete our Walk Entry from the database
```

```
public async Task DeleteWalkEntryAsync(WalkEntries entry)
{
    var url = new Uri(_baseUri, string.Format("/tables/walken
                      tries/{0}", entry.Id));
    await SendRequestAsync<WalkEntries>(url,HttpMethod.Delete
    , _headers);
}
}
}
```

In the preceding code snippet, we began by implementing each of the instance methods that we defined within our `IWalkDataService` interface class. We used the `SendRequestAsync` method on our base class, and passed in the API details, along with the `HttpMethod` type, and the `zumo-api-version` header information. You will have noticed that we passed in the `WalkEntries` data model object. This is so that the object can be serialized and added to the HTTP request message content.

 If you are interested in learning more HTTP, please refer to the Hypertext Transfer Protocol guide located at
`https://en.wikipedia.org/wiki/Hypertext_Transfer_Protocol`.

The HTTP class exposes several different types of HTTP methods that are used by the `HttpMethod` class, which are explained in the following table.

HTTP methods	Description
GET	This type tells the `HttpMethod` class protocol that we are ready to request message content over HTTP to retrieve information from our API, and return this information back, based on the representation format specified within the API.
POST	This type tells the `HttpMethod` class protocol that we want to create a new entry within our table, as specified within our API.
DELETE	This type tells the `HttpMethod` class protocol that we want to delete an existing entry within our table, as specified within our API.

 If you are interested in learning more about client and server versioning in Mobile Apps and Mobile Services, please refer to the Microsoft Azure documentation located at
`https://azure.microsoft.com/en-us/documentation/articles/app-ser vice-mobile-client-and-server-versioning/`.

In the next section, we will update our `WalkBaseViewModel` so that it can use our `DataService` API class, and initialize our Microsoft Azure `TrackMyWalks` database.

Updating the WalkBaseViewModel to use our DataService API

In the previous sections, we created the interfaces classes that will be used by our `WalkWebService` and `WalkDataService` class to enable our `TrackMyWalks` application to communicate with the database that is stored within the Microsoft Azure platform.

Our next step is to begin implementing the code that will be required to make a connection to our `TrackMyWalks` Microsoft Azure database so that our app uses live data instead of the local, hard-coded data that we currently have in place.

Let's look at how we can achieve this, by following the steps:

1. Ensure that the `WalkBaseViewModel.cs` file is displayed within the code editor, and enter in the following highlighted code sections as shown in the code snippet:

```
//
//  WalkBaseViewModel.cs
//  TrackMyWalks Base ViewModel
//
//  Created by Steven F. Daniel on 22/08/2016.
//  Copyright © 2016 GENIESOFT STUDIOS. All rights reserved.
//
using System;
using System.ComponentModel;
using System.Runtime.CompilerServices;
using System.Threading.Tasks;
using TrackMyWalks.Services;
namespace TrackMyWalks.ViewModels
{
    public abstract class WalkBaseViewModel :
      INotifyPropertyChanged
    {
        protected IWalkNavService NavService {
          get; private set; }

        bool _isProcessBusy;
        public bool IsProcessBusy
        {
            get { return _isProcessBusy; }
```

```
          set
          {
              _isProcessBusy = value;
              OnPropertyChanged();
              OnIsBusyChanged();
          }
      }
```

2. Next, we'll create a `IWalkDataService` interface property called `_azureDatabaseService`. Tis will store and retrieve the value of our `TrackMyWalks` Azure database URL. The `AzureDatabaseService` property contains both the getter (`get`) and setter (`set`) implementations that. When we set the `AzureDatabaseService` property, we assign this value to our `_azureDatabaseService` variable, and then call the `OnPropertyChanged` instance methods to tell the `ViewModels` that a change has been made:

```
IWalkDataService _azureDatabaseService;
public IWalkDataService AzureDatabaseService
{
    get { return _azureDatabaseService; }
    set
    {
        _azureDatabaseService = value;
        OnPropertyChanged();
    }
}
```

3. Then, we'll need to modify the `WalkBaseViewModel` class constructor and create an instance to our `WalkDataService` class, that inherits from the `IWalkDataService` interface class, and then assign this to our `AzureDatabaseService` property so that it can be used throughout each of our `ViewModels`:

```
protected WalkBaseViewModel(IWalkNavService navService)
{
    // Declare our Navigation Service and Azure Database URL
    var WALKS_URL = "https://trackmywalks.azurewebsites.net";
    NavService = navService;
    AzureDatabaseService = new WalkDataService(new
      Uri(WALKS_URL, UriKind.RelativeOrAbsolute));
}

public abstract Task Init();

public event PropertyChangedEventHandler PropertyChanged;
```

```
protected virtual void OnPropertyChanged([CallerMemberName]
             string propertyName = null)
{
    var handler = PropertyChanged;
    if (handler != null)
    {
        handler(this, new PropertyChangedEventArgs(
            propertyName));
    }
}

protected virtual void OnIsBusyChanged()
{
    // We are processing our Walks Trail Information
}
}

public abstract class WalkBaseViewModel<WalkParam> :
    WalkBaseViewModel      {
protected WalkBaseViewModel(IWalkNavService navService) :
  base(navService)
{
}

public override async Task Init()
{
    await Init(default(WalkParam));
}

public abstract Task Init(WalkParam walkDetails);
}
}
```

In the preceding code snippet, we begin by creating a AzureDatabaseService property that inherits from our IWalkDataService class, and then created its associated getter and setter qualifiers. Next, we updated the WalkBaseViewModel class constructor to set the AzureDatabaseService property to an instance of WalkDataService class so that it can be used throughout each of our ViewModels.

Updating the WalkEntryViewModel to use our DataService API

Now that we have modified our `WalkBaseViewModel` class so that it will be used by any ViewModel that inherits from this base class, our next step is to begin modifying the `WalkEntryViewModel` that will utilize our `WalkDataService` class, so that any new walk information that is entered will be saved back to our Azure database. Once that's done we can begin storing walk entry information when the **Save** button is pressed.

Let's look at how we can achieve this with the following steps:

1. Ensure that the `WalkEntryViewModel.cs` file is displayed within the code editor, and enter in the following highlighted code sections as shown in the code snippet:

```
//
//  WalkEntryViewModel.cs
//  TrackMyWalks ViewModels
//
//  Created by Steven F. Daniel on 22/08/2016.
//  Copyright © 2016 GENIESOFT STUDIOS. All rights reserved.
//
    using System.Threading.Tasks;
    using TrackMyWalks.Models;
    using TrackMyWalks.Services;
    using TrackMyWalks.ViewModels;
    using Xamarin.Forms;
    using System;

    namespace TrackMyWalks
    {
      public class WalkEntryViewModel : WalkBaseViewModel
      {
          IWalkLocationService myLocation;

          string _title;
          public string Title
          {
            get { return _title; }
            set
            {
                _title = value;
                OnPropertyChanged();
                SaveCommand.ChangeCanExecute();
            }
          }
```

```
            }
    . . .
    . . .
```

2. Next, locate and modify the `ExecuteSaveCommand` instance method to include a check to see if our `ImageUrl` field contains a value, otherwise store an empty placeholder image for the `ImageUrl` property when the **Save**`ToolBarItem` has been pressed. Proceed and enter in the following highlighted code sections:

```
async Task ExecuteSaveCommand()
{
    // Check to see if we are in the middle of processing
    // a request.
    if (IsProcessBusy)
        return;

    // Initialise our Walk Entry Model to state that we are
    // in the middle of updating details to the database.
    IsProcessBusy = true;

    // Set up our New Walk item model
    var newWalkItem = new WalkEntries
    {
        Title = this.Title,
        Notes = this.Notes,
        Latitude = this.Latitude,
        Longitude = this.Longitude,
        Kilometers = this.Kilometers,
        Difficulty = this.Difficulty,
        Distance = this.Distance,
        ImageUrl = (this.ImageUrl == null ?
        new Uri("https://heuft.com/upload/image/4
          00x267/no_image_placeholder.png") :
          new Uri(this.ImageUrl))
    };

    // Upon exiting our New Walk Entry Page, we need to
    // stop checking for location updates
    myLocation = null;
```

[271]

3. Then, we'll make a call to our AddWalkEntryAsync instance method, contained within the AzureDatabaseService class to store the newly entered information. We'll include a reference to our NavService.PreviousPage method, which is declared within the IWalkNavService interface class to allow our WalkEntryPage to navigate back to the previous calling page, before finally initializing our IsProcessBusy indicator to false to inform our ViewModel that we are no longer processing. Proceed and enter in the following highlighted code sections:

```
try
{
    // Save the details entered to our Azure Database
    await AzureDatabaseService.AddWalkEntryAsync(newWalkItem);
    await NavService.PreviousPage();
}
finally
{
    // Re-Initialise our Process Busy Indicator
     IsProcessBusy = false;
}
}

// method to check for any form errors
bool ValidateFormDetails()
{
    return !string.IsNullOrWhiteSpace(Title);
}

public override async Task Init()
{
    await Task.Factory.StartNew(() =>
    {
        Title = "New Walk";
        Difficulty = "Easy";
        Distance = 1.0;
    });
}
}
}
```

In the preceding code snippet, we modified the ExecuteSaveCommand instance method to include a check to see if our ImageUrl field contains a value prior to storing the information within the ImageUrl property. If we have determined that this property is empty, we proceed to assign an empty placeholder image for the ImageUrl property to avoid our application performing unexpected results.

In the next step, we attempt to make a call to our `AddWalkEntryAsync` instance method, contained within our `AzureDatabaseService` class to store the newly entered information.

Next, we'll include a reference to our `NavService.PreviousPage` method, which is declared within the `IWalkNavService` interface class to allow our `WalkEntryPage` to navigate back to the previous calling page when the **Save** button has been pressed. Finally, we'll initialize our `IsProcessBusy` indicator to `false` to inform our ViewModel that we are no longer processing.

Updating the WalksPageViewModel to use our DataService API

In this section, we will proceed to update our `WalksPageViewModel` ViewModel to reference our `WalkDataService` class. Since our `WalksPageViewModel` is used to display information from our `WalkEntries` model, we will need to update this so that it retrieves this information from the `TrackMyWalks` database, located within our Microsoft Azure platform, and display this within the `ListView` control.

Let's look at how we can achieve this with the following steps:

1. Ensure that the `WalksPageViewModel.cs` file is displayed within the code editor, and enter in the following highlighted code sections as shown in the following code snippet:

```
//
//  WalksPageViewModel.cs
//  TrackMyWalks ViewModels
//
//  Created by Steven F. Daniel on 22/08/2016.
//  Copyright © 2016 GENIESOFT STUDIOS. All rights reserved.
//
    using System;
    using System.Collections.ObjectModel;
    using System.Threading.Tasks;
    using TrackMyWalks.Models;
    using TrackMyWalks.Services;
    using Xamarin.Forms;

    namespace TrackMyWalks.ViewModels
    {
        public class WalksPageViewModel : WalkBaseViewModel
```

```
    {
        ObservableCollection<WalkEntries> _walkEntries;

        public ObservableCollection<WalkEntries> walkEntries
        {
            get { return _walkEntries; }
            set
            {
                _walkEntries = value;
                OnPropertyChanged();
            }
        }
    }
...
...
```

2. Next, locate and modify the `LoadWalkDetails` instance method to check to see if we are already in the middle of processing walk trail items within the `ListView`. Next we'll proceed to populate our `WalkEntries` array with items retrieved from our `GetWalkEntriesAsync` Azure web service instance method call to populate our `WalkEntries` asynchronously and use the `await` keyword to wait until the `Task` completed. Finally, we'll initialize our `IsProcessBusy` indicator to `false` to inform our ViewModel that we are no longer processing. Proceed and enter in the following highlighted code sections:

```
public async Task LoadWalkDetails()
{
    // Check to see if we are already processing our
     // Walk Trail Items
    if (IsProcessBusy)
       { return; }
    // If we aren't currently processing, we need to
     // initialise our variable to true
     IsProcessBusy = true;
    try
    {
        // Populate our Walk Entries array with items
         // from our Azure Web Service
        walkEntries = new ObservableCollection<WalkEntries>
        (await AzureDatabaseService.GetWalkEntriesAsync());
    }
    finally
    {
        // Re-initialise our process busy value back to false
        IsProcessBusy = false;
    }
}
```

. . .
. . .

3. Then, create the DeleteWalkItem command property within our class, that will be used within our WalksPage to handle whenever we click on a walk item within our ListView. The DeleteWalkItem property will then run an action, whenever the Delete option has been chosen from the ActionSheet, to delete the chosen item as determined by our trailDetails to permanently remove the record from our TrackMyWalks database located within our Microsoft Azure platform. Proceed and enter in the following highlighted code sections:

```
Command _deleteWalkItem;
public Command DeleteWalkItem
{
    get
    {
        return _deleteWalkItem ?? (_deleteWalkItem =
        new Command(async (trailDetails) =>
        await AzureDatabaseService.
        DeleteWalkEntryAsync((WalkEntries)trailDetails)));
    }
}
}
```

In the preceding code snippet, we modified our LoadWalkDetails instance method to check to see if we are already in the middle of processing walk trail items within the ListView. Then, we proceeded to populate our WalkEntries array with items retrieved from our GetWalkEntriesAsync Azure web service instance method call to populate our WalkEntries asynchronously and use the await keyword to wait until the Task completed.

In the next step, we initialized the IsProcessBusy indicator to false, to inform our ViewModel that we are no longer processing.

Finally, we created a `Command` property within our class that will be used to permanently handle the deletion of the chosen walk entry within our `ListView` and our `TrackMyWalks` Microsoft Azure database.

Updating the WalksPage to use the updated ViewModel

In this section, we need to update our `WalksPageContentPage` so that it can reference the updated changes within our `WalksPageViewModel`. We will need to apply additional logic to handle deletions of walk entry information from our `WalkEntries` model so that it can retrieve newly updated information from our `TrackMyWalks` database located within our Microsoft Azure platform, and display this within the `ListView` control.

Let's look at how we can achieve this with following steps:

1. Ensure that the `WalksPage.cs` file is displayed within the code editor, and enter in the following highlighted code sections as shown in the code snippet:

```
//
//  WalksPage.cs
//  TrackMyWalks
//
//  Created by Steven F. Daniel on 04/08/2016.
//  Copyright © 2016 GENIESOFT STUDIOS. All rights reserved.
//
using Xamarin.Forms;
using TrackMyWalks.Models;
using TrackMyWalks.ViewModels;
using TrackMyWalks.Services;
using TrackMyWalks.DataTemplates;
using TrackMyWalks.ValueConverters;
using System.Diagnostics;

namespace TrackMyWalks
{
    public class WalksPage : ContentPage
    {
        WalksPageViewModel _viewModel
        {
            get { return BindingContext as
                WalksPageViewModel; }
        }
```

2. Next, modify the `newWalkItem` variable, which is within the `WalksPage` class constructor and update the `Text` property for our `ToolbarItem`. Proceed and enter in the following highlighted code sections:

```
public WalksPage()
{
    var newWalkItem = new ToolbarItem
    {
        Text = "Add"
    };

    // Set up our Binding click event handler
    newWalkItem.SetBinding(ToolbarItem.CommandProperty,
    "CreateNewWalk");

    // Add the ToolBar item to our ToolBar
    ToolbarItems.Add(newWalkItem);

    // Declare and initialise our Model Binding Context
    BindingContext = new WalksPageViewModel(DependencyService
    .Get<IWalkNavService>());
...
...
```

3. Then, we need to modify our `walksList.ItemTapped` method whenever an item within the `ListView` has been selected. Here, we need to display a selection of choices for the user to choose from, using the `DisplayActionSheet` method. When the user chooses the `Proceed With` option, the user will be navigated to the `WalksTrail` page within our ViewModel, and pass in the item that has been selected. Alternatively, if the user chooses the `Delete` button, a call is made to our `DeleteWalkItem` command that is included within our `WalksPageViewModel` class, so that it can then permanently delete the Walk Entry from our `TrackMyWalks` Azure database. Once the walk entry has been deleted from the database, the user will receive a pop-up notification telling them that the item has been deleted. Proceed and enter in the following highlighted code sections:

```
// Initialize our event Handler to use when the
// item is tapped
walksList.ItemTapped += async (object sender,
ItemTappedEventArgs e) =>
{
    // Get the selected item by the user
    var item = (WalkEntries)e.Item;
```

```
                // Check to see if we have a value for our item
            if (item == null) return;

          // Display an action sheet with choices
             var action = await DisplayActionSheet("Track My Walks
             - Trail Details", "Cancel","Delete",
             "Proceed With " + item.Title + " Trail");
             if (action.Contains("Proceed"))
             {
                _viewModel.WalkTrailDetails.Execute(item);
             }
          // If we have chosen Delete, delete the item from
            // our database and refresh the ListView
            else if (action.Contains("Delete"))
            {
                _viewModel.DeleteWalkItem.Execute(item);
                await DisplayAlert("Track My Walks - Trail Details",
                item.Title +
                " has been deleted from the database.", "OK");
                await _viewModel.Init();                         }
            // Initialise our item variable to null
            item = null;
        };
     . . .
     . . .
   }
 }
```

In the preceding code snippet, we modified our `newWalkItem` variable, which is within the
`WalksPage` class constructor and updated the `Text` property for our `ToolbarItem`.

Next, we modified our `walksList.ItemTapped` method to handle situations when an item
has been selected from the `ListView`, which will display a selection of choices for the user
to choose from. We accomplished this by using the `DisplayActionSheet` method. When
the user chooses the `Delete` button, a call is made to our `DeleteWalkItem` command that
is included within our `WalksPageViewModel` class, so that it can then permanently delete
the walk entry from our `TrackMyWalks` Azure database, and use the `await` keyword to
wait until the `Task` has completed before displaying a pop-up notification telling them that
the item has been deleted.

Updating the custom picker renderer class for the iOS platform

Now that we have modified our `WalkEntries` database model, we will need to update the `DifficultyPickerCellRenderer` class which will be used by our iOS portion of the `DifficultyPickerEntryCell` class.

This custom picker will be used to obtain the item chosen from the custom list of entries defined within the `DifficultyPicker` class and store this within the `Difficulty` property that will then be written to our `TrackMyWalks` Microsoft Azure database.

Let's look at how we can achieve this with the following steps:

1. Open the `TrackMyWalks.iOS` project located within our `TrackMyWalks` solution, and expand the `Renderers` folder.

2. Next, select the `DifficultyPickerCellRenderer.cs` file and ensure that it is displayed within the code editor, and enter in the following highlighted code sections in the code snippet:

```
//
//   DifficultyPickerCellRenderer.cs
//   TrackMyWalks CustomRenderer for UIPickerView Entry Cells (iOS)
//
//   Created by Steven F. Daniel on 01/10/2016.
//   Copyright © 2016 GENIESOFT STUDIOS. All rights reserved.
//
using Xamarin.Forms.Platform.iOS;
using UIKit;
using TrackMyWalks.Controls;
using Xamarin.Forms;
using TrackMyWalks.iOS.Renderers;

[assembly: ExportRenderer(typeof(
  DifficultyPickerEntryCell),
typeof(DifficultyPickerCellRenderer))]
namespace TrackMyWalks.iOS.Renderers
{
    public class DifficultyPickerCellRenderer :
      EntryCellRenderer
    {
        public override UITableViewCell GetCell(
          Cell item, UITableViewCell reusableCell,
            UITableView tv)
        {
            var cell = base.GetCell(item, reusableCell, tv);
```

```
var entryPickerCell = (EntryCell)item;

UITextField textField = null;

if (cell != null)
 textField = (UITextField)cell.ContentView.Subviews[0];

// Create our iOS UIPickerView Native Control
 var difficultyPicker = new UIPickerView
 {
     AutoresizingMask =
       UIViewAutoresizing.FlexibleWidth,
     ShowSelectionIndicator = true,
     Model = new DifficultyPickerModel(),
     BackgroundColor = UIColor.White,
 };
```

3. Next, we need to modify the `EntryCellRendererGetCell` method so that it can update the `Difficulty` property for the `EntryCell` we are currently on when the `Done` button has been pressed. It will update it with the value from the `difficultyPicker` object and then dismiss the custom picker control. Proceed and enter in the following highlighted code sections:

```
// Create a toolbar with a done button that will
// set the selected value when closed.
var done = new UIBarButtonItem("Done",
        UIBarButtonItemStyle.Done, (s, e) =>
{
    // Update the Difficulty property on the Cell
     if (entryPickerCell != null)
        entryPickerCell.Text = DifficultyPickerModel.
        difficulty[difficultyPicker.
        SelectedRowInComponent(0)];

    // Update the value of the UITextField within the
    // Cell
    if (textField != null)
    {
        textField.Text = DifficultyPickerModel.difficulty
        [difficultyPicker.SelectedRowInComponent(0)];
        textField.ResignFirstResponder();
    }
});
...
...
 }
}
```

}

Now that we have applied the code changes required to the
`DifficultyPickerCellRenderer` class for our iOS portion of our `TrackMyWalks` app,
the next step is to make changes to our `WalkEntryContentPage` so that it will retrieve the
correct difficulty value that is returned from our custom picker, and the `Difficulty`
property value.

Updating the WalksEntryPage to use the updated custom picker

In the previous section, we modified our `DifficultyPickerCellRenderer` class, as well
as defining the various methods that will handle the display of the `UIPickerView` control
when an `EntryCell` within the ViewModel has been tapped.

In this section, we'll look at making the necessary code changes required so that our
`WalkEntryPageContentPage` correctly retrieves the level of difficulty chosen from our
custom `UIPickerViewDifficultyPickerCellRenderer` class.

Let's look at how we can achieve this with the following steps:

1. Ensure that the `WalkEntryPage.cs` file is displayed within the code editor, and
   enter in the following highlighted code sections as shown in the code snippet:

```
//
//   WalkEntryPage.cs
//   TrackMyWalks
//
//   Created by Steven F. Daniel on 04/08/2016.
//   Copyright © 2016 GENIESOFT STUDIOS. All rights reserved.
//
using Xamarin.Forms;
using TrackMyWalks.Services;
using TrackMyWalks.Controls;

namespace TrackMyWalks
{
    public class WalkEntryPage : ContentPage
    {
        WalkEntryViewModel _viewModel
        {
            get { return BindingContext as WalkEntryViewModel; }
        }
```

```
public WalkEntryPage()
{
    // Set the Content Page Title
    Title = "New Walk Entry";

    // Declare and initialise our Model Binding Context
    BindingContext = new WalkEntryViewModel(
    DependencyService.Get<IWalkNavService>());

    // Define our New Walk Entry fields
    var walkTitle = new EntryCell
    {
        Label = "Title:",
        Placeholder = "Trail Title"
    };
    walkTitle.SetBinding(EntryCell.TextProperty, "Title",
    BindingMode.TwoWay);
    ...
    ...
```

2. Next, locate and modify the `walkDifficultyEntryCell` property so that it can correctly return the value of the `Difficulty` property from our `WalkEntries` ViewModel, that is updated by our `DifficultyPickerEntryCell` class. Proceed and enter in the following highlighted code sections:

```
var walkDifficulty = new DifficultyPickerEntryCell
{
    Label = "Difficulty Level:",
    Placeholder = "Walk Difficulty"
};
walkDifficulty.SetBinding(EntryCell.TextProperty,
  "Difficulty", BindingMode.TwoWay);

    ...
    ...
    }
  }
}
```

In this section, we looked at the steps involved in modifying our `WalkEntryPage` so that it correctly returns the level of difficulty that has been chosen from our `DifficultyPickerEntryCell` class custom renderer. We looked at updating our `walkDifficulty` object variable to reference the `DifficultyPickerEntryCell` class, and updated the `setBinding` to return the value of the `Difficulty` property that is implemented within the `WalkEntries` ViewModel class.

Now that we have finished building all the necessary components for our `TrackMyWalks` application, the next step is to finally build and run the `TrackMyWalks` application within the iOS simulator. When compilation completes, the iOS Simulator will appear automatically and the `TrackMyWalks` application will be displayed, as shown in the following screenshot:

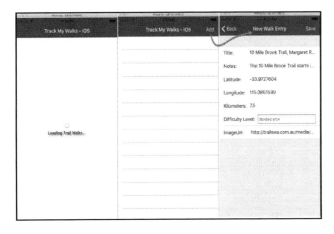

As you can see from the preceding screenshot, this currently displays our `ActivityIndicator` spinner control, with the associated **Loading Trail Walks...** text, after which this will display the `ListView` that will contain our list of trail walks from our `DataTemplate` control. Since we don't have any walk entries contained within our Microsoft Azure `TrackMyWalks` database, the **New Walk Entry** screen displays entries being entered:

The preceding screenshot, shows the updated ListView control displaying information from our TrackMyWalks Microsoft Azure database. You will notice, that upon selecting a Walk entry item from the ListView control, it will pop up with several choices for you to choose from. If you click on the **Delete** button, it will call the DeleteWalkEntryAsync API and pass in the Identifier for the selected item that is to be permanently deleted from the database.

Upon successful deletion, you will be presented with a dialog box telling you that the walk entry has been deleted. When clicking on the **OK** button, the ListView control will be refreshed and display all entries, except for the one that you had just deleted. Alternatively, if you click on the **Proceed With ...** button, it will navigate to the walks **Trail Details** page where you can begin your trail, by clicking on the **Begin this Trail** button.

Summary

In this chapter, you learned about Microsoft Azure App services and how you can use this platform to get information from a remote data source by creating your very first API within the cloud to connect to, and store and retrieve information from, all within the TrackMyWalks app. You learned how to create a live, cloud-based backend service and API using the Microsoft's Azure App services platform to store and retrieve WalkEntry information, as well as creating a DataService class that will be used to handle all the communication between the cloud and the TrackMyWalks app.

In the next chapter, you'll learn how to create a sign-in page that will allow the user to sign into the TrackMyWalks app using their Facebook credentials. You'll learn how you can take advantage of the Facebook SDK and essentially post walk data to your Facebook profile page so you can show off your progress to your friends and/or work colleagues.

8
Making Our App Social - Using the Facebook API

handle the storing of the user token details, when our app determines that we have

In the previous chapter, you learned how you can use Microsoft Azure App services to create your very first live, cloud-based, backend HTTP web service to handle all the communication between the cloud and our app. Now, you will also learn how to create a `DataService` API that will allow our app to consume the API, so that we can have the ability to retrieve, store, and delete walk trail information from the cloud, all within the `TrackMyWalks` app.

On May 24th, 2007, Mark Zuckerberg announced the Facebook platform, a development platform for programmers to create social applications within Facebook. When Facebook launched the development platform, numerous applications had been built and already had millions of users playing them. The social networking application utilizes the Facebook collection of APIs that enables developers to connect to the Facebook platform and send application requests.

In this chapter, you'll learn how you can use both `Xamarin.Auth` and Facebook SDK, which will allow you to incorporate social networking features within the `TrackMyWalks` app to obtain information about a Facebook user, as well as post information to their Facebook wall.

You'll learn how to create a sign-in page that will allow the user to sign in to the `TrackMyWalks` app using their Facebook credentials. You will also create a `FacebookApiUser` class that will be used to store information about the logged-in user, as well as using the **Open Graph** API to retrieve certain information about the user and display this within the `TrackMyWalks` app. To end this chapter, you will see how you can leverage the Facebook library, essentially to post walk data to your Facebook profile page, so you can show off your progress to your friends and/or work colleagues.

This chapter will cover the following points:

- Setting up our `TrackMyWalks` app within the Facebook Developer portal
- Adding the `Xamarin.Auth` and Facebook SDK packages to the solution
- Creating the `FacebookApiUser` and `FacebookCredentials` class
- Creating the `FBSignInPage` and `FBSignInPageRenderer` classes
- Updating the `TrackMyWalksViewModels` to use the Facebook API
- Using the Open Graph API to read JSON data
- Run the `TrackMyWalks` app within the simulator

Setting up and registering the TrackMyWalks app with Facebook

In this section, we will begin by setting up our `TrackMyWalks` app and registering it with the Facebook platform, so that we can begin communicating and interacting with Facebook, and have the ability to retrieve user information, as well as allowing the user to post walk information to their Facebook wall.

Let's now start to implement the code required for our `FacebookApiUser` class model, by performing the following steps:

1. Launch your web browser and type in `https://developers.facebook.com/apps`.
2. Next, either sign up for Facebook if you are not a registered user, or enter your Facebook account credentials.

2. Then, click on the **Create a New App** button, which will display the **Create a New App ID** screen, as shown in the following screenshot:

3.

4. Next, enter TrackMyWalks for the **Display Name** field and provide your **Contact Email** address so that Facebook can contact you if they need to.

5. Then, within the **Category** section, select a category from the **Choose a Category** dropdown, and click on the **Create App ID** button to create our TrackMyWalks app, as shown in the preceding screenshot.

6. Next, you will be prompted to enter the **Security Check** answer before you can proceed to the next step:

7. Then, enter the text displayed on your screen and click on the **Submit** button to continue.

If you enter the text incorrectly, you may end up with your account being blocked. If this is the case, you will need to contact Facebook directly to have this unblocked.

Now that we have created our `TrackMyWalks` Facebook App ID, our next step is to begin setting up the **Client OAuth Settings**, which will be used by our `OAuth2Authenticator` class within our `TrackMyWalks` app:

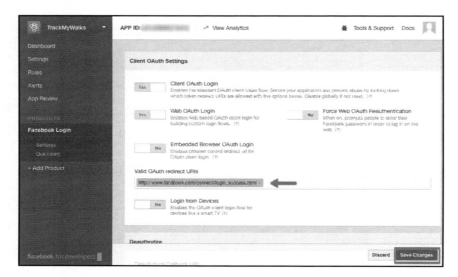

8. Next, from the **Valid OAuth redirect URIs** section located within the **Client OAuth Setting** screen, enter
   `https://www.facebook.com/connect/login_success.html` as the URL to use whenever we detect that we have successfully signed into Facebook from within our app.

9. Then, click on the **Save Changes** button to save our changes within this screen.

10. Next, choose the **App Review** menu item located under the **Dashboard**, as can be seen in the following screenshot:

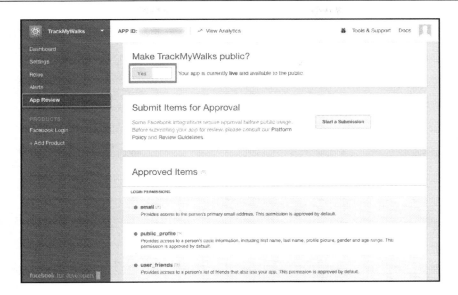

11. Then, ensure that you have chosen **Yes** for the **Make TrackMyWalks public?** question.

Essentially, the **APP ID** is an important field that we will use within our iOS and Android application to communicate with Facebook.

Whenever you enable the **Make TrackMyWalks public?** option, this will make your app live to the public on Facebook, so that your friends and family can see your walk information posted on your Facebook wall. You will notice that, when you enable this option, the list of **Approved Items** will be enabled by default, as well as their login permissions.

If you are interested in learning more about the various types of login permissions, please refer to the Permissions Reference – Facebook Login which can be accessed at `https://developers.facebook.com/docs/facebook-login/permissions`.

Now that we have successfully setup our `TrackMyWalks` app name within the Facebook platform, we can begin making our app communicate with the Facebook APIs to obtain user information, as well as posting messages to the currently logged-in user's Facebook wall. In our next section, we will begin to add the `Xamarin.Auth` .NET Framework library, as well as the Facebook SDK, to connect our `TrackMyWalks` app to Facebook and authenticate users with Facebook, so that we can post status messages directly from within our app and more.

Adding the Xamarin.Auth NuGet package to the TrackMyWalks app

Now that we have setup our Facebook **App ID**, our next step is to add the `Xamarin.Auth` NuGet package to our `TrackMyWalks` Portable Class Library project. The `Xamarin.Auth` package will allow our app to authenticate a user who requires access to use the Facebook platform by using `OAuth 2.0` authentication.

These Authenticators are responsible for managing the user interface and communicating with authentication services. Authenticators take a variety of parameters; in this case, the application's ID, its authorization scope, as well as Facebook's various service locations are required.

Let's look at how to add the `Xamarin.AuthNuGet` package to our `TrackMyWalks` Portable Class Library by performing the following steps:

1. Right-click on the `Packages` folder, which is contained within the `TrackMyWalks` Portable Class Library project, and choose the **Add Packages...** menu option, as shown in the following screenshot:

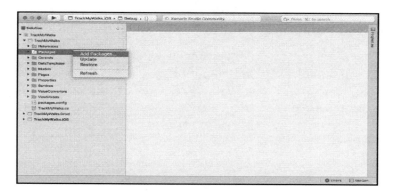

2. This will display the **Add Packages** dialog. Enter `Xamarin.Auth` within the search dialog and select the **Xamarin.Auth** option within the list, as shown in the following screenshot:

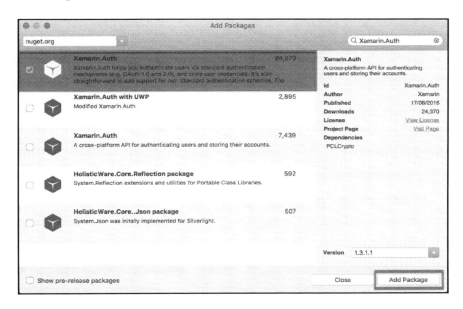

3. Finally, click on the **Add Package** button to add the `NuGet` package to the `Packages` folder, which is contained within the `TrackMyWalks` Portable Class Library project.

Now that we have added the `Xamarin.Auth` NuGet Package, our next step is to add the Facebook Framework to our `TrackMyWalks` Portable Class Library, which we will be covering in the next section.

Adding the FaceBook SDK library to the TrackMyWalks app

In the previous section, we added our `Xamarin.AuthNuGet` package to our `TrackMyWalks` solution; this means that our next step is to add the Facebook library to our `TrackMyWalks` solution.

Since we are using both .NET and C# to build our `Xamarin.Forms` application, we can leverage a library developed by a company called *The Outercurve Foundation*. This library is essentially a Facebook SDK that helps .NET developers build applications that integrate with Facebook.

The Facebook SDK framework contains all the method objects and APIs that are required to enable you to interact with Facebook and send notification requests, or simply post messages to the current user's wall page using the single sign-on feature of Facebook SDK. This simply lets your users sign in to your app using their Facebook identity, and will display an inline dialog box comprising a WebView container in which the authorization UI will be shown to the user, which requires them to enter their credentials to gain access to your app.

Let's look at how we can add the Facebook SDK library to our `TrackMyWalks` Portable Class Library by performing the following steps:

1. Launch your web browser, and type the following URL, `https://components.xamarin.com/view/facebook-sdk`, and log in to the Xamarin portal using your Xamarin credentials.
2. Next, from the **Facebook SDK** section, ensure that you have selected version **6.2.2** as the latest version to download from under the **Versions** section.

2. Then, proceed to click on the **Download** button to download the **Facebook SDK** library, as shown in the following screenshot:

 Once you have downloaded the Facebook SDK, extract the Zip archive package contents. The default download location is `~/Downloads/facebook-sdk-6.2.2.zip`.

4. Next, right-click on the `References` folder, which is contained within the `TrackMyWalks` Portable Class Library project, and choose the **Edit References...** menu option, as shown in the following screenshot:

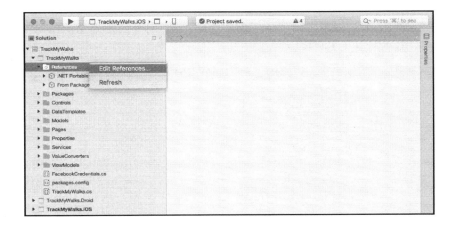

5. Then, ensure that the **.Net Assembly** tab has been selected, and click on the **Browse** button to choose the `Facebook.dll` for either the Android or iOS platform:

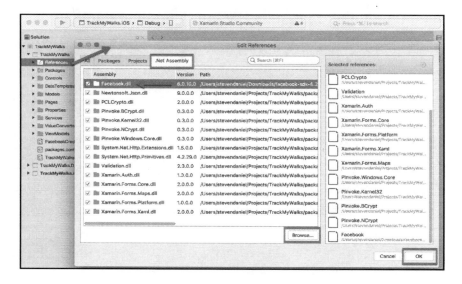

6. Finally, ensure that you have selected the `Facebook.dll` assembly within the **.Net Assembly** tab, click on the **OK** button add the new assembly to the references section of your `TrackMyWalks` Portable Class Library, and close the **Edit References** dialog.

Incorporating and using the Facebook SDK within your applications allows you to do what is described in the following table:

FACEBOOK SDK Types	Description
Authentication and authorization	This prompts your users to sign in to Facebook and grant permissions to your application.
Make API calls	This allows you to fetch user-profile data, as well as any information that relates to the user's friends, using the JSON API calls.
Display dialog	This allows you to interact with the user via a WebView container object, which is extremely useful for enabling interactions with Facebook, without the need for requiring upfront permissions.

Now that we have added both the `Xamarin.Auth` NuGet package and Facebook **Dynamic-Link Library** (**DLL**) packages to our solution, we can now begin utilizing these framework libraries as we progress throughout this chapter.

Creating a Facebook user model for the TrackMyWalks app

In the previous section, we added both of our `Xamarin.Auth` and Facebook SDK .NET Assembly packages to our `TrackMyWalks` Portable Class Library. This will essentially be used by each of our `ViewModels` along with the Views (pages).

In this section, we will begin by creating our `FacebookApiUser` data model, which will be used to store our Facebook login information from when we create our backend service calls, and then the `FacebookCredentials.cs` and `FBSignInRenderer.cs` files will communicate and interact with our Facebook TrackMyWalks App ID to retrieve Facebook related information, as well as allowing the user to post walk information to their Facebook wall.

Let's now start to implement the code required for our `FacebookApiUser` class model by performing the following steps:

1. Create an empty class within the `Models` folder by choosing **Add | New File...**. If you can't remember how to do this, you can refer to the section entitled *Creating the Track My Walks Model* within `Chapter 1`, *Creating the TrackMyWalks Native App*.

2. Then, enter `FacebookApiUser` for the name of the new class that you want to create, and click on the **New** button to allow the wizard to proceed and create the new file.

3. Next, ensure that the `FacebookApiUser.cs` file is displayed within the code editor, and enter the following code snippet:

```
//
//  FacebookApiUser.cs
//  TrackMyWalks
//
//  Created by Steven F. Daniel on 07/11/2016.
//  Copyright © 2016 GENIESOFT STUDIOS. All rights reserved.
//
using System;
using Xamarin.Auth;
using Newtonsoft.Json.Linq;
```

```
namespace TrackMyWalks.Facebook
{
```

4. Next, we need to implement the `FacebookApiUser` class that will contain the various property methods used to store the currently logged-in user, their Facebook Id, and the properties that will be used to store and retrieve the user's Facebook details. To proceed, enter the following code snippet:

```
public class FacebookApiUser
{
    // Store the currently logged in user
    public static bool IsLoggedIn
    {
        get { return !string.IsNullOrWhiteSpace
          (FaceBookApiAuthToken.GetAuthToken);
        }
    }
    // Define our Facebook Id property
    public static string FacebookId
    {
        get { return "<YOUR_FACEBOOK_ID>"; }
    }

    // Retrieve our user details
    static JObject _userDetails;
    public static JObject GetUserDetails
    {
        get { return _userDetails; }
    }
    // Store our user details
    public static void SaveUserDetails(JObject userDetails)
    {
        _userDetails = userDetails;
    }
}
```

5. Next, we need to implement the `FacebookApiAuthToken` class that will contain the various property methods that will be used to store and retrieve our Facebook authentication Token on successfully logging in to our `TrackMyWalks` app. These properties will be used throughout our application to retrieve our Facebook user details, and when we post walk information to our Facebook wall. To proceed, enter the following code snippet:

```
// Facebook API authentication Token
public class FacebookApiAuthToken
{
```

```
// Property to point to the Api user
public FacebookApiUser User { get; set; }

// Get our Facebook authentication Token
static string _authToken;
public static string GetAuthToken
{
    get { return _authToken; }
}
// Store our authentication Token
public static void StoreAuthToken(string authToken)
{
    _authToken = authToken;
}
// Get our Facebook authentication Account Details
static AuthenticatorCompletedEventArgs _authAccount;
public static EventArgs GetAuthAccount
{
    get { return _authAccount; }
}
// Store our Facebook authentication Account Details
public static void StoreAuthAccount
    (AuthenticatorCompletedEventArgs authAccount)
{
    _authAccount = authAccount;
}
    }
}
```

In the preceding code snippet, we begin by implementing the various property methods that will be required to handle communication between our TrackMyWalks app and Facebook, to allow our app to successfully log in. The FacebookApiUser class method is responsible for handling the information relating to the Facebook user who will be logging in. It contains a property called IsLoggedIn that will be used throughout our app to determine if the user has logged in; this is determined by checking to see if we have received a valid authentication token back from Facebook.

The FacebookId property is essentially the user's Facebook Id. You will need to replace this with your own Facebook ID so that you can post walk trail information to your Facebook wall. The GetUserDetails and SaveUserDetails properties are used to store the user information that will be displayed within the DistanceTravelled page. The FaceBookApiAuthToken method contains the various properties that will be used to handle the storing of the user token details, when our app determines that we have successfully been authenticated with Facebook.

Creating a FacebookCredentials class for the TrackMyWalks app

In our previous section, we created our `FacebookApiUser` class model, which will provide us with a mechanism for storing our Facebook credentials, that we can use throughout our `TrackMyWalks` app.

In this section, we will begin by creating a `FacebookCredentials` class that will allow us to make API calls, so that we can retrieve user profile information back from our API, in JSON format, and store this information to be used later. Our `FacebookCredentials` class contains a method that allows our app to post walk trail information to the user's Facebook page wall.

Let's now start to implement the code required for our `FacebookCredentials` class by performing the following steps:

1. Create an empty class within the `Services` folder. If you can't remember how to do this, you can refer to the section entitled *Creating the Navigation Service Interface for the TrackMyWalks app* within `Chapter 3`, *Navigating within the MVVM Model – The Xamarin.Forms Way*.

2. Next, enter the `FacebookCredentials` for the name of the new class that you want to create, and click on the **New** button to allow the wizard to proceed and create the file.

3. Then, ensure that the `FacebookCredentials.cs` file is displayed within the code editor, and enter the following code snippet:

```
//
//  FacebookCredentials.cs
//  Stores the credentials to be used for Facebook
//
//  Created by Steven F. Daniel on 09/11/2016.
//  Copyright © 2016 GENIESOFT STUDIOS. All rights reserved.
//
    using TrackMyWalks.Models;
    using Facebook;
    using Xamarin.Auth;
    using System;
    using System.Threading.Tasks;
    using Newtonsoft.Json.Linq;
    using System.Collections.Generic;
    using TrackMyWalks.Facebook;

    namespace TrackMyWalks
```

```
    {
        public class FacebookCredentials
        {
```

4. Next, implement the `PostWalkInformation` instance method that will be used to post information relating to the currently active walk trail to the user's Facebook page wall. We define an `fb` variable that instantiates a new `FacebookClient` object using the authorization token `GetAuthToken` from our `FacebookAuthToken` class, which we obtained upon achieving a successful login from Facebook.

5. We use the `PostTaskAsync` method and pass in the Graph API `me/feed` syntax value as the first parameter, followed by a `message` parameter, along with the message details that we want to post to the user's Facebook wall. To proceed, enter the following code snippet:

```
// Post information to the user's Facebook Wall
public static void PostWalkInformation(string Title,
                    double Kilometers, string Difficulty,
                    string Notes, string trailPictureUrl)
{
    FacebookClient fb = new FacebookClient(FacebookApiAuthToken.
                    GetAuthToken);

    // The message to post as a key/value pair
    string postMessage = "TrackMyWalks App - Trail Completed -
                    Results.";
    postMessage +="\n\nTitle: " + Title;
    postMessage +="\nKilometers: " + Kilometers;
    postMessage +="\nDifficulty: " + Difficulty;
    postMessage +="\nNotes: " + Notes;
    postMessage +="\nTrail Image: " + trailPictureUrl;

    fb.PostTaskAsync("me/feed", new { message = postMessage }).
    ContinueWith(t =>
    {
        if (t.IsFaulted)
        {
            // Catch any errors that occur here.
        }
    });
}
```

The Graph API is the primary way in which we can get data in and out of Facebook's social graph, and is essentially a low-level HTTP-based API that is used to query data, post new stories, and upload photos.
If you are interested in finding our more information about the Facebook Graph API framework classes, please refer to the Facebook Developer documentation located at
https://developers.facebook.com/docs/graph-api/using-graph-api/.

6. Then, implement the GetProfileInformation instance method that will be used to retrieve information relating to the currently active Facebook user. We define a request object that initializes a new instance of the OAuth2Request class, and accepts the HTTP method type, along with the URL, and a list of parameters. The final parameter is our obtained Facebook account details that will be used to authenticate our request.

7. We then use the GetResponseAsync method to make an asynchronous web request call to retrieve the information, as specified by our request object, and then use the GetReponseText method to return a JSON object, containing the Facebook user details as specified in our URL string, and then parse this using the JObject.Parse method to convert the details to a JSON object and assign this to our obj variable.

8. Next, we check to ensure that we have the information returned by our web request, and then pass the JSON object details, as defined by our obj variable, to our SaveUserDetails property, which is contained within our FacebookApiUser class. To proceed, enter the following code snippet:

```
// Retrieve Facebook information pertaining to the user.
public static async Task GetProfileInformation(AuthenticatorCompl
etedEventArgs eventArgs)
{
    // Make a request to retrieve our items based on the list of
    // parameters below.
    var request = new OAuth2Request("GET",
    new Uri("https://graph.facebook.com/me?fields=id,name,
    first_name,last_name,gender,picture,email,devices,education"),
    null, eventArgs.Account);
    var response = await request.GetResponseAsync();
    var obj = JObject.Parse(response.GetResponseText());

    // Check to see if we have returned any information
    if (obj != null)
    {
        try
        {
```

```
        // Store our user profile information into our property.
            FacebookApiUser.SaveUserDetails(obj);
        }
        catch (Exception e)
        {
            // Handle any errors that fall in here.
        }
      }
    }
  }
}
```

In the preceding code snippet, we begin by implementing the methods that are required to post and retrieve our Facebook information using the `FacebookClient` class that is used to make synchronous requests to the Facebook server. The `PostWalkInformation` instance method is used to post information relating to the currently active user to the user's Facebook page wall.

The `GetProfileInformation` instance method is used to retrieve information associated with the currently logged-in Facebook user, using the `OAuth2Request` class and the Facebook Graph API, which accepts a URL, containing a list of parameters that we would like our method to return and that will be stored within our `SaveUserDetails` property, which is defined within our `FacebookApiUser` class.

 If you are interested in finding out more information about the `OAuth2Request` and the `Xamarin.Auth` classes, please refer to the Xamarin developer documentation located at `https://components.xamarin.com/gettingstarted/xamarin.auth`.

Creating the Facebook Sign In to use within our TrackMyWalks app

In our previous section, we created and implemented our `FacebookCredentials` wrapper class that will be used by our `TrackMyWalks` application to handle the retrieving of our Facebook user details, as well as providing the ability to post walk trail information directly to our Facebook wall so that our friends and family can track our progress.

Our next step is to begin creating a Facebook Sign In page that will be hooked up to a custom renderer page that will be used to display the Facebook login page within a web container.

Let's now start to implement the code required for our `FBSignInPageContentPage` by performing the following steps:

1. Create an empty Forms `ContentPage` within the `Pages` folder. If you can't remember how to do this, you can refer to the section entitled *Creating the walks main page* within `Chapter 1`, *Creating the TrackMyWalks Native App.*

2. Next, enter `FBSignInPage` for the name of the new `ContentPage` that you want to create, and click on the **New** button to allow the wizard to proceed and create the file.

3. Then, ensure that the `FBSignInPage.cs` file is displayed within the code editor and enter the following code snippet:

```
//
//  FBSignInPage.cs
//  TrackMyWalks Facebook SignIn Page
//
//  Created by Steven F. Daniel on 09/11/2016.
//  Copyright © 2016 GENIESOFT STUDIOS. All rights reserved.
//

using Xamarin.Forms;

namespace TrackMyWalks
{
  public class FBSignInPage : ContentPage
  {
  }
}
```

In the preceding code snippet, our `ContentPage` contains the bare-bones implementation. This is intentional, as, in our next section, we will be creating a custom class renderer that will use our `FBSignInPageContentPage` to instantiate an instance of the Facebook login web page.

Creating the Facebook Sign In Class for TrackMyWalks (iOS) app

In our previous section, we created our `FBSignInPage` content page that will be used as a placeholder for our Facebook Sign In class custom renderer. In this section, we will build the custom Facebook sign-in page renderer, which will be used by the iOS and Android portions of our app to handle the signing in to Facebook via the `FacebookApiAuthToken` model, to store the received Facebook token that will be used throughout the `TrackMyWalks` application.

Let's look at how we can achieve this by performing the following steps:

1. Create an empty class within the `Renderers` folder for our `TrackMyWalks.iOS` project. If you can't remember how to do this, you can refer to the section entitled *Creating the custom picker renderer class* for the iOS platform within `Chapter 5`, *Customizing the User Interface*.

2. Next, enter `FBSignInPageRenderer` for the name of the new class that you want to create, and click on the **New** button to allow the wizard to proceed and create the file.

3. Then, ensure that the `FBSignInPageRenderer.cs` file is displayed within the code editor and enter the following code snippet:

```
//
//  FBSignInPageRenderer.cs
//  TrackMyWalks Facebook SignIn Page (iOS)
//
//  Created by Steven F. Daniel on 09/11/2016.
//  Copyright © 2016 GENIESOFT STUDIOS. All rights reserved.
//
    using System;
    using Xamarin.Forms;
    using TrackMyWalks;
    using Xamarin.Forms.Platform.iOS;
    using Xamarin.Auth;
    using TrackMyWalks.Facebook;
```

4. Next, we need to initialize our `FBSignInPageRenderer` class being marked as an `ExportRenderer` by including the `ExportRenderer` assembly attribute to the top of our class definition. This lets our class know that it inherits from the `ViewRenderer` class.

```
[assembly: ExportRenderer(typeof(FBSignInPage),
typeof(TrackMyWalks.iOS.FBSignInPageRenderer))]
```

```
namespace TrackMyWalks.iOS
{
    public class FBSignInPageRenderer : PageRenderer
    {
```

Then, we declare an `IsVerified` Boolean variable that will be used to determine if a successful to Facebook has happened. Next, we implement the `ViewDidAppear` method that will be launched upon the `ContentPage` becoming visible, and then call the `FacebookSignIn` instance method:

```
bool IsVerified = false;

public override void ViewDidAppear(bool animated)
{
    base.ViewDidAppear(animated);

    if (!IsVerified)
    {
        FacebookSignIn();
    }
}
```

5. Next, we need to create the `FacebookSignIn` instance method that will be called whenever the user hasn't signed in to Facebook. We use the `OAuth2Authenticator` method, which will be responsible for managing the user interface and handling the communication with the Facebook authentication services.

6. The `OAuth2Authenticator` class accepts the user's Facebook ID, which is stored within the `FacebookId` property that is declared within the `FacebookApiUser` class. The `OAuth2Authenticator` class also accepts the authorization scope and the Facebook service locations to authenticate and determine what to do when a successful login happens:

```
void FacebookSignIn()
{
    string AccessToken = String.Empty;

    var auth = new OAuth2Authenticator(FaceBookApiUser.FacebookId,
    "publish_actions",
    new Uri("https://m.facebook.com/dialog/oauth/"),
    new Uri("https://www.facebook.com/connect/login_success.html")
     );

    // Prevent our form from being dismissed by the user.
    auth.AllowCancel = false;
```

7. Then, before we present the Facebook UI to the user, we need to start listening to the `Completed` event of the `OAuth2Authenticator` instance, which fires up whenever the user successfully authenticates or cancels, and then check the `IsAuthenticated` property of the `eventArgs` property to properly determine if the authentication has succeeded.

8. If we have determined that a successful login has happened, we make a call to the `DismissViewController` method to dismiss the currently presented Facebook UI and then call the `RemoveFBSignInPage` instance method from our `TrackMyWalks` app class, within Portable Class Library, to remove our `FBSignInPage` from memory:

```
auth.Completed += async (sender, eventArgs) =>
{
    if (eventArgs.IsAuthenticated)
    {
        // Dismiss our Facebook Authentication UI Dialog
        DismissViewController(true, null);

        // Remove our Facebook SignIn Page View from memory.
        App.RemoveFBSignInPage();
```

9. Next, we proceed to retrieve the access token from the Facebook session of the successfully logged-in user, and proceed to store the values within the `StoreAuthToken` and `StoreAuthAccount` details within our `FacebookApiAuthToken` class. Finally, we call our `NavigateToWalksPage` Action within our `TrackMyWalks` App class:

```
// Retrieve our access token for our Facebook session.
eventArgs.Account.Properties.TryGetValue("access_token",
    out AccessToken);
FacebookApiAuthToken.StoreAuthToken(AccessToken);
FacebookApiAuthToken.StoreAuthAccount(eventArgs);

// Navigate To Walks List method from our main class.
await App.NavigateToWalksPage();
}
else
{
    // The user cancelled the Facebook Login UI
    Console.WriteLine("You are not authorised to use
    the TrackMyWalks app");
    IsVerified = false;
    return;
}
};
```

10. Then, we present the Facebook login UI by using the `PresentViewController` method, and call the `GetUI` method returns `UINavigationControllers` on iOS and intents on Android. On Android, we would write the following code to present the UI from the `OnCreate` method:

```
IsVerified = true;
PresentViewController(auth.GetUI(), true, null);
   }
  }
}
```

In the preceding code snippet, we begin by initializing our `FBSignInPageRenderer` class, being marked as an `ExportRenderer`, to let our class know that it inherits from the `ViewRenderer` class, and then declare an `IsVerified` Boolean variable that will be used to determine if a successful login to Facebook has happened. We then proceed and implement the `ViewDidAppear` method, which will be launched when the `ContentPage` becomes visible, and then call the `FacebookSignIn` instance method, which will be called whenever the user hasn't signed in to Facebook, and use the `OAuth2Authenticator` method, which will be responsible for managing the user interface and handling the communication with the Facebook authentication services.

Finally, we present the Facebook login UI, retrieve the access token from the Facebook session of the successfully logged-in user, and proceed to store the values within the `StoreAuthToken` and `StoreAuthAccount` details within our `FacebookApiAuthToken` class:

 The Android version of the `FBSignInPageRenderer` class is available in the companion source code for this book, which can be located within the `TrackMyWalks.Droid` project.

Updating the NavigationService Interface for the TrackMyWalks app

In this section, we will proceed to update our `IWalkNavService` Interface to contain a new method of implementation that will allow our app to clear all previously created views from the `NavigationStack`. Since this abstract Interface class will act as the base `NavigationService` class that each of our `ViewModels` will inherit from, they will be able to access each of the class members contained within this Interface.

Let's look at how we can achieve this by performing the following steps:

Ensure that the IWalkNavService.cs file is displayed within the code editor and enter the highlighted code sections shown in the following code snippet:

```
//
//   IWalkNavService.cs
//   TrackMyWalks Navigation Service Interface
//
//   Created by Steven F. Daniel on 03/09/2016.
//   Copyright © 2016 GENIESOFT STUDIOS. All rights reserved.
//

using System.Threading.Tasks;
using TrackMyWalks.ViewModels;

namespace TrackMyWalks.Services
{
    public interface IWalkNavService
    {
        // Navigate back to the Previous page
           in the NavigationStack
        Task PreviousPage();

        // Navigate to the first page within
           the NavigationStack
         Task BackToMainPage();

        // Navigate to a particular ViewModel
           within our MVVM Model,
        // and pass a parameter
         Task NavigateToViewModel<ViewModel,
           WalkParam>(WalkParam parameter)
          where ViewModel : WalkBaseViewModel;

        // Clear all previously created views
          from the NavigationStack
          void ClearAllViewsFromStack();
    }
}
```

In the preceding code snippet, we implement a new class member ClearAllViewsFromStack method that will be used to clear all previously created views from the NavigationStack. This is because, upon successfully logging in to our TrackMyWalks app after the Facebook UI login has been dismissed, we need to have the ability to remove the FBSignInPage from the NavigationStack.

Updating the NavigationService class for the TrackMyWalks app

In the previous section, we updated the base Interface class for our `NavigationService`, as well as defining a new class member that will be used to handle the removing of all previously created views from our `NavigationStack` within our MVVM ViewModel.

These will be used by each of our `ViewModels`, and the Views (pages) will implement those `ViewModels` and use them as their `BindingContext`.

Let's look at how we can achieve this by performing the following steps:

1. Ensure that the `WalkNavService.cs` file is displayed within the code editor, and enter the highlighted code sections shown in the following code snippet:

```
//
// WalkNavService.cs
// TrackMyWalks Navigation Service Class
//
// Created by Steven F. Daniel on 03/09/2016.
// Copyright © 2016 GENIESOFT STUDIOS. All rights reserved.
//
    using System;
    using Xamarin.Forms;
    using System.Collections.Generic;
    using System.Threading.Tasks;
    using System.Reflection;
    using System.Linq;
    using TrackMyWalks.ViewModels;
    using TrackMyWalks.Services;

    [assembly: Dependency(typeof(WalkNavService))]
    namespace TrackMyWalks.Services
    {
        public class WalkNavService : IWalkNavService
        {
            public INavigation navigation { get; set; }
            readonly IDictionary<Type, Type>
            _viewMapping = new
            Dictionary<Type, Type>();

    // Register our ViewModel and View within our Dictionary
            public void RegisterViewMapping(
            Type viewModel, Type view)
            {
                _viewMapping.Add(viewModel, view);
```

```
    }

    // Instance method that allows us to move back to
       the previous page
       public async Task PreviousPage()
       {
    // Check to see if we can move back to the previous page
       if (navigation.NavigationStack != null &&
        navigation.NavigationStack.Count > 0)
        {
            await navigation.PopAsync(true);
        }
    }

    // Instance method that takes us back to the
       main Root WalksPage
       public async Task BackToMainPage()
       {
           await navigation.PopToRootAsync(true);
       }

    // Instance method that navigates to a specific ViewModel
    // within our dictionary viewMapping.
       public async Task NavigateToViewModel
       <ViewModel, WalkParam> (WalkParam parameter)
    where ViewModel : WalkBaseViewModel
    {
       Type viewType;

    if (_viewMapping.TryGetValue(typeof(ViewModel),
        out viewType))
    {
        var constructor = viewType.GetTypeInfo()
          .DeclaredConstructors
          .FirstOrDefault(dc => dc.GetParameters()
          .Count() <= 0);

        var view = constructor.Invoke(null) as Page;
        await navigation.PushAsync(view, true);
    }

    if (navigation.NavigationStack.Last().BindingContext is
        WalkBaseViewModel<WalkParam>)
        await ((WalkBaseViewModel<WalkParam>)(navigation.Navigation
        Stack.Last().BindingContext)).Init(parameter);
}
```

2. Next, we need to create the `ClearAllViewsFromStack` instance method for our `WalkNavService` class, which will be used to remove all previously created views from the `NavigationStack` by first checking the `NavigationStack` property for the `navigation` property `INavigation` interface to see if any items already have been pushed onto the `NavigationStack`. This is to ensure that a crash doesn't happen within our app.

3. In our next step, we proceed to iterate through each item that is contained in our `NavigationStack` and call the `RemovePage`, method to remove each page:

```
// Instance method to remove all previously created views from
// the Navigation Stack.
   public void ClearAllViewsFromStack()
   {
     // Check to see if any items have already been pushed
     // onto the NavigationStack.
     if (navigation.NavigationStack.Count <= 1)
        return;
     for (var i = 0; i < navigation.NavigationStack.Count - 1; i++)
        navigation.RemovePage(navigation.NavigationStack[i]);
   }
 }
}
```

In the preceding code snippet, we implement a new class member `ClearAllViewsFromStack` instance method within our `WalkNavService` class, to handle the clearing of all previously created Views (pages) from the `NavigationStack`.

Updating the WalksPage to properly handle Facebook Sign In

In this section, we need to update our `WalksPageContentPage` so that it can reference the updates within our `WalksPageViewModel`. We will need to apply additional logic to update the `NavigationBar` Title once we have dismissed our Facebook Sign In dialog.

Let's look at how we can achieve this by performing the following steps:

Ensure that the `WalksPage.cs` file is displayed within the code editor, and enter the highlighted code sections shown in the following code snippet:

```
//
// WalksPage.cs
// TrackMyWalks
```

```
//
//   Created by Steven F. Daniel on 04/08/2016.
//   Copyright © 2016 GENIESOFT STUDIOS. All rights reserved.
//
using Xamarin.Forms;
using TrackMyWalks.Models;
using TrackMyWalks.ViewModels;
using TrackMyWalks.Services;
using TrackMyWalks.DataTemplates;
using TrackMyWalks.ValueConverters;

namespace TrackMyWalks
{
    public class WalksPage : ContentPage
    {
        WalksPageViewModel _viewModel
        {
            get { return BindingContext
                as WalksPageViewModel; }
        }

        public WalksPage()
        {
            var newWalkItem = new ToolbarItem
            {
                Text = "Add"
            };

        if (Device.OS == TargetPlatform.iOS)
        {
            Title = "Track My Walks - iOS";
        }
        else if (Device.OS == TargetPlatform.Android)
        {
            Title = "Track My Walks - Android";
        }
...
...
...
...
```

In the preceding code snippet, we begin by checking the Device.OS class, to determine what OS Xamarin.Forms is running on, and then use the TargetPlatform class to determine if our app is running on the Android or iOS platform. If we have determined that our app is running on Android, we set the Title property for our ContentPage; alternatively, if we are running on iOS, we set the Title property as well.

Updating the WalksPage ViewModel to use our FaceBookApiUser

In this section, we will proceed to update our `WalksPageViewModel` ViewModel, so that it has the ability to display our Facebook Sign In page if it determines that we haven't already logged in.

Let's look at how we can achieve this by performing the following steps:

Ensure that the `WalksPageViewModel.cs` file is displayed within the code editor, and enter the highlighted code sections shown in the following code snippet:

```
//
//   WalksPageViewModel.cs
//   TrackMyWalks ViewModels
//
//   Created by Steven F. Daniel on 22/08/2016.
//   Copyright © 2016 GENIESOFT STUDIOS. All rights reserved.
//
using System;
using System.Collections.ObjectModel;
using System.Threading.Tasks;
using TrackMyWalks.Models;
using TrackMyWalks.Services;
using Xamarin.Forms;
using TrackMyWalks.Facebook;

namespace TrackMyWalks.ViewModels
{
    public class WalksPageViewModel :
      WalkBaseViewModel
    {
        ObservableCollection<WalkEntries>
          _walkEntries;

        public ObservableCollection<WalkEntries>
          walkEntries
        {
          get { return _walkEntries; }
          set
          {
              _walkEntries = value;
              OnPropertyChanged();
          }
        }
```

```
public WalksPageViewModel
  (IWalkNavService navService) :
base(navService)
{
    walkEntries = new ObservableCollection
      <WalkEntries>();
  }


public override async Task Init()
  {
// Check if we have logged in and that we are running our
 // device on iOS
if (!FacebookApiUser.IsLoggedIn &&
Device.OS == TargetPlatform.iOS)
{
    await App.Current.MainPage.Navigation
    .PushModalAsync(new FBSignInPage());
}
else {
    await LoadWalkDetails();
    await NavService.ClearAllViewsFromStack();
}
}
. . .
. . .
. . .
. . .
```

In the preceding code snippet, we begin by modifying the Init method to include a check
to see if we have already logged in to Facebook, by checking the IsLoggedIn property of
the FacebookApiUser class, and whether we are running on a device running iOS. If we
determine that the IsLoggedIn property doesn't contain a value, we call the
PushModalAsync method on the Navigation property from the MainPage to display our
FBSignInPageContentPage. Alternatively, if the user has logged in, we proceed to load
our walk entry details using the LoadWalkDetails instance method, and call the
ClearAllViewsFromStack instance method that is located within our WalkNavService
class.

Updating the DistanceTravelledPage for the TrackMyWalks app

In this section, we need to update our `DistanceTravelledPageContentPage`, so that it can make use of our Facebook API and retrieve the currently logged-in Facebook user, as well as providing the ability to post Walk Trail information to the user's Facebook wall.

Let's look at how we can achieve this by performing the following steps:

1. Ensure that the `DistanceTravelledPage.cs` file is displayed within the code editor, and enter the highlighted code sections shown in the following code snippet:

```
var postToFacebook = new Button
{
    BackgroundColor = Color.FromHex("#455c9f"),
    TextColor = Color.White,
    Text = "Post to Facebook"
};
postToFacebook.Effects.Add(Effect.Resolve(
  "com.geniesoftstudios.ButtonShadowEffect"));
```

2. Next, we create a `Clicked` handler method for our `postToFacebook` button, so that whenever the **Post to Facebook** is pressed we display a selection of choices for the user to choose from, using the `DisplayActionSheet` method:

```
// Set up our event handler
postToFacebook.Clicked += async (sender, e) =>
{
    if (_viewModel.WalkEntry == null) return;
    // Display our list of choices to choose from
    var action = await DisplayActionSheet(
      "Track My Walks - Trail Details",
      "Cancel", "Display User Details",
      "Post to Facebook Wall");
```

3. Then, we use the `Contains` property of the `action` variable to determine if the `Post` option has been selected, and, if so, we call the `PostWalkInformation` instance method of our `FacebookCredentials` class; pass in the `Title`, `Kilometers`, `Difficulty`, `Notes`, and `ImageUrl` as parameters to the class; and then display an alert dialog box telling the user that their walk information has been posted to their Facebook wall:

```
if (action.Contains("Post"))
```

[314]

```
{
    // Declare an instance to our Facebook Credentials Class
    FacebookCredentials.PostWalkInformation(
    _viewModel.WalkEntry.Title,
    _viewModel.WalkEntry.Kilometers,
    _viewModel.WalkEntry.Difficulty,
    _viewModel.WalkEntry.Notes,
    _viewModel.WalkEntry.ImageUrl.AbsoluteUri);
    // Display an alert dialog letting the user know that
    // their information has been posted to their Facebook
    // Wall.
    await DisplayAlert("Post to Facebook","Trail
    information has been posted to your wall!", "OK");
}
```

4. Next, we use the `Contains` property of the `action` variable to determine if the `User Details` option has been selected, and, if so, we call the `GetProfileInformation` instance method of our `FacebookCredentials` class, and pass in the `GetAuthAccount` property from our `FacebookApiAuthToken` class to retrieve our currently logged-in Facebook user's details and assign the value to our `objUserDetails` variable. We then proceed to construct our `userDetails` string with the information extracted from the `objUserDetails` dictionary, and display the information within an alert dialog box:

```
else if (action.Contains("User Details"))
{
    // Declare an instance to our Facebook Credentials Class
    await FacebookCredentials.GetProfileInformation((Xamarin
    .Auth.AuthenticatorCompletedEventArgs)
    FacebookApiAuthToken.GetAuthAccount);
    // Construct our Facebook User details based on
    // information stored within each of the properties
    var objUserDetails = FacebookApiUser.GetUserDetails;
    var userDetails = objUserDetails.GetValue("id").ToString();
    userDetails +="\n"+objUserDetails.GetValue("name").ToString();
    userDetails +="\n"+ objUserDetails.GetValue("first_name")
    .ToString();
    userDetails +="\n"+ objUserDetails.GetValue("last_name")
    .ToString();
    userDetails +="\n"+ objUserDetails.GetValue("gender")
    .ToString();
    userDetails += "\n"+ objUserDetails.GetValue("devices")
    .ToString();
    // Display an Alert Dialog that will display
    // information from our user properties
    await DisplayAlert("Facebook User Details",
```

```
        userDetails, "OK");
      }
   };
```

In the preceding code snippet, we create our `postToFacebook` button and begin applying the `ButtonShadowEffect` class to our control, so that it can take advantage of the nice platform-specific rendering effects for visual control elements.

Next, we modify the `Clicked` method to handle each press of the button, so that we can display a selection of options for the user to choose from. We accomplish this by using the `DisplayActionSheet` method. When the user chooses the `Post` button, a call is made to our `FacebookCredentials` class and the `PostWalkInformation` method to submit the current walk information to the user's Facebook page. Alternatively, if the user chooses the `User Details` option, we make a call to our `FacebookCredentials` class, but this time we call the `GetProfileInformation` method to return a JSON dictionary that contains the currently logged-in Facebook user's details, which we assign to an object variable called `objUserDetails`.

Finally, we create a `userDetails` variable that we construct by extracting each of the values for `name`, `last_name`, `first_name`, etc. and display this information within an alert dialog box using the `DisplayAlert` method.

Updating the Xamarin.Forms App class to handle Facebook Sign In

In this section, we need to update our `Xamarin.Forms.App` class by modifying the constructor in the main `App` class to include additional property and action methods that will help with navigating to our `WalksPageContentPage` after our `TrackMyWalks` app has successfully signed in to Facebook.

Let's look at how we can achieve this by performing the following steps:

1. Open the `TrackMyWalks.cs` file, located within the `TrackMyWalks` Portable Class Library project solution.
2. Next, ensure that the `TrackMyWalks.cs` file is displayed within the code editor, locate the `App` method, and enter the highlighted code sections shown in the following code snippet:

```
//
//  TrackMyWalks.cs
//  TrackMyWalks
```

```
//
//   Created by Steven F. Daniel on 04/08/2016.
//   Copyright © 2016 GENIESOFT STUDIOS. All rights reserved.
//
     using System;
     using System.Threading.Tasks;
     using TrackMyWalks.Services;
     using TrackMyWalks.ViewModels;
     using Xamarin.Forms;

     namespace TrackMyWalks
     {
        public class App : Application
        {
           public App()
           {
            // Check the Device Target OS Platform
            if (Device.OS == TargetPlatform.Android)
            {
             // Set the root page of your application
             MainPage = new SplashPage();
            }
            else if (Device.OS == TargetPlatform.iOS)
            {
             // Set our Walks Page to be the root page of our
             // application.
             var mainPage = new NavigationPage(new WalksPage()
             {
               Title = "Track My Walks – iOS",
             });
           ...
           ...
           ...
           ...
        }
     }
```

3. Next, create the RemoveFBSignInPage action property method, which will be used to handle the removal of the FBSignInPage once we have successfully signed in to Facebook, as determined by the FBSignInPageRenderer class. We then call the PopModalAsync property of the Navigation property on the MainPage to pop the last page off the NavigationStack:

```
// Property method instance to remove our FBSignInPage
   public static Action RemoveFBSignInPage
   {
      get
```

```
        {
            return new Action(() => App.Current.
            MainPage.Navigation.PopModalAsync());
        }
    }
```

4. Then, create the `NavigateToWalksPage` instance method; this will be used to handle navigating to the `WalksPage` ViewModel within the `NavigationStack` by calling the `PushAsync` property on the `Navigation` property on the `MainPage`:

```
// Handle navigating to our Walks Page when
   we have successfully
 // signed into Facebook.
public async static Task NavigateToWalksPage()
{
    await App.Current.MainPage.Navigation.PushAsync
    (new WalksPage());
}
}
```

In the preceding code snippet, we begin by implementing the methods that will be required to remove an instance of `FBSignInPage`, as determined by the `RemoveFBSignInPage` property `Action` method that will be used to handle removal of the `FBSignInPage` once we have successfully signed into Facebook, as determined by the `FBSignInPageRenderer` class. We then call the `PopModalAsync` property of the `Navigation` property on the `MainPage` to pop the last page off the `NavigationStack`.

The `NavigateToWalksPage` instance method will be used to handle the navigation to our `Walks Page` ViewModel upon successfully being logged in to Facebook via the `TrackMyWalks` app; this is done by using the `PushAsync` property on the `Navigation` property.

Enabling Facebook functionality within the TrackMyWalks app

When working with the Facebook SDK and the `Xamarin.Auth` framework, we need to make some additional changes to our iOS project solution property list to enable **SSO** (**Single Sign-On**) support when the application runs.

Let's look at how we can achieve this by performing the following steps:

1. Double-click on the `Info.plist` file that is contained within the `TrackMyWalks.iOS` project, and ensure that the **Advanced** tab is showing.
2. Next, scroll down to the bottom of the page, and expand the **URL Types** section.
3. Then, within the **Identifier** field, provide your Facebook Id whilst prefixing it with `fb` as the first two characters that is `fb1234567890`:

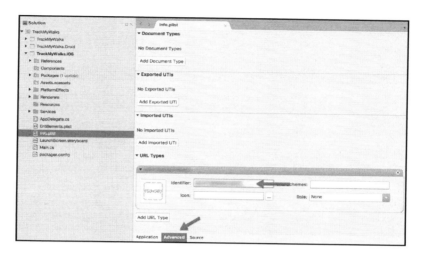

 The URL types section is a single array sub-item that needs your Facebook App ID to be prefixed with `fb`. This is used to ensure the application will receive the call-back methods of the URL and the web-based OAuth flow.

Now that we have modified our `TrackMyWalks.iOS` project to allow our app to receive the call-back methods of the URL and the web-based OAuth flow, we need to do one more thing, and set up our Facebook App ID and application name that we configured within the app dashboard:

1. Ensure that the `Info.plist` file is displayed within the Xamarin IDE, and that the **Source** tab is showing.
2. Next, create the `FacebookAppID` and `FacebookDisplayName` keys by clicking within the **Add new entry** section of the `Info.plist`.

2. Then, enter your Facebook App ID as the string description for the **Value** field, as shown in the following screenshot. You will notice here that we don't need to provide the `fb` prefix as we did for our **URL types** section.

3. Next, enter `TrackMyWalks` as the string description for the **Value** field, as shown in the following screenshot:

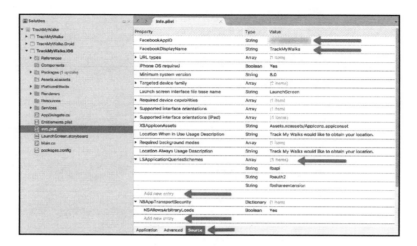

5. Then, create the `LSApplicationQueriesScenes` array keys, and add the string description fields and their values, using **fbapi**, **fbauth2**, and **fbshareextension** as the **Value** fields, as shown in the preceding screenshot.

   Apple introduced the **App Transport Security** protocol with iOS 9 to enforce secure connections between Internet connections, as well as with any app that communicates using the HTTPS protocol. It requires that information is encrypted using the TLS version 1.2. We need to disable and opt out of ATS entirely by configuring our local `Info.plist` file within the `TrackMyWalks.iOS` project solution, so that it can communicate over HTTPS without any issues.

6. Next, with the `Info.plist` file still open within the Xamarin IDE environment, create the `NSAppTransportSecurity` dictionary array.

7. Next, add the `NSAllowArbitraryLoads` Boolean value, setting it to **Yes**, as shown in the preceding screenshot.

If you are interested in finding out more information on the App Transport Security and `NSAppTransportSecurity` class, refer to the Xamarin developer documentation located at `https://developer.xamarin.com/guides/ios/platform_features/intro duction_to_ios9/ats/`.

Now that we have finished building all the components for our `TrackMyWalks` application necessary to enable integration with Facebook, we can build and run the `TrackMyWalks` application within the iOS simulator. When compilation completes, the iOS Simulator will appear automatically and the `TrackMyWalks` application will be displayed, as shown in the following screenshot:

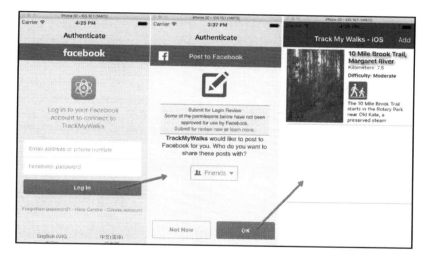

As you can see from the preceding screenshot, this currently displays our Facebook Sign In page, which tells the user to **Log in to your Facebook account to connect to TrackMyWalks** application. To proceed, provide your **Email address or phone number** and your **Facebook password**, and click on the **Log In** button.

Upon successfully determining that your details have been validated by Facebook, you will be presented with a **Post to Facebook** authentication screen, asking you who you would like to share your posts with; you have the option to choose either **Friends, Public,** or **Only Me**. Once you have made your choice, click on the **OK** button to dismiss the **Post to Facebook** dialog and display the `ListView` that will contain our list of walk trails from our `DataTemplate` control:

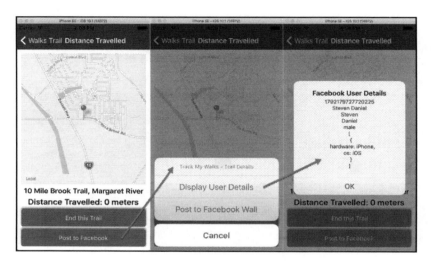

The preceding screenshot shows the **Distance Travelled** page that includes our **Post to Facebook** button, and you will notice that, upon clicking on this button, several choices will pop up for you to choose from. If you proceed and click on the **Display User Details** button, this will make a call to the `GetProfileInformation` method that is located within our `FacebookCredentials` class, and will pass the `GetAuthAccount` account information to obtain the user details, which are located within our `FacebookApiAuthToken`, using the Open Graph API platform. Upon successfully obtaining the user's Facebook details, you will be presented with a dialog box containing each of our user's field details:

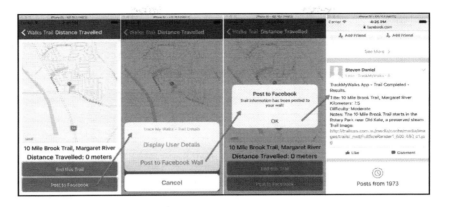

The preceding screenshot shows the **Distance Travelled** page that includes our **Post to Facebook** button, and you will notice that, upon clicking on this button, several choices will pop up for you to choose from. If you click on the **Post to Facebook Wall** button, this will make a call to the `PostWalkInformation` method that is located within our `FacebookCredentials` class, and will pass the currently chosen walk trail information, as determined by our ViewModel. Upon successfully posting to the user's Facebook wall, you will be presented with a dialog box telling you that the walk entry has been posted to the user's Facebook wall.

Summary

In this chapter, we updated our `TrackMyWalks` application to allow us to use Facebook to sign in to our app. You learned how you can use both the `Xamarin.Auth` and the Facebook SDK to authenticate whether the user is a valid Facebook user. Next, you learned how to create a custom `FacebookApiUser` model and a `FacebookCredentials` class that are used to store the user's credentials, so that these can be used throughout our app to obtain information about the user.

As we progressed throughout the chapter, you created a Facebook Sign In content page and a custom page renderer class that will allow the user to sign in to the `TrackMyWalks` app using their Facebook credentials, and updated the ViewModel and content pages so that they can utilize the Facebook functionality appropriately. You learned how to take advantage of the Facebook SDK and post walk data to your Facebook profile page, so you can show off your progress to your friends and/or work colleagues.

In the next chapter, you'll learn how to create and run unit tests within the Xamarin Studio IDE, using the UITest framework, before moving on to learn how to profile our application using the Xamarin Profiler, and how to use the Xamarin Inspector to inspect and debug our user interfaces visually, and fix UI-related problems.

9
Unit Testing Your Xamarin.Forms Apps Using the NUnit and UITest Frameworks

In our previous chapter, we updated our `TrackMyWalks` application to allow us to use Facebook to sign into our app. You learned how you can use both the `Xamarin.Auth` and Facebook SDK to authenticate if the user is a valid Facebook user. Next, you learned how to create a custom `FacebookApiUser` model and `FacebookCredentials` class that will be used to store the user's credentials, so that these can be used throughout our app to obtain information about the user, as well as post information to their Facebook wall.

During the development of our `TrackMyWalks` app, we have designed and implemented various design patterns and best practices, with the intention of making it easier to maintain and test our app by separating the user interface and business logic.

In this chapter, you'll learn how to create and run unit tests using the **NUnit** and **UITest** testing frameworks right within the Xamarin Studio IDE. You'll learn how to write unit tests for our ViewModels that will essentially test the business logic to validate that everything is working correctly, before moving on to testing the user interfaces portion using automated UI testing.

This chapter will cover the following topics:

- Creating a unit testing solution using the popular NUnit testing framework
- Adding the **Moq NuGet** package to the unit testing solution
- Adding the **Xamarin Test Cloud Agent NuGet** package to the UITest solution
- Successfully learning how to test your ViewModels

- Running unit tests and UITests using the Xamarin Studio IDE
- Understanding the common types of UITest testing methods
- Creating a unit testing solution using the UITest framework
- Successfully learning how to test your ContentPages (Views)

Creating a unit test solution folder using Xamarin Studio

During the development of our TrackMyWalks application, we have designed the user interfaces, ViewModels, and ContentPages. As developers, there may be times when we would like to obtain feedback to let us know when our application logic is working as expected. We can use the NUnit testing framework to provide us with that confirmation.

In this section, you'll begin by adding a new solution folder to our existing TrackMyWalks Portable Class Library solution. This new solution folder will be used to separate each of our NUnit and UITests from our main solution.

The good news is that Xamarin Studio has built in support for the NUnit framework that we can run our unit tests from, and then have our results displayed, right within the Xamarin Studio IDE.

Let's look at how to add a new Solution folder to our TrackMyWalks Portable Class Library, by performing the following steps:

1. Right-click on the TrackMyWalks solution project and choose the **Add** | **Add Solution Folder** menu option, as shown in the following screenshot:

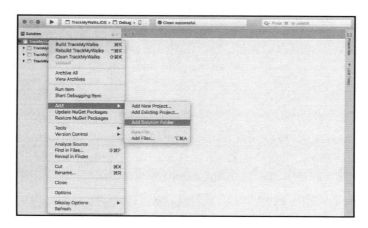

2. Next, enter in `TrackMyWalks.Tests` for the name of the solution folder.

Now that you have created the `TrackMyWalks.Tests` solution within the main `TrackMyWalks` solution project, our next step is to create a new unit test project solution, that will be responsible for testing the business logic within our `TrackMyWalksViewModels`.

Creating a unit test project using Xamarin Studio

In the previous section, we created the unit testing `Solution` folder within our `TrackMyWalks` main project solution that will be used to separate the unit tests from our main iOS and Android project solutions. This is so that we can run these independently from the main solution.

One of the great benefits of using Xamarin Studio to handle your tests is that it leverages the popular NUnit testing framework for performing unit tests. We will begin by creating the NUnit test project within the `TrackMyWalks.Tests` solution that we've previously created.

Let's start by creating a new NUnit project within our `TrackMyWalks.Tests` project solution, by performing the following steps:

1. Right-click on the `TrackMyWalks.Tests` solution project and choose the **Add** | **Add New Project...** menu option, as shown in the following screenshot:

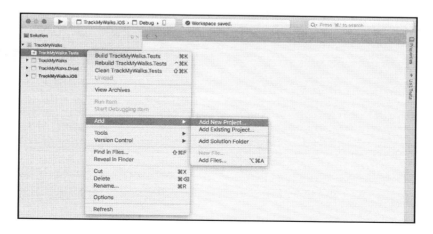

2. Next, choose the **NUnit Library Project** option located within the **General** section under the **Other** | **.NET** section; ensure you have selected **C#** as the programming language to use, as shown in the following screenshot:

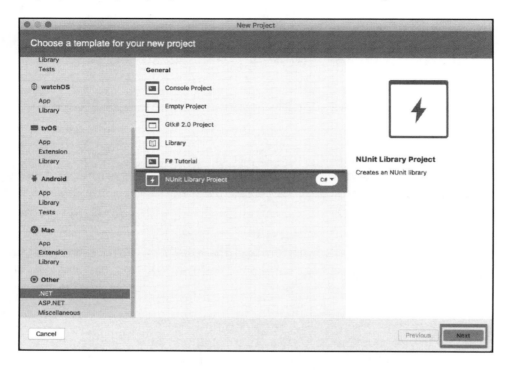

3. Then, click on the **Next** button to proceed to the next step in the wizard.
4. Next, enter `TrackMyWalks.UnitTests` to use as the name for your new project in the **Project Name** field.

5. Then, ensure that the **Create a project directory within the solution directory.** has been selected, as shown in the following screenshot:

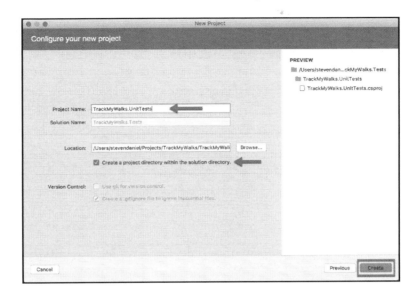

6. Finally, click on the **Create** button to save your project at the specified location.

Once your project has been created, you will be presented with the Xamarin Studio development environment, with your new projected created within the `TrackMyWalks.Tests` solution folder.

In the next section, we will begin to add the Moq (pronounced as mock) framework library that will be responsible for allowing us to test our `ViewModels` within the `TrackMyWalks` solution.

Adding the Moq NuGet package to the unit test project

Now that you have set up and created a new unit test project, our next step is to add the Moq (pronounced as Mock) NuGet package to the `TrackMyWalks.UnitTests` solution. This library is essentially one of the most popular and friendly mocking framework libraries for the .NET platform, and we will use this to test some of our `ViewModels` within our `TrackMyWalks` app.

Let's look at how to add the Moq NuGet package to our `TrackMyWalks.UnitTests` project solution, by performing the following steps:

1. Right-click on the `Packages` folder that is contained within the `TrackMyWalks.UnitTests` solution, and choose the **Add Packages...** menu option, as shown in the following screenshot:

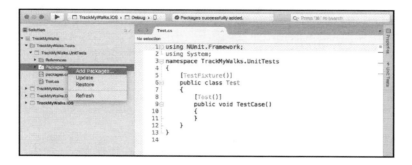

2. This will display the **Add Packages** dialog, enter in moq within the search dialog, and select the **Moq: an enjoyable mocking library** option within the list, as shown in the following screenshot:

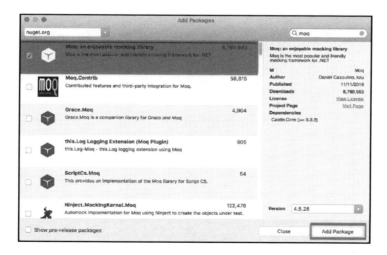

3. Finally, click on the **Add Package** button to add the `NuGet` package to the `Packages` folder contained within the `TrackMyWalks.UnitTests` solution.

Now that you have added the Moq NuGet package, our next step is to begin writing the test case scenarios for our ViewModels, which we will be covering in the next section.

Adding the TrackMyWalks project to TrackMyWalks.UnitTests

In the previous section, we added the Moq NuGet package to our `TrackMyWalks` solution. The next step is to add a reference to the `TrackMyWalks` core library to our `TrackMyWalks.UnitTests` solution.

Since we will be testing our `ViewModels`, you will need to ensure that you have applied all of the cumulative code changes to the `TrackMyWalks` solution project throughout this book to avoid any issues, as we will essentially need to break each of the tests into individual classes representing each ViewModel and the accompanying unit test class that we want to test the business logic on. To successfully test our `ViewModels`, we will first need to include a reference to the `TrackMyWalks` project within our `TrackMyWalks.UnitTests` solution project.

Let's look at how we can achieve this, by performing the following steps:

1. Right-click on the `References` folder that is contained within the `TrackMyWalks.UnitTests` project solution, and choose the **Edit References...** menu option, as shown in the following screenshot:

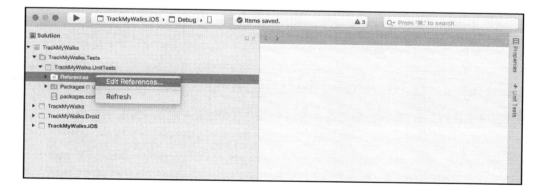

2. Then, ensure that the **Projects** tab has been selected and choose the **TrackMyWalks** project to include our Android and iOS platform solution projects within our `TrackMyWalks.UnitTests` project solution:

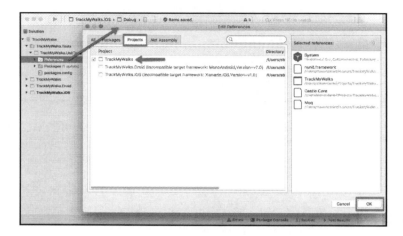

3. Next, ensure that you have selected the `TrackMyWalks` project within the **Projects** tab, click on **OK** to add the project reference to your `References` section of your `TrackMyWalks.UnitTests` project solution, and close the **Edit References** dialog.

In the next section, we will begin by creating our first unit test which will be responsible for validating the `WalkEntry` model to ensure that after the ViewModel has been initialized, it will contain walk information.

Creating and implementing the WalksTrailViewModel NUnit test class

Now that you have incorporated the `TrackMyWalks` project into the `TrackMyWalks.UnitTests` solution, our next step is to create the unit test for our `WalksTrailViewModel`. These tests will be used to help us check to see when our ViewModel passes or fails under these test conditions.

Let's now start to implement the code required for our `WalksTrailViewModelTest` class, by performing the following steps:

1. Create an empty class within the `TrackMyWalks.UnitTests` project solution folder, by choosing **Add | New File...**. If you can't remember how to do this, you can refer to the section entitled *Creating the TrackMyWalks model*, within `Chapter 1`, *Creating the TrackMyWalks Native App*.

2. Then, enter `WalksTrailViewModelTest` for the name of the new class that you want to create, and click on the **New** button to allow the wizard to proceed and create the new file.

3. Next, ensure that the `WalksTrailViewModelTest.cs` file is displayed within the code editor, and enter in the following code snippet:

```
//
//    WalksTrailViewModelTest.cs
//    WalksTrailViewModel Testing Framework
//
//    Created by Steven F. Daniel on 23/09/2016.
//    Copyright © 2016 GENIESOFT STUDIOS. All rights reserved.
//
    using NUnit.Framework;
    using TrackMyWalks.ViewModels;
    using TrackMyWalks.Services;
    using Moq;
    using System.Threading.Tasks;

    namespace TrackMyWalks.Tests
    {
```

4. Next, we need to modify the `WalksTrailViewModelTest` class constructor by adding the `[TestFixture]` attribute which sets up our class to be an instance of the `TestFixture` testing class. Proceed and enter in the following code snippet:

```
[TestFixture]
public class WalksTrailViewModelTest
{
    WalksTrailViewModel _vm;
```

5. Then, create the `Setup` instance method that will be responsible for creating a new instance of our ViewModel for each of the tests that are declared within the class. This is to ensure that each test is run using a clean instance of the ViewModel. We then proceed to declare a `navMock` variable instance of the `Mock` class from our Moq library to create a new instance of the `IWalkNavService` and instantiate the `WalksTrailViewModel`, using the `navMock` instance. Proceed and enter in the following code snippet:

```
[SetUp]
public void Setup()
{
    var navMock = new Mock<IWalkNavService>().Object;
    _vm = new WalksTrailViewModel(navMock);
}
```

6. Next, we need to implement the `CheckIfWalkEntryIsNotNull` instance method that will check to see if our `WalksTrailViewModel` has been properly initialized when the `Init` method is called. We declare the `[Test]` attribute which is essentially an abstract class that represents a test within the `NUnit.Test` framework. We proceed to initialize our `WalkEntry` model to `null`, and then call the `Init` method to check to see if the `WalkEntry` model has been properly set to the value provided in the `Init` method's parameter and then use the `IsNotNull` method on the `Assert` class to display a message should the test fail. This is so that you can troubleshoot the code at a later point. Proceed and enter in the following code snippet:

```
[Test]
public async Task CheckIfWalkEntryIsNotNull()
{
    // Arrange
    _vm.WalkEntry = null;

    // Act
    await _vm.Init();

    // Assert
    Assert.IsNotNull(_vm.WalkEntry, "WalkEntry is null
    after being initialized with a valid WalkEntries object.");
    }
  }
}
```

In the preceding code snippet, we began by implementing the various instance methods that will be required to perform each test for our `WalksTrailViewModel`. We added the `[TestFixture]` attribute at the beginning of our class constructor so that it will be an instance of the `TestFixture` testing class. We then proceeded to create the `Setup` instance method so that it will be responsible for creating a new instance of our ViewModel for each of the tests that are declared within the class, using the `[Test]` attribute. This is essentially an abstract class that represents a test within the `NUnit.Test` framework, and ensures that each test is run using a clean instance of the ViewModel.

Next, we used the `Mock` class from our Moq library to create a new instance of the `IWalkNavService` when instantiating the `WalksTrailViewModel`.

In the next step, we implemented the `CheckIfWalkEntryIsNotNull` instance method that will perform a check to see if our `WalksTrailViewModel` has been properly initialized whenever the `Init` method has been called. Again, we declared the `[Test]` attribute prior to initializing our `WalkEntry` model to `null`, and prior to calling the `Init` method to check to see if the `WalkEntry` model has been properly set to the value provided in the `Init` method's parameter. After that, we used the `IsNotNull` method on the `Assert` class to display a message should the test fail. This is so that you can troubleshoot the code at a later point.

In the next section, we will begin by creating the second unit test which will be responsible for validating information contained within our `WalkEntryViewModel` to ensure that after our ViewModel has been initialized, we receive the expected results returned.

Creating and implementing the WalkEntryViewModel NUnit test class

In the previous section, we created the NUnit test for our `WalksTrailViewModel` which checked to ensure that the `WalksEntry` model was properly initialized after the `Init` method was called. In this section, we will create another NUnit test that will check to see if certain properties within our `WalksEntryViewModel` have been set up and initialized.

Let's now start to implement the code required for our `WalkEntryViewModelTest` class by performing the following steps:

1. Create an empty class within the `TrackMyWalks.UnitTests` project solution folder, by choosing **Add | New File...**. If you can't remember how to do this, you can refer to the section entitled *Creating and implementing the WalksTrailViewModel NUnit test class*, within this chapter.

2. Then, enter in `WalkEntryViewModelTest` for the name of the new class that you want to create, and click on the **New** button to allow the wizard to proceed and create the new file.

3. Next, ensure that the `WalkEntryViewModelTest.cs` file is displayed within the code editor, and enter in the following code snippet:

```
//
//   WalkEntryViewModelTest.cs
//   WalkEntryViewModel Testing Framework
//
//   Created by Steven F. Daniel on 23/09/2016.
//   Copyright © 2016 GENIESOFT STUDIOS. All rights reserved.
//
    using NUnit.Framework;
    using TrackMyWalks.ViewModels;
    using TrackMyWalks.Services;
    using Moq;
    using System.Threading.Tasks;

    namespace TrackMyWalks.UnitTests
    {
```

4. Next, we need to modify the `WalkEntryViewModelTest` class constructor by adding the `[TestFixture]` attribute just as we did in the previous section. This sets up our class to be an instance of the `TestFixture` testing class. Proceed and enter in the following code snippet:

```
[TestFixture]
public class WalkEntryViewModelTest
{
   WalkEntryViewModel _vm;
```

5. Then, create the `Setup` instance method that will be responsible for creating a new instance of our ViewModel for each of the tests that are declared within the class. This is to ensure that each test is run using a clean instance of the ViewModel. We then use the `Mock` class from our Moq library to create a new instance of the `IWalkNavService` when instantiating the `WalkEntryViewModel`. Proceed and enter in the following code snippet:

```
[SetUp]
public void Setup()
{
   var navMock = new Mock<IWalkNavService>().Object;
   _vm = new WalkEntryViewModel(navMock);
}
```

6. Next, we need to implement the `CheckIfEntryTitleIsEqual` instance method that will check to see if our `Title` property has been properly initialized when the `Init` method has been called. We'll declare the `[Test]` attribute just as we did in the previous test, and then we'll proceed to initialize the `Title` property and call the `Init` method to check whether the `Title` property has been initialized correctly to the value provided in the `Init` method's parameter.

7. Next, we use the `AreEqual` method on the `Assert` class to check to see if the `Title` property has been initialized correctly, and then display a message containing the value of the `Title` property from the ViewModel, should the test fail. Proceed and enter in the following code snippet:

```
[Test]
public async Task CheckIfEntryTitleIsEqual()
{
  // Arrange
  _vm.Title = "New Walk";

  // Act
  await _vm.Init();

  // Assert
  Assert.AreEqual("New Walk", _vm.Title);
}
```

8. Then, we need to implement the `CheckIfDifficultyIsEqual` instance method and declare the `[Test]` attribute, prior to initializing our `Difficulty` property to a string value, and then calling the `Init` method. In the next step, we use the `AreEqual` method on the `Assert` class to check whether the `Difficulty` property has been initialized correctly, and display a message containing the value of the `Difficulty` property from the ViewModel, should the test fail. Proceed and enter in the following code snippet:

```
[Test]
public async Task CheckIfDifficultyIsEqual()
{
  // Arrange
  _vm.Difficulty = "Easy";

  // Act
  await _vm.Init();

  // Assert
  Assert.AreEqual("Easy", _vm.Difficulty);
}
```

9. Next, we need to implement the `CheckIfKilometersIsNotEqual` instance method that declares the `[Test]` attribute just as we did in the previous test. We then initialize our `Kilometers` property to a `Double` value, and call the `Init` method. In the next step, we use the `AreEqual` method on the `Assert` class to check to see if the `Kilometers` property has been initialized correctly, and display a message containing the value of the `Kilometers` property from the `ViewModel`, should the test fail. Proceed and enter in the following code snippet:

```
[Test]
public async Task CheckIfKilometersIsNotEqual()
{
    // Arrange
    _vm.Kilometers = 40.0;

    // Act
    await _vm.Init();

    // Assert
    Assert.AreNotEqual(40.0, _vm.Kilometers);
}


}
}
```

In the preceding code snippet, we began by implementing the various instance methods that will be required to perform each test for our `WalkEntryViewModel`. We added the `[TestFixture]` attribute at the beginning of the class constructor so that it will be an instance of the `TestFixture` testing class; and then proceeded to create the `Setup` instance method so that it will be responsible for creating a new instance of our ViewModel for each of the tests that is declared within the class, using the `[Test]` attribute which is essentially an abstract class that represents a test within the `NUnit.Test` framework, and ensures that each test is run using a clean instance of the ViewModel.

Next, we used the `Mock` class from our Moq library to create a new instance of the `IWalkNavService` when instantiating the `WalkEntryViewModel`. In the next step, we implemented the `CheckIfEntryTitleIsEqual` instance method that will perform a check to see if the `Title` property has been properly initialized whenever the `Init` method has been called. Again, we declare the `[Test]` attribute prior to initializing the `Title` property of the `WalksEntry` model, and prior to calling the `AreEqual` method on the `Assert` class to check to see if the `Title` property has been initialized correctly. We then displayed a message containing the value of the `Title` property from the ViewModel, should the test fail.

Next, we implemented the `CheckIfDifficultyIsEqual` instance method that will initialize the `Difficulty` property to a string value, and then call the `Init` method of the `WalkEntryViewModel`. We called the `AreEqual` method on the `Assert` class to confirm that, after we call the `Init` method, the value of the `Difficulty` property from the ViewModel is the value that we expect to come back from the provided `Mock` instance. If the value is not what we expect, the test will fail and will display a message containing the value of the `Difficulty` property from the `ViewModel`.

In our final step, we implemented the `CheckIfKilometersIsNotEqual` instance method that initializes our `Kilometers` property to a `Double` value, and then calls the `Init` method. Just as we did in our `CheckIfDifficultyIsEqual` instance method, we used the `AreNotEqual` method on the `Assert` class to confirm that, after we call the `Init` method, the value of the `Kilometers` property from the ViewModel is the value that we expect to come back from the provided mock instance. If the value is not what we expect, the test will fail and will display a message containing the value of the `Kilometers` property from the ViewModel.

For each test method that you create that will be represented by the NUnit `[Test]` attribute, the **Arrange-Act-Assert** pattern will follow. This is described in the following table:

Test pattern	Description
Arrange	This will essentially perform all the setting up and initialization conditions for your test.
Act	This ensures that your test will successfully interact with the application.
Assert	This will examine the results of the actions that were initially performed within the Act step to verify the results.

You can now see, that by incorporating the `NUnit.Framework` within your applications, as well as adopting the Arrange-Act-Assert pattern, you can essentially perform tests on your ViewModels to ensure that the results you are expecting are returned.

If you are interested in learning more about the `NUnit.Framework.Test` class, and its associated methods, please refer to the information contained at `https://developer.xamarin.com/api/type/NUnit.Framework.Internal.Test/`.

To learn more about the `NUnit.Framework.Assert` class and other methods that you can use to handle the different types of assertions, please refer to the information located at `https://developer.xamarin.com/api/type/NUnit.Framework.Assert/`.

Now that you have created your unit tests, our next step is to begin running our tests right within the Xamarin Studio IDE, which we will be covering in the next section.

Running the TrackMyWalks.UnitTests using Xamarin Studio

In our previous section, we created and implemented unit tests for both the `WalksTrailViewModel` and the `WalkEntryViewModel`. These contained sets of various test conditions that we checked against.

Our next step is to begin running these unit tests directly from within the Xamarin Studio development environment.

Let's look at how we can achieve this with the following steps:

1. To run a unit test, right-click on the `TrackMyWalks.UnitTests` project within the **Solution** pane, and choose the **Run Item** option, as shown in the following screenshot:

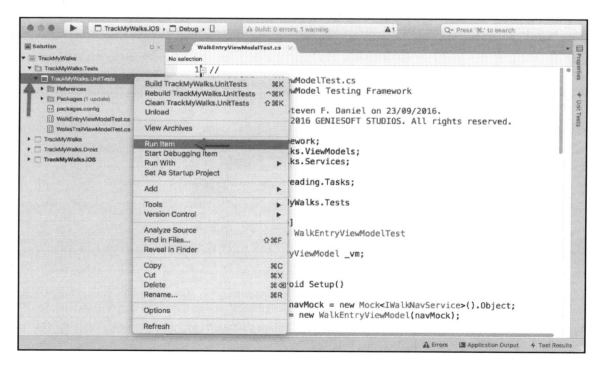

2. Alternatively, you can also run the unit test by selecting the `TrackMyWalks.UnitTests` solution project and then navigating to the **Run** menu option and choosing the **Run Unit Tests** sub-menu item.

When the compilation of the unit tests has completed, you will be presented with a list showing each of your test results that have passed, failed, or were ignored. These are displayed within the **Test Results** pane, as shown in the following screenshot:

Should any of your tests fail, these will be displayed within the **Test Results** pane, along with their associated **Stack Trace**. You will also notice that the message that we provided within the `Assert.AreEqual` method will also be displayed as part of the failure result:

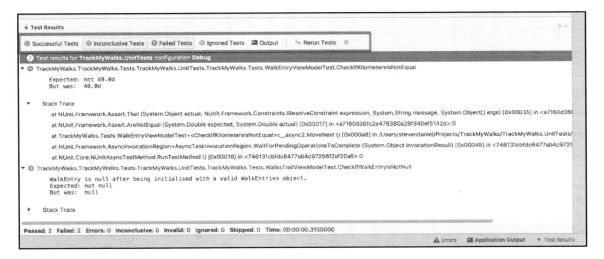

From this screen, you have the option of filtering your test results or re-running your unit test conditions again. These are explained in more detail in the following table:

Test result option	Description
Successful Tests	This will display all the successfully executed tests which passed the conditions as specified within the test case.
Inconclusive Tests	This will display any test results that were found to be inconclusive, meaning that a firm result could not be determined.
Failed Tests	This option displays a list of any tests that did not meet the conditions as specified within the test case scenario.
Ignored Tests	This option displays a list of any tests that were ignored as specified by the [Ignore] attribute.
Output	This option displays a console output for each of the tests that are executed and will contain any tests that have successfully passed, failed, been ignored, or were found to be inconclusive.
Rerun Tests	This option enables you to re-run your tests again, without the need for recompiling your test cases.

Now that you have a good understanding of how to create your own unit tests using the NUnit testing framework, we can now look at how to create another form of unit testing, which is called automated UI testing. This time we will be leveraging the UITest framework which will enable us to perform tests on the user interface portion of our `TrackMyWalks` app which we will be covering over the next sections.

Creating a UI test project using Xamarin Studio

In the previous section, we saw how easy it is to create a set of unit tests that enable us to test our `ViewModels` within the `TrackMyWalks` project. Whilst unit testing ensures that a significant amount of code is tested, it is primarily focused on testing the actual business logic within the app. This leaves the user interface portions of the app still untested, but the beauty of using UI testing allows us to automate specific actions within our app's user interface to ensure that it is working as expected.

Fortunately, Xamarin Studio provides you with a rich set of tools for performing automated UI tests, and these can be both written in C# and make use of the UITest framework. Let's start by creating a new UITest project within our `TrackMyWalks.Tests` project solution, by performing the following steps:

1. Right-click on the `TrackMyWalks.Tests` solution project and choose the **Add |
Add New Project...** menu option. If you can't remember how to do this, you can
refer to the section entitled *Creating a unit test project using Xamarin Studio*, located
within this chapter.

2. Next, choose the **UI Test App** option located within the **Xamarin Test Cloud**
section, under the **Multiplatform | Tests** section. Ensure that you have selected
C# as the programming language to use, as shown in the following screenshot:

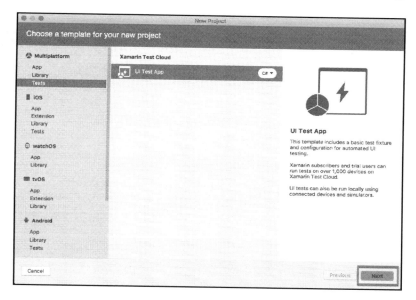

3. Then, click on the **Next** button to proceed to the next step in the wizard.
4. Next, enter `TrackMyWalks.UITests` to use as the name for your new project as
the **Project Name** field.

5. Then, ensure that the **Create a project directory within the solution directory.** has been selected, as shown in the following screenshot:

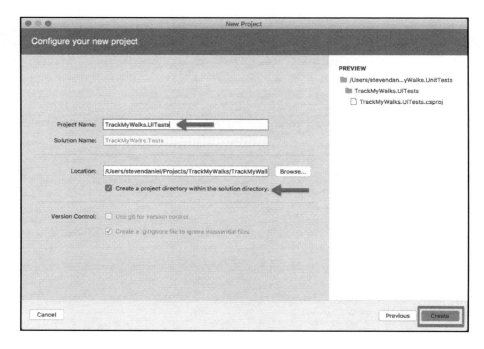

6. Finally, click on the **Create** button to save your project at the specified location.

Once your project has been created, you will be presented with the Xamarin Studio development environment, with your new project created within the TrackMyWalks.Tests solution folder.

You will notice that by default our project has created a file named Test.cs that we can use to write our UITests, as well as a class named AppInitializer.cs that is essentially used by the Test.cs class to create an IApp instance and start the app for each test condition. Since we will only be creating one UITest for this chapter, we can essentially just use the Test.cs file for now.

In an ideal world, you would be creating various tests, one for each test condition, so it would make sense to break each of your UITests into individual files. In the next section, we will learn about some of the commonly used UITest methods that we can use while performing UITests for our application's user interface.

Understanding the commonly used UITest methods

As mentioned previously, in this section, we will learn about some of the commonly used methods that we can use with the UITest framework. The UITest framework provides you with a way of automating the interactions between your iOS, or Android apps using C# and the NUnit testing platform.

We will be using an instance of the `IApp` and `ConfigureApp` classes that will be used to create our iOS and Android `IApp` instances to handle all the interactions within the UI.

As we progress throughout the next couple of sections, we will be taking a closer look at how to create `IApp` instances using the `ConfigureApp` class. The UITest framework provides you with several APIs that you can use to interact with an app's user interface.

The following table describes some of the more commonly used methods and the ones that we will be using to test the `TrackMyWalks` app:

UITest methods	Description
`Screenshot()`	This will essentially take a screenshot of the current state of the app.
`Tap()`	This is used to send a tap interaction to a specific element on the app's current screen.
`EnterText()` and `ClearText()`	These methods are used to add and remove text from input elements such as the entry views used within `Xamarin.Forms`.
`Query()`	This method is essentially used to locate or find elements that are currently displayed within the app's screen.
`Repl()`	This command is commonly used to interact in real-time with the app through the terminal using the UITest API.
`WaitForElement()`	This method is used to pause the test until a specific element appears on the app's current screen within a specific timeout period.

Methods such as the `Query` and `WaitForElement` return an `AppResult[]` object that you can essentially use to determine the results of the call. An example would be that if you used the `Query` method call that returns an empty result set, we can be sure that the element does not exist within the app's current screen.

 It is worth mentioning that currently the UITest framework only provides support for both the iOS and Android platforms and doesn't yet provide support for the Windows Phone platform.

As you will see from the methods displayed in the following table, these are essentially all the members pertaining to the `AppQuery` class that are used by the `Query` and `WaitForElement` method members of the `IApp` methods:

AppQuery class methods	Description
`Class()`	Finds elements on the app's current screen, based on their class type.
`Marked()`	Finds elements within the app's current screen, based on their text or identifier.
`Css()`	Performs CSS selector operations on the contents of a WebView on the app's current screen.

 If you are interested in learning more about the various types of UITest methods, please refer to the Introduction to Xamarin.UITest at `https://developer.xamarin.com/guides/testcloud/uitest/intro-to-u itest/`.

Now that you understand some of the most commonly used UITest methods, we can start to implement some tests which we will be covering over the next couple of sections within this chapter.

Setting up and initializing our TrackMyWalks app for UITest

Prior to starting an app and interacting with it using the UITest framework, we need to do some preliminary initialization steps for which we'll make some modifications within the `AppInitializer` class. The `AppInitializer` class contains a static method called `StartApp`.

This static method is called each time the test's `Setup` method is called to get an `IApp` instance. It currently supports both the `iOSApp` and `AndroidApp` as defined by the `ConfigureApp` class.

One thing that you will notice within the `AppInitializer` class is that the `ApkFile` and the `AppBundle` have both been commented out. You will need to uncomment these if you would like to run the tests locally within the unit test pane using Xamarin Studio.

```
using System;
using System.IO;
```

```
using System.Linq;
using Xamarin.UITest;
using Xamarin.UITest.Queries;

namespace TrackMyWalks.UITests
{
    public class AppInitializer
    {
        public static IApp StartApp(Platform platform)
        {
            ...
            ...
            ...
            if (platform == Platform.Android)
            {
                return ConfigureApp.Android
                    // TODO: Update this path to point
                       to your Android
                    // app and uncomment the code if the
                       app is not
                    // included in the solution.
                    //.ApkFile("../../../Droid/bin/Debug
                      /TrackMyWalks.apk").StartApp();
            }

            return ConfigureApp.iOS
                // TODO: Update this path to point to
                   your iOS app and
                // uncomment the code if the app is
                   not included in the
                // solution.
                //.AppBundle("../../../iOS/bin/
                  iPhoneSimulator/Debug/TrackM
                // yWalks.iOS.app").StartApp();
        }
    }
}
```

As you can see from the preceding code snippet, the `AppInitializer` class contains several different methods that are part of the `ConfigureApp` method. The following table provides a brief description of what each one is used for:

ConfigureApp methods	Description
AppBundle()	This method is used for specifying the path to the app bundle to use during testing.
StartApp()	This method essentially launches the app within the simulator.
Debug()	This method is essentially used to enable debugging and logging of messages and is particularly useful if you need to troubleshoot problems when running the application using the simulator.

DeviceIdentifier()	This method configures the device to use with the device identifier. This can be used to detect iOS simulators using the following command line statement: `xcrun instruments -s devices`
EnableLocalScreenshots	This method is used to enable screenshots when you're running tests locally. By default, screenshots are always enabled whenever tests are being run using Xamarin Test Cloud.
Repl()	This method will essentially pause the test execution and invoke the REPL in a terminal prompt.

As you can see, the `AppInitializer` file doesn't contain much information, but as we work our way through this chapter, we will be adding the `Xamarin.TestCloud.Agent` to the iOS portion of the `TrackMyWalks` app so that we will be able to run our UITests.

Implementing the CreateNewWalkEntry using the UITest.Framework

In the previous section, we looked at some of the different types of methods that we can use to customize the `AppInitializer` class so that we can specify different app bundles to use during testing, as well as to enable screenshots, and provide the ability to debug our unit tests within the Xamarin Studio environment.

In this section, we will begin by implementing a UITest that we can use to handle signing into Facebook and creating a new walk entry using the UITest framework.

Let's now start to implement the code required for our class by performing the following steps:

1. Open the `Test.cs` file which can be located within the `TrackMyWalks.UITests` project as part of the `TrackMyWalks.Tests` solution folder.

2. Next, ensure that the `Test.cs` file is displayed within the code editor, and enter in the following highlighted code sections, as shown in the code snippet:

```
using System;
using System.IO;
using System.Linq;
using NUnit.Framework;
using Xamarin.UITest;
using Xamarin.UITest.Queries;
namespace TrackMyWalks.UITests
{
    [TestFixture(Platform.Android)]
    [TestFixture(Platform.iOS)]
    public class Tests
    {
        IApp app;
        Platform platform;
```

3. Then, modify the `Tests` instance method that will be responsible for creating a new instance of our `IApp` instance. We update our `entryCellPlatformClassName` string variable to return the type of `TextField`, dependent on the platform that we are testing on. Under iOS, we use the `UITextField`, whereas under Android it will use the default `EntryCellEditText` class. Proceed and enter in the highlighted code sections within the following code snippet:

```
string entryCellPlatformClassName;
public Tests(Platform platform)
{
  this.platform = platform;
  entryCellPlatformClassName = platform
    == Platform.iOS ? "UITextField" : "EntryCellEditText";
}
[SetUp]
public void BeforeEachTest()
{
  app = AppInitializer.StartApp(platform);
}
[Test]
public void AppLaunches()
{
    app.Screenshot("First screen.");
}
```

4. Next, create the `SignInToFacebook` instance method that will be responsible for handling the test's steps specifically to the Facebook sign-in process. This uses the user's login credentials to automate the login process prior to carrying out other steps within the UI. Proceed and enter in the highlighted code sections within the following code snippet:

```
// Perform signing in to Facebook
public void SignInToFacebook()
{
    // Set up our Facebook credentials
    var FaceBookEmail = "<Your-Facebook-Email-Address> ";
    var FaceBookPassword = "<Your-Facebook-Password>";
    // Wait for Login button within Facebook oAuth webview
    // to appear.
    app.WaitForElement(x => x.WebView().Css("[name=login]"));
    // Enter text within the webview with name="email"
    app.EnterText(x => x.WebView().Css("[name=email]"),
    FaceBookEmail);
    // Enter text within the webview with name="email"
    app.EnterText(x => x.WebView().Css("[name=pass]"),
```

```
          FaceBookPassword);
          app.ScrollDownTo(x => x.WebView().Css("[name=login]"));
          // Tap the button in the webview with name="login"
          app.Tap(x => x.WebView().Css("[name=login]"));
      }
```

5. Then, create the `PopulateEntryCellFields` instance method that will be responsible for handling the test steps specifically for the creation of a new walk entry. In this method, we make use of both the `ClearText` and `EnterText` methods of the UITest framework that will locate each entry field within the **New Walk Entry** form and populate it with the necessary information. The `DismissKeyboard` method will, as the name suggests, dismiss the keyboard from the view and continue to the next step. Proceed and enter in the highlighted code sections within the following code snippet:

```
   // Populate our EntryCell Fields
   void PopulateEntryCellFields()
   {
     // Clear the default text entry for our Title EntryCell
     app.ClearText(x => x.Class
       (entryCellPlatformClassName).Index(0));
     app.DismissKeyboard();
     // Enter in some default text for our Title EntryCell
     app.EnterText(x => x.Class
       (entryCellPlatformClassName).Index(0),
        "This is a new walk Entry");
     app.DismissKeyboard();
     // Enter in some default text for our Notes EntryCell
     app.EnterText(x => x.Class(entryCellPlatformClassName).Index(1),
     "New Note Entry For Walk Entry");
     app.DismissKeyboard();
     // Clear the default text for our Image Url EntryCell
     app.ClearText(x => x.Class(entryCellPlatformClassName).Index(6));
     app.DismissKeyboard();
     // Enter in some default text Image Url EntryCell
     app.EnterText(x => x.Class(entryCellPlatformClassName).Index(6),"
     https://heuft.com/upload/image/
     400x267/no_image_placeholder.png");
     app.DismissKeyboard();
   }
```

6. Next, create the `ChooseDifficultyPicker` instance method that will be responsible for displaying the difficulty picker that contains various choices of difficulty for the user to choose from. All we are doing here is displaying the picker when the user taps into the cell entry, and dismissing the picker from the view when then user taps the `Done` or `OK` buttons. Proceed and enter the highlighted code sections, as shown within the following code snippet:

```
// Automatically tap into the Difficulty Cell to display the
// Difficulty Picker, and dismiss it by pressing the Done or
// OK button.
 public void ChooseDifficultyPicker()
  {
    // Tap into Difficulty EntryCell
    app.Tap(x => x.Class(entryCellPlatformClassName).Index(5));
    // Tap Done located within the Difficulty Picker Cell
    if (platform == Platform.iOS)
      app.Tap(x => x.Marked("Done"));
    else
      app.Tap(x => x.Marked("OK"));
  }
}
```

7. Then, create the `CreateNewWalkEntry` UITest method that includes the `[Test]` attribute. This is an abstract class that represents a test within the UITest and `NUnit.Test` framework. This method will essentially be the main test driver and will call each of the other instance methods that we've previously declared. Within this method, we call our `SignInToFacebook` method to perform the sign-in to Facebook, using the user's Facebook credentials.

8. Upon successful login, we use the `WaitForElement` method to wait until the main `Track My Walks` screen has been displayed, prior to using the `Assert.IsTrue` method to check to see if the `Track My Walks` screen is displayed. If it's not displayed, our test will fail and display the assigned error message within the **Test Results** screen. Proceed and enter the following code sections shown within the following code snippet:

```
[Test]
public void CreateNewWalkEntry()
{
    // Sign in to Facebook
    SignInToFacebook();
    // Wait for main screen to appear and check for our
    // navigation title.
    var navigationBarTitle = (platform == Platform.iOS ?
    "Track My Walks - iOS" : "Track My Walks - Android");
```

```
var mainScreen = app.WaitForElement(x => x.Marked
(navigationBarTitle).Class("UINavigationBar"));
// Check to see if the Track My Walks - iOS main screen is
// displayed.
Assert.IsTrue(mainScreen.Any(), navigationBarTitle + " screen
wasn't shown after signing in.");
```

9. Next, we use the `Tap` method of the `app` class instance and the `Marked` method to find the `Add` element within the app's current screen, and wait until the `New Walk Entry` page is displayed within the screen. We then proceed to use the `Assert.IsTrue` method to check to see if the `New Walk Entry` screen has been successfully displayed. Alternatively, our test will fail and display the assigned error message within the **Test Results** screen. Proceed and enter in the highlighted code sections shown within the following code snippet:

```
// Click on the Add button from our main screen and wait for
// the New Walk Entry screen to appear.
app.Tap(x => x.Marked("Add"));
var newWalkEntryBarTitle = "New Walk Entry";
var newWalkEntryScreen = app.WaitForElement(x => x.Marked(newWalk
EntryBarTitle));
// Check to ensure that our New Walk Entry screen was displayed.
Assert.IsTrue(newWalkEntryScreen.Any(), newWalkEntryBarTitle + "
screen was not shown after tapping the Add button.");
```

10. Then, we call the `PopulateEntryCellFields` and `ChooseDifficultyPicker` instance methods to populate our entry cell fields and handle the display of the difficulty picker selector. In our final steps, we use the `Tap` method of the `app` class instance, and we use the `Marked` method to find the `Save` element within the app's current screen. We'll wait until the `Track My Walks` page is displayed, before using the `Assert.IsTrue` method to check to see if the `Track My Walks` screen has been successfully displayed. Alternatively, our test will fail and display the assigned error message within the **Test Results** screen. Proceed and enter the following highlighted code sections, as shown within the following code snippet:

```
// Populate our Entry Cell Fields
PopulateEntryCellFields();
// Display our Difficulty Picker selector.
ChooseDifficultyPicker();
// Then tap on the Save button to save the details and exit
// the screen.app.Tap(x => x.Marked("Save"));
// Next, wait for main screen to appear
   mainScreen = app.WaitForElement(x => x.Marked
      (navigationBarTitle).Class("UINavigationBar"));
```

```
// Check to see if the Track My Walks — iOS main screen is
// displayed.
  Assert.IsTrue(mainScreen.Any(), navigationBarTitle
    + " screen wasn't shown after signing in.");}
}
}
```

In the preceding code snippet, we began by implementing the various instance methods that will be required to perform each test for our `CreateNewWalkEntry`. We added the `[Test]` attribute to our `CreateNewWalkEntry` instance method. This method will essentially be the main test driver and call each of the other instance methods that we've previously declared. Within this method, we call our `SignInToFacebook` method to perform the sign-in to Facebook, using the user's Facebook credentials. Upon successful login, we use the `WaitForElement` method to wait until the main `Track My Walks` screen has been displayed.

In the next step, we used the `Tap` method of the `App` class instance, and use the `Marked` method to find the `Add` element within the App's current screen, and wait until the **New Walk Entry** page is displayed within the screen. We then proceed to use the `Assert.IsTrue` method to check to see if the **New Walk Entry** screen was successfully displayed. Alternatively, our test will fail and display the assigned error message within the **Test Results** screen.

Adding the Xamarin Test Cloud Agent to the iOS project

Now that you have created your UITest, the next step is to add the Xamarin Test Cloud Agent NuGet package to our `TrackMyWalks.iOS` project. This library allows you to execute your `Xamarin.UITest`, using C# and the NUnit framework to validate the functionality of iOS and Android apps within the Xamarin Studio development environment.

Let's look at how to add the Xamarin Test Cloud NuGet package to our `TrackMyWalks.iOS` project, by performing the following steps:

1. Right-click on the `Packages` folder that is contained within the `TrackMyWalks.iOS` project, and choose the **Add Packages...** menu option, as you did in the section entitled, *Adding the Moq NuGet package to the unit test project*, located within this chapter.

2. This will display the **Add Packages** dialog. Enter in `Cloud Agent` within the search dialog, and select the **Xamarin Test Cloud Agent** option within the list, as shown in the following screenshot:

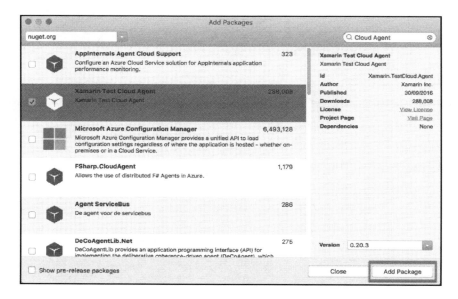

3. Finally, click on the **Add Package** button to add the `NuGet` package to the `Packages` folder contained within the `TrackMyWalks.iOS` project.

Now that you have added the Xamarin Test Cloud Agent NuGet package, our next step is to begin by modifying the `AppDelegate` class within the `TrackMyWalks.iOS` portion of our project. We will be covering this in the next section.

Updating the TrackMyWalks AppDelegate class to handle Xamarin Test Cloud Agent

Prior to running UITests within Xamarin Studio, we will need to add the Xamarin Test Cloud Agent NuGet package to the iOS portion of our `TrackMyWalks` app. Under Android, this is not required as the Xamarin Test Cloud Agent is provided by the UITest framework.

In this section, we need to update the `AppDelegate` class, by modifying the `FinishLaunching` method located within our `TrackMyWalks.iOS` project. This will include a compiler directive that will start the Xamarin Test Cloud Agent.

Let's look at how we can achieve this with the following steps:

1. Open the `AppDelegate.cs` file located within the `TrackMyWalks.iOS` project.
2. Next, ensure that the `AppDelegate.cs` file is displayed within the code editor, and locate the `FinishLaunching` method and enter in the following highlighted code sections:

```
//
//  AppDelegate.cs
//  TrackMyWalks
//
//  Created by Steven F. Daniel on 04/08/2016.
//  Copyright © 2016 GENIESOFT STUDIOS. All rights reserved.
//
using Foundation;
using UIKit;

namespace TrackMyWalks.iOS
{
    [Register("AppDelegate")]
    public partial class AppDelegate : global::Xamarin.Forms.
      Platform.iOS.FormsApplicationDelegate
      {
        public override bool FinishedLaunching
          (UIApplication app, NSDictionary options)
        {
            global::Xamarin.Forms.Forms.Init();

            // Integrate Xamarin Forms Maps
            Xamarin.FormsMaps.Init();

            #if USE_TEST_CLOUD
            Xamarin.Calabash.Start();
            #endif

            LoadApplication(new App());

            return base.FinishedLaunching(app, options);
        }
      }
  }
```

Calabash is basically an Automated UI Acceptance Testing framework that allows you to write and execute tests that validate the functionality of your iOS and Android apps.

In the preceding code snippet, you will notice that we have defined the `USE_TEST_CLOUD` compiler variable that is wrapped within the `#if` and `#endif` directive and includes a call to the `Xamarin.Calabash.Start()` method that will only be started when it has been defined under specific configurations as defined within the compiler configuration settings for the project.

If you are interested in learning more about the Calabash framework, please refer to the section on an *Introduction to Calabash* which is located at `https://developer.xamarin.com/guides/testcloud/calabash/introduction-to-calabash/`.

We have just added in the code that will essentially start our Xamarin Test Cloud functionality. However, for this to work, we will need to perform one additional step, which is to modify the compiler configurations for our `TrackMyWalks.iOS` project. Perform the following to achieve this:

1. Right-click on the `TrackMyWalks.iOS` project, and choose the **Options** menu option.
2. Next, within the **Project Options – TrackMyWalks.iOS** dialog, choose the **Compiler** option located under the **Build** section.
3. Then, ensure that you have chosen debug from the **Configuration** dropdown and that you have chosen **iPhoneSimulator** from the **Platform** dropdown.

4. Next, add the `USE_TEST_CLOUD;` to the list of existing **Define Symbols**, as shown in the following screenshot:

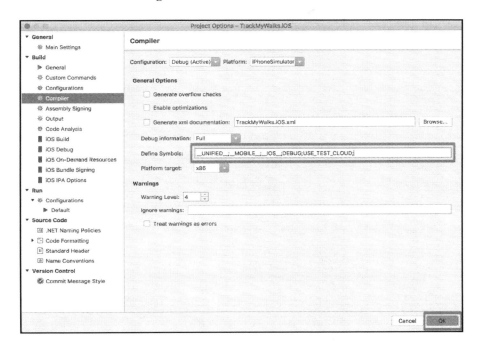

5. Then, click on **OK** to save your changes and close the **Project Options – TrackMyWalks.iOS** dialog.

Now that you have modified the compiler configurations for our iOS portion of the `TrackMyWalks` app, we can finally build and run our UITests using Xamarin Studio, similarly to what we did when executing our NUnit tests. However, this needs to be handled very differently, and we will be covering this in the next section.

Running the TrackMyWalks UITests using Xamarin Studio

Prior to running your UITests within Xamarin Studio, you will need to add your iOS or Android apps to the **Test Apps** node of the **Unit Tests** pane, or alternatively specifying a path to your app within the `AppInitializer` class. If you don't do this, your tests will continue to fail until you add these projects to your solution.

In this section, we will look at how to go about adding your apps to the **Test Apps** node within the **Unit Tests** pane. Let's look at how we can achieve this with the following steps:

1. To add your iOS and Android apps to your `TrackMyWalks.UITests` project, select the **View** menu option, then choose the **Pads** sub-menu item, and then the **Unit Tests** option, as shown in the following screenshot:

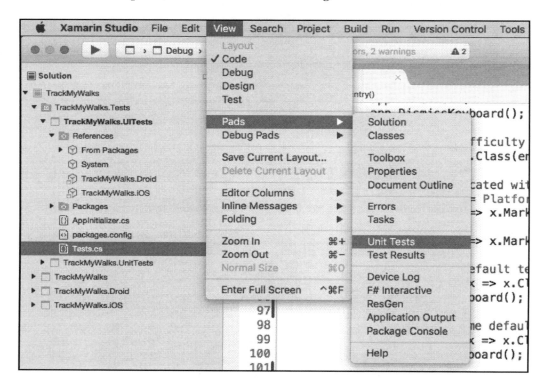

2. Next, right-click on the **Test Apps** item within the **Unit Tests** pane and click on the **Add App Project**. This will display the **Select a project or solution** dialog that allows you to select each of your projects for the various platforms, as shown in the following screenshot:

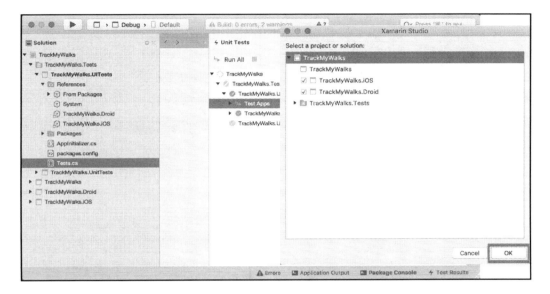

3. Once you have selected the projects that you would like to add to your `TrackMyWalks.UITests` solution, click **OK** and dismiss the dialog.

 If for some reason, you don't see your iOS app project listed, you may have forgotten to add the Xamarin Test Cloud Agent NuGet package to your iOS project.

Once you have successfully added your projects to the `TrackMyWalks.UITests` solution project, our next step is to run our app and see the results:

4. To run your UITests, select the **Run** menu option, then choose the **Run Unit Tests** menu item, as shown in the following screenshot.

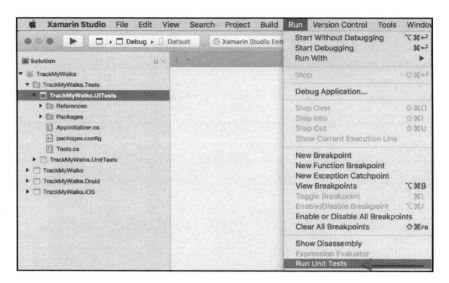

When your app starts to run, the UITest framework will automatically deploy your app to the iOS or Android simulator, and then run the app and process through each of the steps that you have specified within your test methods. The results from each of the tests will appear within the **Test Results** pane within Xamarin Studio.

Summary

In this chapter, we updated the `TrackMyWalks` application by adding a new project solution, `TrackMyWalks.Tests`, so that we can separate our tests from the main Portable Class Library. This gives us the ability to write test cases. We added the Mock framework so that it will provide us with the ability to successfully test our `ViewModels` as well as to provide the business logic behind them.

We then moved onto considering how we can leverage the UITest framework to write, test, and execute UI tests locally by using the Xamarin Test Cloud Agent and the Calabash framework, by adding the iOS and Android projects to the UITest solution project.

In the final chapter, you'll learn how to prepare your iOS app for submission to **iTunes Connect**, and learn how to set up internal and external users within **TestFlight** so that your users can download and test your apps on their iOS devices. To end the chapter, you will learn how to code-sign your Android apps before publishing, and releasing your Android APK file to the Google Play Store.

10
Packaging and Deploying Your Xamarin.Forms Applications

In our previous chapter, we updated our `TrackMyWalks` application to allow us to create and run unit tests using the NUnit and UITest testing frameworks right within the Xamarin Studio IDE. You learned how to write unit tests for our `ViewModels` to test the business logic to validate that everything is working correctly, before moving on to testing the user interfaces portion using automated UI testing.

In this chapter, you'll look at what is required to submit your `TrackMyWalks` iOS app to the Apple App Store, and share your creations with the rest of the community.

You'll learn the steps required to set up your iOS development team, as well as the certificates for both development and distribution, and learn how to create the necessary provisioning profiles for both your development and distribution builds, and create the necessary app IDs for your application.

At the end of the chapter, you will learn how to register your iOS devices so that your users can download and test your apps on their iOS devices and learn how to prepare your `TrackMyWalks` iOS app for submission to iTunes Connect, using the Xamarin Studio IDE.

This chapter will cover the following topics:

- Setting up your iOS development team
- Creating the `TrackMyWalks` iOS development certificate
- Obtaining the development certificate from Apple
- Registering your iOS devices for testing
- Creating your `TrackMyWalks` iOS App ID
- Creating the development provisioning profiles

- Preparing your `TrackMyWalks` iOS app for submission
- Using the provisioning profiles to install the app on the iOS device
- Building and archiving your app for publishing using Xamarin Studio
- Using Xamarin Studio to submit your `TrackMyWalks` iOS app to iTunes Connect

Creating and setting up your iOS development team

You have finally completed building your `TrackMyWalks` app and are ready to release it to the rest of the world; all you need to do is decide how to deploy and market it. Before you can begin submitting your iOS applications to the Apple App Store for approval, you will need to first set up your iOS development team, which can be achieved by following these steps:

1. Log in to the iOS developer portal website at `http://developer.apple.com/`.
2. Click on the **Member Center** link that is located right at the top of the screen.
3. Sign in to your account using your Apple ID and password. This will then display the developer program resources page, as shown in the following screenshot:

4. Next, click on the **iTunes Connect** button, as highlighted in the preceding screenshot. This is where you can check on various things such as **SalesandTrends, Payments and Financial Reports,** and **App Analytics**. Take a look at the following image:

5. Next, click on the **Users and Roles** button, as highlighted in the preceding screenshot. This will bring up the **Users and Roles option** pane from where you can add a new user, as shown in the following screenshot:

The **Users and Roles** screen allows you to add yourself or the people within your organization who will be able to log in to the iOS developer program portal, test apps on iOS devices, and add additional iOS devices to the account.

6. Ensure that you are within the **iTunes Connect Users** section, as highlighted in the preceding screenshot. Then, click on the **+** button to bring up the **Add New User** screen that is shown in the following screenshot.

7. Next, fill in the **User Information** section for the person that you will be adding to your development team. Once you have finished, click on the **Next** button, as shown in the following screenshot:

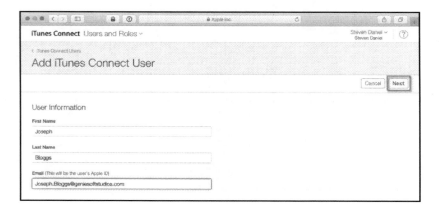

8. Next, under the **Role** section, from the list of roles available, choose what roles the user can perform and then click on the **Next** button, as shown in the following screenshot:

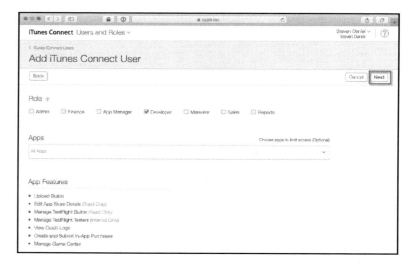

9. Next, from under the **Notifications** and **Settings** sections, this is where you will be assigning the ways in which you want the user to be notified. From this screen, you also have the ability of specifying what information relating to a list of territories you want the user to be notified about, as shown in the following screenshot:

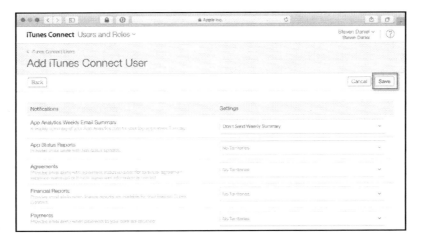

10. Once you have finished specifying each of the different types of notification methods, click on the **Save** button, as shown in the preceding screenshot. The new user account will then be created, along with a confirmation e-mail that will be sent to the users, accounts, requesting them to activate their account:

Now that we have covered the necessary steps required to create and assign roles to new users, as well as setting up which user roles can log into the iOS developer portal to manage new and existing users, view **Sales and Trends** reports, as well as **Payments and Financial** statements, our next step is to look at the steps involved to generate an iOS development certificate.

This certificate is encrypted and serves the purpose as your digital identification signature, and you must sign your apps using this certificate before you can submit your apps to the Apple App Store.

Creating the TrackMyWalks iOS development certificate

In this section, you will learn how to create the iOS development certificate that will enable us to run and test our `TrackMyWalks` app on the iOS device. We will begin by generating the iOS development certificate, which will be encrypted and will serve the purpose of identifying you digitally.

You will then need to sign your apps using this certificate before you can run and test any application that you develop on your iOS device. To begin, perform the following simple steps:

1. Launch the **Keychain Access** application, which can be found in the `/Applications/Utilities` folder.
2. Next, choose the **Request a Certificate From a Certificate Authority...** menu option from the **Keychain Access | Certificate Assistant**, as shown in the following screenshot:

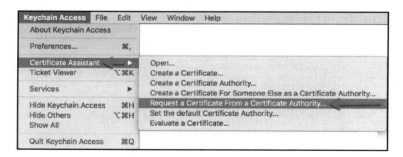

3. Then, we need to provide some information before the certificate can be generated under the **Certificate Information** section.

4. Next, enter in the required information, as shown in the following screenshot, whilst ensuring that you have selected the **Saved to disk** and the **Let me specify key pair information** options:

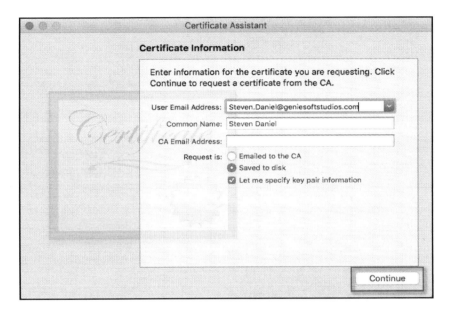

5. Once all the information has been filled out, click on the **Continue** button. You will then be asked to specify a name for the certificate. Accept the default suggested name, and click on the **Save** button.

At this point the certificate is being created at the location specified. You will then be asked to specify the **Key Size** and **Algorithm** to use.

6. Next, accept the default of **2048** bits and **RSA** algorithm. We need to provide some information before the certificate can be generated under the **Certificate Information** section, as shown in the following screenshot:

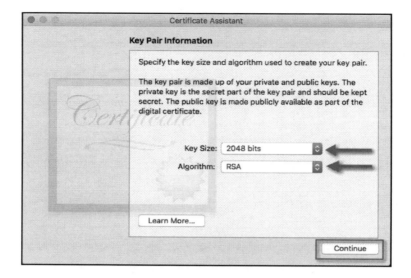

7. Click on the **Continue** button and then click on the **Done** button when the final screen appears.

Up until now, you learned how to generate a certificate request for iOS development, using the **Certificate Signing Request (CSR)** using the pre-installed Mac OS X Keychain Access application, so that we have the ability of code-signing our applications, which will enable us to deploy our applications to the iOS device for both development and testing.

In our next step, we will learn how to request a development certificate from Apple that will provide us with the ability of code-signing our applications using our generated certificate information file that we created in this section.

Obtaining the iOS development certificate from Apple

In this section, we will learn how to obtain the development certificate from Apple, to enable us to begin developing apps.

Before you can begin submitting your application to the Apple App Store, you will need to obtain your own copy of the iOS development certificate. This certificate is basically your unique identity for each of your apps that you submit for approval, so let's get started:

1. Log in to the iOS developer portal website at `http://developer.apple.com/`.
2. Click on the **Member Center** link that is located right at the top of the screen.
3. Sign in to your account using your Apple ID and password. This will then display the developer program resources page, as shown in the following screenshot:

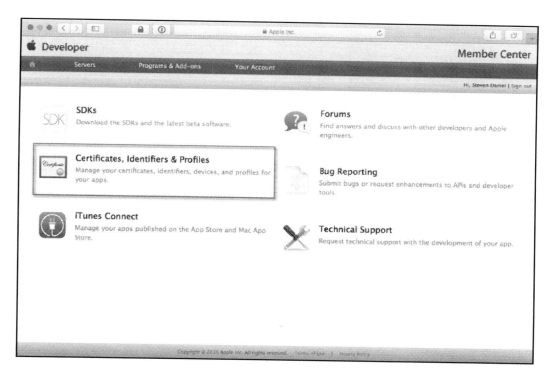

4. Next, click on the **Certificates, Identifiers & Profiles** button, as highlighted in the preceding screenshot.

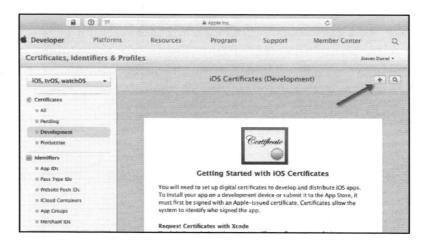

5. Then, click on the + button, as highlighted in the preceding screenshot.

6. Next, choose the **iOS App Development** option under the **Development** section, as highlighted in the preceding screenshot, and click on the **Continue** button to proceed to the next step, as displayed further down the page:

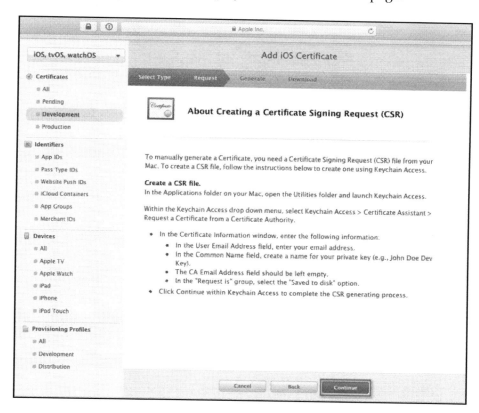

7. Then, click on the **Continue** button, as highlighted in the preceding screenshot, to proceed to the next step.

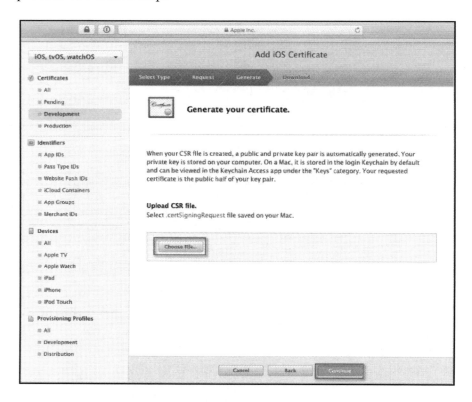

8. Next, click on the **Choose File...** button, as highlighted in the preceding screenshot.
9. Then, select the `CertificateSigningRequest.certSigningRequest` file that you created in the previous sections and click on the **Continue** button to proceed to the next step in the wizard.
10. After a few seconds, the page will refresh and the certificate will be ready and you will be able to download it.

In this section, we considered the steps involved in requesting a certificate from Apple that will be used to provide us with the ability of code-signing our applications required to deploy onto the iOS device and the Apple App Store.

We then moved on to learn how to use the generated certificate request file that we created in our previous section, *Creating the TrackMyWalks iOS development certificate*, to generate the development certificate.

Creating the App ID for the TrackMyWalks (iOS) application

In previous sections, we have learned how to request a certificate from Apple to provide us with the ability of code-signing our applications, as well as learning how to use the generated certificate request file to generate our deployment certificate.

In this section, we will be looking at how to create the application App IDs so that we can use these to deploy our applications to test on an iOS device:

1. Log in to the iOS developer portal website at `http://developer.apple.com/`.
2. Click on the **Member Center** link that is located right at the top of the screen.
3. Sign in to your account using your Apple ID and password. This will then display the developer program resources page, as shown in the following screenshot:

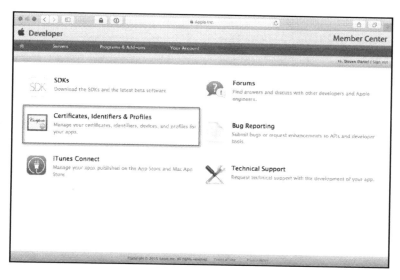

4. Next, click on the **Certificates, Identifiers & Profiles** button, as highlighted in the preceding screenshot.

5. Then, click on the **App IDs** item located underneath the **Identifiers** group at the left-hand side of the page and click on the + button to display the **Register iOS App IDs** section, as highlighted in the following screenshot:

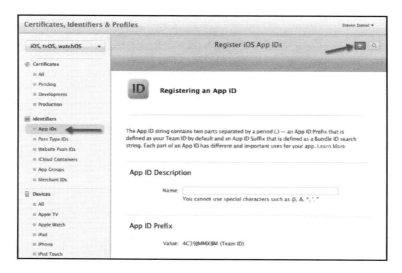

6. Next, provide a description for the **App ID Description** field that will be used to identify your app, as shown in the preceding screenshot.

7. Then, provide a name for the **Bundle ID** field. This needs to be the same as your application's bundle identifier.

The **Bundle ID** for your app needs to be unique. Apple recommends that you use the reverse domain style (for example, com.domainName.appName).

Consider the following screenshot:

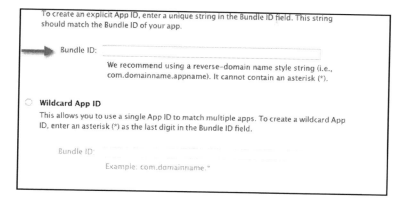

8. Next, choose from the list of **App Services** that you would like to enable for your app, and then click on the **Continue** button, as shown in the following screenshot:

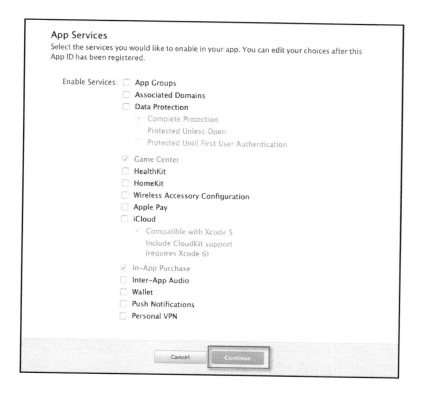

9. Then, from the **Confirm your App ID** screen, click on the **Register** button.

In this section, we covered the necessary steps required to create the App ID for our application. Creation of **App IDs** are required for each application that you create and must contain a unique application ID that identifies itself. The App ID is part of the provisioning profile and identifies an App or a suite of related applications.

These are used when your applications communicate with the iOS hardware accessories, the **Apple Push Notification Service** (**APNS**), and when sharing of data happens between each of your applications.

Creating the TrackMyWalks development provisioning profile

In this section, we will learn how to create the development provisioning profiles so that your applications can be installed on the iOS device so that you can deploy and test your applications prior to deploying your app to the Apple App Store:

1. Log back in to the iOS developer portal at `http://developer.apple.com/`.
2. Click on the **Member Center** link that is located right at the top of the screen.
3. Sign in to your account using your Apple ID and password. This will then display the developer program resources page, as shown in the following screenshot:

4. Next, click on the **Certificates, Identifiers & Profiles** button, as done previously.

5. Then, click on the **All** item located under the **Provisioning Profiles** section located at the left-hand side of the page.

6. Next, click on the + button to display the **Add iOS Provisioning Profiles** section, as highlighted in the following screenshot:

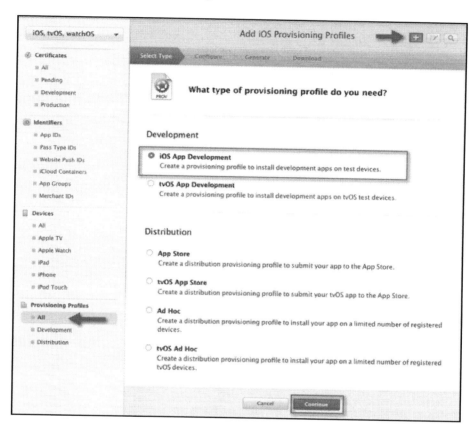

7. Then, choose the **iOS App Development** option from the **Development** section, and then click on the **Continue** button to proceed to the next step, as shown in the preceding screenshot.

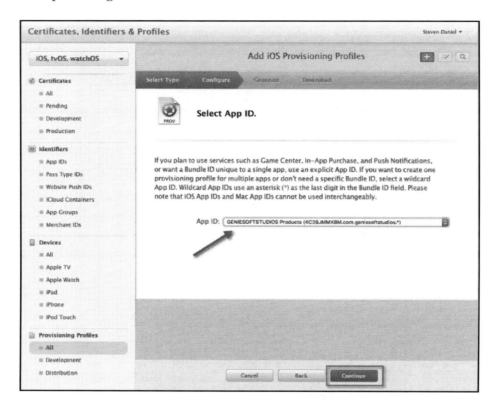

8. Next, select your **App ID** from the drop-down list available, as shown in the preceding screenshot, and click on the **Continue** button to proceed to the next step in the wizard:

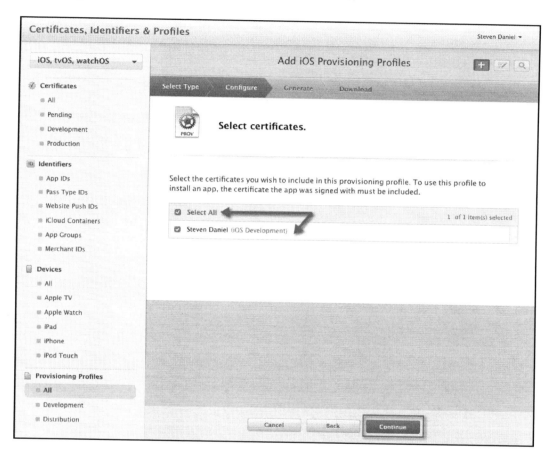

9. Then, choose your certificate from the list of available certificates that you would like to include to be part of the **Provisioning Profiles**, and click on the **Continue** button to proceed to the next step, as shown in the preceding screenshot.

10. Next, choose from the list of devices that you would like to include as part of the **Provisioning Profiles** that you are about to create, and click on the **Continue** button to proceed to the next step, as shown in the preceding screenshot.

For more information about how to register iOS devices using the **Member Center**, please refer to the Apple distribution guide documentation using the following link: `https://developer.apple.com/library/ios/documentation/IDEs/C onceptual/AppDistributionGuide/MaintainingProfiles/MaintainingPr ofiles.html#//apple_ref/doc/uid/TP40012582-CH30-SW10`.

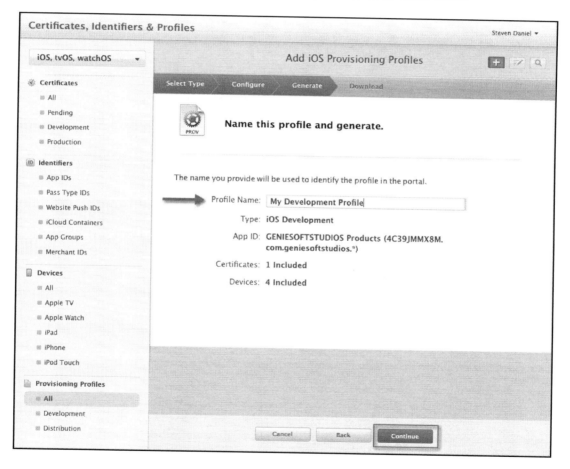

11. Then, specify a name for the **Profile Name** field to be used to identify the provisioning profile within the iOS developer portal, and click on the **Continue** button to proceed to the next step, as shown in the preceding screenshot.

12. Finally, your provisioning profile has been created and is ready to be used. You can choose to **Download** your provisioning profile from here, or you can let Xcode handle this for you, which we will be covering in the next sections.

13. To close this screen, and take you back to the list of **Provisioning Profiles**, click on the **Done** button, as shown in the preceding screenshot.

In this section, we learned how to create a provisioning profile that will allow your applications to be installed onto a real iOS device. This will give you the ability to assign team members who are authorized to install and test an application onto each of their devices.

Whenever you deploy an application onto an iOS device, this will contain the iOS development certificate for each team member, as well as the **Unique Device Identifier (UDID)**, which is a sequence of 40 letters and numbers that are specific to your device, and the App id.

Preparing the TrackMyWalks (iOS) app for submission

Now that you have tested your application to ensure that everything works fine and is free from errors, you will want to start preparing your application so that it is ready for submission to the Apple App Store.

In this section, we will need to use Xcode and sign in with our Apple ID so that we can download our provisioning profiles for both development and distribution. This is mainly since Xamarin Studio uses Xcode to perform its compilation, and if we don't set this up, we won't be able to submit our TrackMyWalks iOS app to the App Store and iTunes Connect.

To begin preparing your application using Xcode, follow these simple steps:

1. Ensure that you have launched the Xcode development IDE and it is displayed.
2. Next, choose the **Preferences...** menu option from the **Xcode | Preferences...** menu, or alternatively press *command + ,* as shown in the following screenshot:

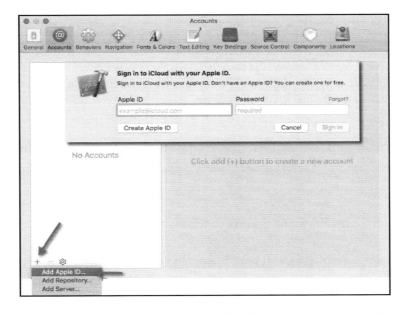

3. Next, ensure that the **Accounts** button has been selected, then click on the **+** button, and choose the **Add Apple ID...** menu option, as shown in the preceding screenshot.

4. Then, enter in your **Apple Developer** credentials by specifying both the **Apple ID** and **Password**, as can be seen in the preceding screenshot.

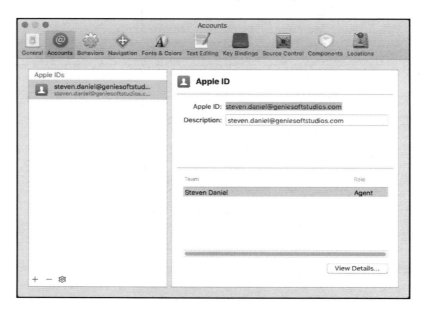

 Once Xcode has validated your Apple credentials, you will be presented with a screen like the one shown in the preceding screenshot. This screen shows you the team that you belong to, as well as your role within the team. You can also add multiple Apple IDs to this screen.

Now that we have set up our Xcode development IDE to use our iOS development and distribution provisioning profiles, our next step is to create an entry for our application within iTunes Connect.

This is so that when we begin to submit our app using Xamarin Studio and the **Application Loader** application to the Apple App Store using iTunes Connect, we won't run in to any issues:

1. Log back in to the iOS developer portal at `http://developer.apple.com/`.
2. Click on the **Member Center** link that is located right at the top of the screen.
3. Sign in to your account using your Apple ID and password. This will then display the developer program resources page.

4. Next, click on the **My Apps** button, as shown in the following screenshot:

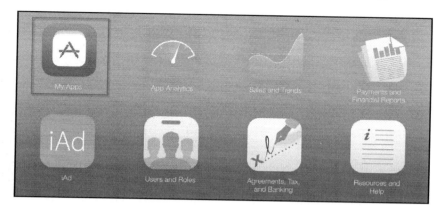

5. Then, click on the + button and then choose the **New App** menu option, as shown in the following screenshot:

6. Next, proceed to enter in the application details for the application that we are uploading. The **SKU** number field is a unique identifier that you create for your app:

The **Bundle ID** suffix that you provide must match the same one that you used within your `TrackMyWalks.iOS` app's `info.plist`; otherwise, you will run into issues when submitting your apps to the App Store and iTunes Connect.

7. Then, click on the **Create** button to create your app and proceed to the next step.

8. Next, choose the **Pricing and Availability** menu option, located underneath the **APP STORE INFORMATION** section, on the left-hand side panel.

9. Then, from the **Pricing and Availability** section, specify the values for our **Price Schedule** as well as the **Start Date** and **End Date** for our application. This will determine when our application will be made available for download, as shown in the following screenshot:

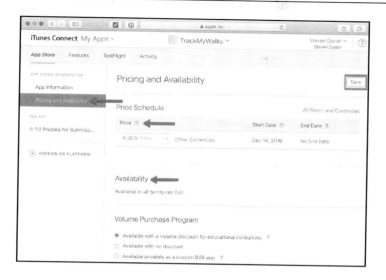

10. Next, click on the **Save** button to save any changes made within this screen.

There are more than 100 pricing tiers to choose from, including an option for selling your application for free.

In this section, we learned the steps involved in preparing our application for submission to the Apple App Store using iTunes Connect. We also learned that before submitting our apps for approval, you must ensure that everything works properly, and is free from problems, and the iOS simulator is a good place to start.

Although, not everything can be tested within the iOS simulator, it proves a good starting point. Apple suggests that you should always deploy your apps to a real iOS device running the latest iOS release, so that you can test your app for a few days to ensure that all issues are ironed out, prior to submitting your app to the Apple App Store. Next, we looked at how to create a new application ID for the application that will be uploaded to the Apple App Store, as well as providing detailed information about the application, and specifying a date when the application will become available.

For more information on how to go about submitting and managing your apps using iTunes Connect, you can refer to the following link at this location: `https://developer.apple.com/library/ios/documentation/ID Es/Conceptual/AppDistributionGuide/UsingiTunesConnect/UsingiTune sConnect.html#//apple_ref/doc/uid/TP40012582-CH22-SW3`.

Submitting the TrackMyWalks (iOS) app to iTunes Connect using Xamarin Studio

In the previous section, we began by creating the `TrackMyWalks` App within iTunes Connect and learned that before submitting apps for approval, you must ensure that everything is working properly, and is free from problems.

In this section, we will begin getting our `TrackMyWalks.iOS` app ready for submission to the Apple App Store, using Xamarin Studio IDE.

To begin submitting your application, follow these simple steps:

1. Ensure that the `TrackMyWalks.sln` project is already open within Xamarin Studio IDE.
2. Next, right-click on the `TrackMyWalks.iOS` project, choose the **Options** menu option, and choose the **iOS Bundle Signing** located under the **Build** section within the left pane.
3. Then, within the **iOS Bundle Signing** section, choose **Release** for the **Configuration** and **iPhone** for the **Platform** and ensure that you have chosen the **Distribution (Automatic)** option within the **Signing Identity** dropdown that will be used to sign our `TrackMyWalks` app with.
4. Next, ensure that you have chosen the **Automatic** option to use for our **Provisioning Profile,** and click on the **OK** button to save the settings and dismiss the **Project Options – TrackMyWalks.iOS** dialog.

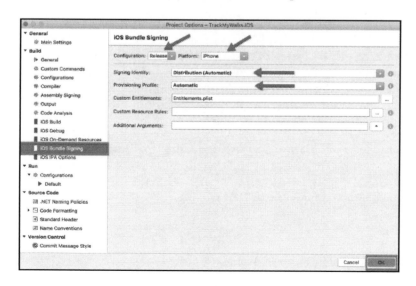

Your iOS provisioning certificate will be shown in bold, with your provisioning profile in gray. If you don't import a valid provisioning certificate, you won't be able to deploy or upload your `TrackMyWalks` iOS application to the Apple App Store.

5. Then, ensure that you have chosen **Release | iPhone** to use as the iOS device prior to choosing the **Archive for Publishing** option within the **Build** menu, as shown in the following screenshot:

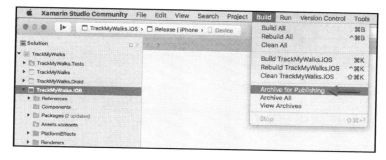

6. Next, provide a comment for your application, by clicking within the **Comment** field, and then click on the **Sign and Distribute...** button to have Xamarin sign and prepare your app for submission, as shown in the following screenshot:

Once you click on the **Sign and Distribute...** button, you will be presented with the **Select iOS Distribution Channel** dialog, where you can choose your distribution channel to create a package for your app.

7. Then, since we want to publish our `TrackMyWalks` app to the App Store, choose the **App Store** option within the list and click on the **Next** button to proceed to the next step within the wizard, as shown in the following screenshot:

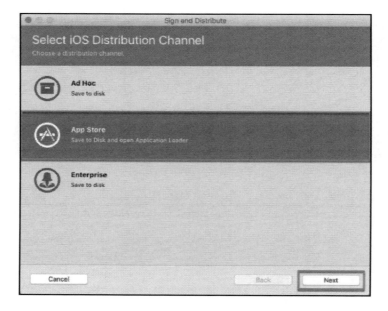

8. Next, you will be presented with the **Provisioning profile** screen where you can select your signing identity and provisioning profile, or re-sign using a different identity. Click on the **Next** button to proceed to the next step within the wizard, as shown in the following screenshot.

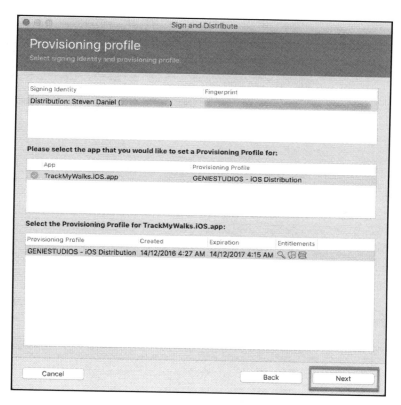

9. Upon clicking on the **Next** button, Xamarin Studio will proceed to collect all the necessary files, and create a `TrackMyWalks.ipa` file which, by default, will be saved within your `TrackMyWalks` folder.

10. You will be presented with the **Publish to App Store** dialog, where you will be presented with the ability of publishing your app to the app store, as shown in the following screenshot:

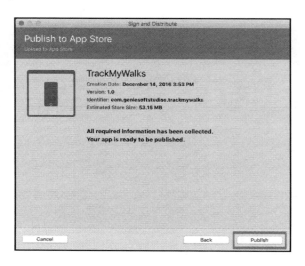

11. Then, click on the **Publish** button to proceed to the next step within the wizard where you can then upload your binary archive.

12. Once you have clicked on the **Publish** button, and everything passes, you will be presented with the **Publishing Succeeded** dialog where you can begin uploading your binary archive by clicking on the **Open Application Loader** button, as can be seen in the preceding screenshot.

> For more information on how to go about deploying your Xamarin.Forms Android app, please refer to the section on *Preparing an Application for Release* at the following link: https://developer.xamarin.com/guides/android/deployment,_tes ting,_and_metrics/publishing_an_application/part_1_- _preparing_an_application_for_release/.

This will then launch the Application Loader application, as shown in the following screenshot, where you will need to sign-in to iTunes Connect using your iTunes Connect credentials.

13. Next, choose the **Deliver Your App** option and click on the **Choose** button, as shown in the following screenshot:

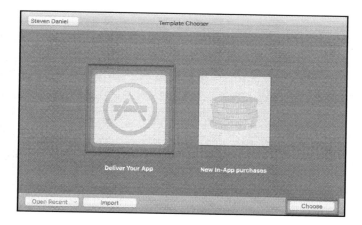

14. Once you have clicked on the **Choose** button, you will be presented with the Deliver Your App dialog where you will need to choose the `TrackMyWalks.ipa` file that was generated during the **Sign and Distribute** process within the *Submitting the TrackMyWalks (iOS) app to iTunes Connect using Xamarin Studio* section located within this chapter.

15. Then, select and choose the **TrackMyWalks.ipa** file, and click on the **Open** button, as shown in the preceding screenshot.

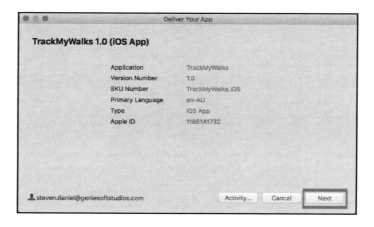

The Application Loader will read the information contained within the `TrackMyWalks.ipa` binary file, populated from iTunes Connect, and display the **Application name**, **Version Number**, **SKU Number**, **Primary Language**, **Type**, and the user's **Apple ID**, as shown in the preceding screenshot.

16. Next, click on the **Next** button to proceed to the next step within the wizard, as shown in the preceding screenshot.

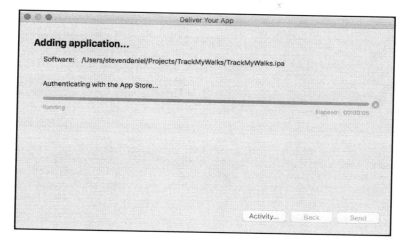

In the preceding screenshot, the Application Loader application will begin by authenticating your app with the Apple App Store and iTunes Connect, and then validating to ensure that everything passes, at which point your binary archive will begin uploading.

 For information on how to use the Application Loader to publish your `Xamarin.iOS` apps, you can refer to *Publishing to the App Store Guide* from the Xamarin developer documentation, which can be accessed by using the following
link: `https://developer.xamarin.com/guides/ios/deployment,_testing ,_and_metrics/app_distribution/app-store- distribution/publishing_to_the_app_store/`.

Summary

In this chapter, you learned how to create and set up your iOS development team and the associated iOS development certificate that will enable you to run and test your apps on an iOS device. We then moved on to describe how to create an App ID for our `TrackMyWalks` app.

These special App IDs are used both within Xamarin and Xcode to associate your app with the one assigned as part of your iOS provisioning profiles. Once we created all the necessary development certificates and provisioning profiles, you learned how to package, sign, and distribute your app using Xamarin Studio IDE, and deploy it to iTunes Connect using the Application Loader application, where you can then download and test your app on a real iOS device.

This was the final chapter, and I sincerely hope that you had lots of fun developing apps throughout our journey working through this book. You now have enough knowledge and expertise to understand what it takes to build rich and engaging apps for the Xamarin.Forms platform, by using a host of exciting concepts and techniques that are unique to the Xamarin.Forms platform.

You have enough knowledge to get your Xamarin.Forms projects off to a great start, and I can't wait to see what you build. Thank you so much for purchasing this book and I wish you the very best of luck with your Xamarin.Forms adventures.

Index

PlatformEffects, creating with 186

47817404R00235

Made in the USA
San Bernardino, CA
08 April 2017